CLIFFS

Advanced Placement
# Chemistry
Examination

# PREPARATION GUIDE

*by*

**Gary S. Thorpe, M.S.**

*Series Editor*
Jerry Bobrow, Ph.D.

**Cliffs Notes**
INCORPORATED
LINCOLN, NEBRASKA   68501

# ACKNOWLEDGMENTS

*I would like to thank my wife, Patti, for her patience and understanding while I was writing this book. I would also like to thank the Beverly Hills High School Advanced Placement Chemistry Class of 1992–93 for offering many valuable suggestions. And special thanks go to Ali Zarrinpar of Harvard University for his input, proofreading, and suggestions.*

ISBN 0-8220-2309-1

SECOND EDITION

# CONTENTS

## PART III: AP CHEMISTRY PRACTICE TEST

# PREFACE

The AP chemistry exam is coming up! Your thorough understanding of months and months of college-level chemistry lectures, tests, quizzes, homework problems, lab write-ups, and notes are to be evaluated in a 3-hour examination. It's just you and the AP exam. In preparing to do the very best job possible, you have four options:

1. Read all of your textbook again.
2. Do all of your homework problems again.
3. Buy a test preparation guide that has every conceivable type of problem in it *and* that in many cases is thicker than your textbook *and* that you will never be able to finish *and* that does not explain how to do well on the essay portion of the exam.
4. Use the *Cliffs AP Chemistry Examination Preparation Guide.*

I'm glad you chose option 4. I have taught chemistry for about 20 years. I've put together for this book, in a reasonable number of pages, what I feel are the best examples of problems to help you prepare for the exam. With other AP exams to study for and other time commitments, you need a quick and neat book that you can finish in a few weeks and that covers just about everything you might expect to find on the exam. You have that book in your hands.

This guide is divided into three parts:

*Part I: Introduction*

Part I contains the following sections: Questions Commonly Asked About the AP Chemistry Exam, Strategies for Taking the AP Chemistry Exam, Methods for Writing the Essays, Mathematical Operations, and Mathematics Self-Test.

## Part II: Specific Topics

Each chapter lists key vocabulary words, formulas, and equations and provides about ten completely worked-out multiple-choice questions and solutions for two or more free-response questions. Self-contained chapters cover gravimetrics, thermochemistry, gases, the structure of atoms, covalent bonding, ionic bonding, liquids and solids, solutions, kinetics, equilibrium, acids and bases, energy, organic chemistry, nuclear chemistry, and writing and predicting chemical equations.

## Part III: AP Chemistry Practice Test

A complete exam consisting of both multiple-choice and free-response questions. All solutions are fully worked out.

*This book is not a textbook.* The last thing you need right now is another chemistry textbook. However, if you have forgotten concepts or if something is new to you, use this preparation guide *with* your textbook to prepare for the AP chemistry exam. Now turn to the Study Guide Checklist on page viii and check each item, in order, as you complete the task. When you have checked all the items, you will be ready for the AP chemistry exam. Good Luck!

# STUDY GUIDE CHECKLIST

____ 1. Read the *Advanced Placement Course Description—Chemistry* (also commonly known as the "Acorn Book") published by Educational Testing Service (ETS) and available from your AP chemistry teacher, testing office, or counseling center or directly from ETS.

____ 2. Read the Preface to this Cliffs preparation guide.

____ 3. Read "Questions Commonly Asked about the AP Chemistry Exam."

____ 4. Read "Strategies for Taking the AP Chemistry Exam."

____ 5. Read "Methods for Writing the Essays."

____ 6. Review "Mathematical Operations" and take the "Mathematics Self-Test."

____ 7. Go through each of the chapters listed below, carefully reviewing each key term, each key concept, and all the worked-out examples of multiple-choice and free-response questions.

   **Key Terms.** You should be familiar with the meanings of these words and with the principles underlying them. They can serve as foundations for your essays. The more of these key terms (provided that they are relevant) that you can use effectively in your explanations, the better your free-response answers will be.

**Key Concepts.** These are formulas, constants, and equations used in the chapter. You should be completely familiar with them.

**Examples.** Do not go on to a new example until you thoroughly understand the example you are currently working on. If you do not understand an example after considerable thought, ask your AP chemistry teacher or fellow classmates how they approached the problem. Be sure to work each example with pencil and paper as you go through the book. Write out your answer to every free-response question. Practice makes perfect!

\_\_\_\_ Gravimetrics
\_\_\_\_ Thermochemistry
\_\_\_\_ The Gas Laws
\_\_\_\_ Electronic Structure of Atoms
\_\_\_\_ Covalent Bonding
\_\_\_\_ Ionic Bonding
\_\_\_\_ Liquids and Solids
\_\_\_\_ Solutions
\_\_\_\_ Kinetics
\_\_\_\_ Equilibrium
\_\_\_\_ Acids and Bases
\_\_\_\_ Energy and Spontaneity
\_\_\_\_ Reduction and Oxidation
\_\_\_\_ Organic Chemistry
\_\_\_\_ Nuclear Chemistry
\_\_\_\_ Writing and Predicting Chemical Reactions

\_\_\_\_ 8. Take the Practice Test.

\_\_\_\_ 9. Analyze any remaining weaknesses that the Practice Test reveals.

\_\_\_\_ 10. Read "The Final Touches."

# FORMAT OF THE AP CHEMISTRY EXAM

**Section I: Multiple-Choice Questions**

| 90 minutes | 75 questions | 45% of total grade |
|---|---|---|

Periodic table provided; no calculators allowed; no table of equations and constants provided.

**Section II: Free-Response (Essay) Questions**

| 95 minutes | 6 questions | 55% of total grade |
|---|---|---|

Part A: 10 minutes; no calculators allowed. A periodic table is provided. Select 5 of 8 chemical reactions and determine the formulas of the reactants and products.                8%

Parts B, C, and D: 85 minutes. Table of equations and constants, table of standard half-cell potentials, and a periodic table provided. Calculators are allowed (you will **not** be required to clear the memory of the calculator).

Part B: Answer 1 question involving equilibrium (no choice).                11%

Part C: Select 1 of 2 questions involving math computations.                11%

Part D: Write on 3 of 5 essay questions, 1 required, 2 selected.                25%

Format and allotment of time may vary slightly from year to year.

### Brief Description / Analysis of Section II

- **Part A:** 8% of total grade. You are given 8 chemical reactions. You are to choose 5 to answer in 10 minutes. You may **not** use a calculator. A periodic table will be provided. For each reaction, you are to write the formulas of the reactants and predict the formulas of the products. You do not need to balance the equations. After 10 minutes, this part of Section II will be collected.

*Example: Concentrated ammonia is added to a solution of zinc hydroxide.*

$$Answer: Zn(OH)_2 + NH_3 \rightarrow Zn(NH_3)_4^{2+} + OH^-$$

You will have 85 minutes to complete Parts B, C, and D. You will be given a table of equations and constants, a table of standard half-cell potentials, and a periodic table. You may use any programmable or graphing calculator, except those with type-writer-style keyboards (qwerty), to answer Parts B, C, and D. You will not be required to clear the memory of the calculator. Calculators may not be shared. It is vital that you show all steps in solving mathematical problems since partial credit is awarded in each problem for showing how the answer was obtained.

- **Part B:** 11% of total grade. 1 question. *Always* an equilibrium problem ($K_c$, $K_p$, $K_a$, $K_b$, or $K_{sp}$).

- **Part C:** 11% of total grade. You are given 2 questions. You are to choose 1 to answer. The questions in this section involve mathematical computations. Each problem has 4 to 5 components.

- **Part D:** 25% of total grade. You are given 5 essay questions, 1 of which you will be required to answer. From the 4 that remain, you choose 2 to answer. These questions involve concepts and theories of chemistry; no mathematical computations are necessary.

# Part I: Introduction

# QUESTIONS COMMONLY ASKED ABOUT THE AP CHEMISTRY EXAM

*What is the AP chemistry exam?*

The AP chemistry exam is given once a year to high school students and tests their knowledge of concepts in first-year college-level chemistry. The student who passes the AP exam may receive one year of college credit for taking AP chemistry in high school. Passing is generally considered to be achieving a score of 3, 4, or 5. The test is administered each May. It has two sections.

- Section I, worth 45% of the total score, is 90 minutes long and consists of 75 multiple-choice questions. The total score for Section I is the number of correct answers minus $\frac{1}{4}$ for each wrong answer. If you leave a question unanswered, it does not count at all. A student generally needs to answer from 50% to 60% of the multiple-choice questions correctly to obtain a 3 on the exam. The multiple-choice questions fall into three categories.

*Calculations:* These questions require you to quickly calculate mathematical solutions. Since beginning in 1996 you will not be able to use a calculator for the multiple-choice questions, the questions requiring calculations have been limited to simple arithmetic so that they can be done quickly, either mentally or with paper and pencil. Also, in some questions, the answer choices differ by several orders of magnitude so that the questions can be answered by estimation.

*Conceptual:* These questions ask you to consider how theories, laws, or concepts are applied.

*Factual:* These questions require you to quickly recall important chemical facts.

- Section II, worth 55% of the total score, is 95 minutes long and consists of four parts—writing and predicting chemical equations, an equilibrium problem, mathematical essays, and nonmathematical essays.

### What are the advantages of taking AP chemistry?

- Students who pass the exam may, at the discretion of the college in which the student enrolls, be given full college credit for taking the class in high school.

- Taking the exam improves your chance of getting into the college of your choice. Studies show that students who successfully participate in AP programs in high school stand a much better chance of being accepted by selective colleges than students who do not.

- Taking the exam reduces the cost of a college education. In the many private colleges that charge upward of $500 a unit, a first-year college chemistry course could cost as much as $3000! Taking the course during high school saves money.

- Taking the exam may reduce the number of years needed to earn a college degree.

- If you take the course and the exam while still in high school, you will not be faced with the college course being closed or overcrowded.

- For those of you who are not going on in a science career, passing the AP chemistry exam may fulfill the laboratory science requirement at the college, thus making more time available for you to take other courses.

- Taking AP chemistry greatly improves your chances of doing well in college chemistry. You will already have covered most of the topics during your high school AP chemistry program, and you will find yourself setting the curve in college!

### Do all colleges accept AP exam grades for college credit?

No. College policies in awarding credit for passing AP exams vary. For a complete list of colleges that accept AP scores for college credit, you can ask your chemistry teacher for the *Advanced Placement Course Description—Chemistry*. Commonly known as the "Acorn Book," it is published each year by Educational Testing Service (ETS). If you need more information, you can call the college you are interested in and speak to someone in the registrar's office.

*How is the AP exam graded and what do the scores mean?*

The AP exam is graded on a five-point scale:

**5:** Extremely well qualified. About 12% of the students who take the exam earn this grade.

**4:** Well qualified. Roughly 17% earn this grade.

**3:** Qualified. Generally, 30% earn this grade.

**2:** Possibly qualified. Generally considered "not passing." About 25% of the students who take the exam earn this grade.

**1:** Not qualified. About 16% earn this grade.

Section I, the multiple-choice section, is machine graded. Each question has five answers to choose from. Remember, there is a penalty for guessing: ¼ of a point is taken off for each wrong answer. A student generally needs to correctly answer 50 to 60% of the multiple-choice questions to obtain a 3 on the exam. Each answer in Section II, the free-response section, is read several times by different chemistry instructors who pay great attention to consistency in grading.

*Are there old exams out there that I could look at?*

Yes! Questions (and answers) from previous exams are periodically published by ETS. Request an order blank by writing to the Advanced Placement Program, Dept. E-22, P.O. Box 6670, Princeton, NJ 08541-6670 or by calling (609) 771-7243.

*What materials should I take to the exam?*

Be sure to take with you your admission ticket, some form of photo and signature identification, your social security number, several sharpened No. 2 pencils, a good eraser, a watch, and a scientific calculator with fresh batteries. You may bring a programmable calculator (it will **not** be erased or cleared), but it must **not** have a typewriter-style (qwerty) keyboard. You may use the calculator only in Section II, Parts B, C, and D.

### When will I get my score?

The exam itself is generally given in the second or third week of May. The scores are usually available during the second or third week of July.

### Should I guess on the test?

Except in certain special cases explained later in this book, you should *not* guess. There is a penalty for guessing on the multiple-choice section of the exam. As for the free-response section, it simply comes down to whether you know the material or not.

### Suppose I do terribly on the exam. May I cancel the test and/or the scores?

Yes. You can cancel all records of an exam by writing a letter to ETS. There is no canceling fee, but the test fee is not refunded. If you want to redesignate the colleges that will receive your score, or if you want to prevent the designated college from receiving your score, use the form included with your AP candidate pack (given to all students who take the exam) and mail it to the address given. The deadline is usually within a month of the test date.

### May I write on the test?

Yes. Because scratch paper is not provided, you'll need to write in the test booklet. Make your notes in the booklet near the questions so that if you have time at the end, you can go back to your notes to try to answer the question.

### How do I register or get more information?

Information is available at each school where AP chemistry is taught. The head counselor or chemistry teacher can answer your questions or give you information about registering for the exam. If you need further information, contact the College Board National Office at 45 Columbus Avenue, New York, New York 10023-6992. You can also call ETS at (212) 713-8000 for more information or for the regional office located nearest you.

# STRATEGIES FOR TAKING THE AP CHEMISTRY EXAM

## SECTION I: THE MULTIPLE-CHOICE SECTION

### The "Plus-Minus" System

Many students who take the AP chemistry exam do not get their best possible score on Section I because they spend too much time on difficult questions and fail to leave themselves enough time to answer the easy ones. Don't let this happen to you. Because every question within each section is worth the same amount, consider the following guidelines.

1. Note in your test booklet the starting time of Section I. Remember that you have just over 1 minute per question.

2. Go through the entire test and answer all the easy questions first. Generally, the first 25 or so questions are considered by most to be the easiest questions, with the level of difficulty increasing as you move through Section I. Most students correctly answer approximately 60% of the first 25 multiple-choice questions, 50% of the next 25 questions, and only 30% of the last 25 questions (the fact that most students do not have time to finish the multiple-choice questions is factored into the percentages).

3. When you come to a question that seems impossible to answer, mark a large minus sign ($-$) next to it in your test booklet. You are penalized for wrong answers, so do not guess at this point. Move on to the next question.

4. When you come to a question that seems solvable but appears too time-consuming, mark a large plus sign ($+$) next to that question in your test booklet. Do not guess. Then move on to the next question.

7

5. Your time allotment is just over 1 minute per question, so a "time-consuming" question is one that you estimate will take you several minutes to answer. Don't waste time deciding whether a question gets a plus or a minus. Act quickly. The intent of this strategy is to save you valuable time.

   After you have worked all the easy questions, your booklet should look something like this:

   > 1.
   > +2.
   > 3.
   > −4.
   > 5.
   > etc.

6. After doing all the problems you can do immediately (the easy ones), go back and work on your "+" problems.

7. If you finish working your "+" problems and still have time left, you can do either of two things:

   Attempt the "−" problems, but remember not to guess under any circumstance.

   Forget the "−" problems and go back over your completed work to be sure you didn't make any careless mistakes on the questions you thought were easy to answer.

   You do not have to erase the pluses and minuses you made in your question booklet.

### The Elimination Strategy

Take advantage of being able to mark in your test booklet. As you go through the "+" questions, eliminate choices from consideration by marking them out in your question booklet:

(A)
?(B)
(C)
(D)
?(E)

Mark with question marks any choices you wish to consider as possible answers. This technique will help you avoid reconsidering those choices that you have already eliminated and will thus save you time. It will also help you narrow down your possible answers.

If you are able to eliminate all but two possible answers, answers such as (B) and (E) in the foregoing example, you may want to guess. Under these conditions, you stand a better chance of raising your score by guessing than by leaving the answer sheet blank.

## SECTION II: THE FREE-RESPONSE (ESSAY) SECTION

Many students waste valuable time by memorizing information that they feel they should know for the AP chemistry exam. Unlike the history exam, for which you need to have memorized hundreds of dates, battles, names, and treaties, the AP chemistry exam requires you to have memorized comparatively little. Rather, it is generally testing whether you can *apply* given information to new situations. You will be frequently asked to *explain, compare,* and *predict* in the essay questions.

Section II of the AP chemistry exam comes with

- a periodic table (page 334)
- an $E^\circ_{red}$ table (page 336)
- a table of equations and constants (page 337)

See the pages given above for examples of these tables and charts.

# METHODS FOR WRITING THE ESSAYS

## The Restatement

In the second section of the AP exam, you should begin all questions by numbering your answer. You do not need to work the questions in order. However, the graders must be able to identify quickly which question you are answering. You may wish to underline any *key words* or *key concepts* in your answer. Do not underline too much, however, because doing so may obscure your reasons for underlining. In free-response questions that require specific calculations or the determination of products, you may also want to underline or draw a box around your final answer(s). In Part II of this guide, we indicate the answers to such free-response questions in **boldface type.**

After you have written the problem number, restate the question in as few words as possible, but do not leave out any essential information. Often a diagram will help. By restating, you put the question in your own words and allow time for your mind to organize the way you intend to answer the questions. As a result, you eliminate a great deal of unnecessary language that clutters the basic idea. Even if you do not answer the question, a restatement may be worth 1 point.

If a question has several parts, such as (a), (b), (c), and (d), do *not* write all of the restatements together. Instead, write each restatement separately when you begin to answer that part. In this book, you will see many examples of the use of restatements.

## Four Techniques for Answering Free-Response Questions

When you begin Section II, the essays, the last thing you want to do is start writing immediately. Take a minute and scan the questions. Find the questions that you know you will have the most success with, and put a star (*) next to them in your booklet. *You do not have to answer the questions in order;* however, you must number them clearly in your response book.

After you have identified the questions that you will eventually answer, the next step is to decide what format each question lends itself to. There are four basic formats. Let's do an actual essay question to demonstrate each format.

### The Chart Format

In this format, you fill in a chart to answer the question. When you draw the chart, use the edge of your calculator case to make straight lines. Fill in the blanks with symbols, phrases, or *incomplete* sentences. The grid forces you to record all answers quickly and makes it unlikely that you will forget to give any part of the answer.

*Essay 1*

**Given the molecule $SF_6$, $XeF_4$, $PF_5$, and $ClF_3$:**
**(a) Draw a Lewis structure for each molecule.**
**(b) Identify the geometry for each molecule.**
**(c) Describe the hybridization of the central atom for each molecule.**
**(d) Give the number of unshared pairs of electrons for each molecule.**

*Answer*

1. Restatement: Given $SF_6$, $XeF_4$, $PF_5$, and $ClF_3$. For each, supply
   (a) Lewis structure
   (b) geometry
   (c) hybridization
   (d) number of unshared pairs of electrons

| | SF$_6$ | XeF$_4$ | PF$_5$ | ClF$_3$ |
|---|---|---|---|---|
| Lewis structure | | | | |
| Geometry | Octahedral | Square planar | Triangular bypyramidal | T-shaped |
| Hybridization | $sp^3d^2$ | $sp^3d^2$ | $sp^3d$ | $sp^3d$ |
| Unshared pairs | 0 | 2 | 0 | 2 |

### The Bullet Format

The bullet format is also a very efficient technique because it, like the chart format, does not require complete sentences. In using this format, you essentially provide a list to answer the question. A • is a bullet, and each new concept receives one. Try to add your bullets in a logical sequence. And leave room to add more bullets; you may want to come back later and fill them in. Don't get discouraged if you do not have as many bullets as the examples contain—it takes practice. Reviewing the key terms at the beginning of each chapter may suggest additional points that you can incorporate.

### Essay 2

**As one examines the periodic table, one discovers that the melting points of the alkali metals increase as one moves from cesium to lithium, whereas the melting points of the halogens increase from fluorine to iodine.**
**(a) Explain the phenomenon observed in the melting points of the alkali metals.**
**(b) Explain the phenomenon observed in the melting points of the halogens.**
**(c) Given the compounds CsI, NaCl, LiF, and KBr, predict the order of their melting points (from high to low) and explain your answer using chemical principles.**

*Answer*

2. Given—melting points:    alkali metals increase from Cs → Li
                            halogens increase from F → I

    (a)  Restatement: Explain alkali metal trend.

- Observed melting point order: Li > Na > K > Rb > Cs
- All elements are metals
- All elements contain metallic bonds
- Electrons are free to migrate in a "sea"
- As one moves down the group, size (radius) of the atoms increases
- As volume of atom increases, charge density decreases
- Attractive force between atoms is directly proportional to melting point
- Therefore, as attractive forces decrease moving down the group, melting point decreases

    (b)  Restatement: Explain halogen trend.

- Observed melting point order: I > Br > Cl > F
- All halogens are nonmetals
- Intramolecular forces = covalent bonding
- Intermolecular forces = dispersion (van der Waals) forces, which exist between molecules
- Dispersion forces result from "temporary" dipoles caused by polarization of electron clouds
- As one moves up the group, the electron clouds become smaller
- Smaller electron clouds result in higher charge density
- As one moves up the group, electron clouds are less readily polarized
- Less readily polarized clouds result in weaker dispersion forces holding molecules to other molecules
- Therefore, attractive forces between molecules decrease as one moves up the group, resulting in lower melting points
- Added to these is the effect of the increasing molecular weight of the elements

(c) Restatement: Predict melting point order (high to low) CsI, NaCl, LiF, and KBr and explain.

- LiF > NaCl > KBr > CsI
- All compounds contain a metal and a nonmetal
- Predicted order has ionic bonds
- Larger ionic radius results in lower charge density
- Lower charge density results in smaller attractive forces
- Smaller attractive forces result in lower melting point

### The Outline Format

This technique is similar to the bullet format, but instead of bullets it uses the more traditional outline style that you may have used for years: roman numerals, letters, etc. The advantages of this format are that it does not require full sentences and that it progresses in a logical sequence. The disadvantage is that it requires you to spend more time thinking about organization. Leave plenty of room here because you may want to come back later and add more points.

### Essay 3

The boiling points and electrical conductivities of six aqueous solutions are as follows:

| Solution | Boiling Point | Relative Electrical Conductivity |
|---|---|---|
| 0.05 m $BaSO_4$ | 100.0254°C | 0.03 |
| 0.05 m $H_3BO_3$ | 100.0387°C | 0.78 |
| 0.05 m NaCl | 100.0485°C | 1.00 |
| 0.05 m $MgCl_2$ | 100.0689°C | 2.00 |
| 0.05 m $FeCl_3$ | 100.0867°C | 3.00 |
| 0.05 m $C_6H_{12}O_6$ | 100.0255°C | 0.01 |

Discuss the relationship among the composition, the boiling point, and the electrical conductivity of each solution.

*Answer*

3. Given: Boiling point data and electrical conductivities of six aqueous solutions, all at 0.05 m.

   Restatement: Discuss any relationships between B.P. and electrical conductivities.

   I. $BaSO_4$ (*If you have a highlighter with you, highlight the main categories.*)

      A. $BaSO_4$ is an ionic compound.

      B. According to known solubility rules, $BaSO_4$ is not very soluble.

         1. If $BaSO_4$ were totally soluble, one would expect its B.P. to be very close to that of NaCl because $BaSO_4$ would be expected to dissociate into two ions ($Ba^{2+}$ and $SO_4^{2-}$) just as NaCl would ($Na^+$ and $Cl^-$). The substantial difference between the B.P. of the NaCl solution and that of the $BaSO_4$ solution suggests that the dissociation of the latter is negligible.

         2. The electrical conductivity of $BaSO_4$ is closest to that of $C_6H_{12}O_6$, an organic molecule, which does not dissociate; this observation further supports the previous evidence of the weak-electrolyte properties of $BaSO_4$.

   II. $H_3BO_3$

      A. $H_3BO_3$ is a weak acid.

      B. In the equation $\Delta t = i \cdot m \cdot K_b$, where $\Delta t$ is the boiling-point elevation, $m$ is the molality of the solution, and $K_b$ is the boiling-point-elevation constant for water, $i$ (the van't Hoff factor) would be expected to be 4 if $H_3BO_3$ were completely ionized. According to data provided, $i$ is about 1.5. Therefore, $H_3BO_3$ must have a relatively low $K_a$.

III. NaCl, $MgCl_2$, and $FeCl_3$

   A. All three compounds are chlorides known to be completely soluble in water, so they are strong electrolytes and would increase electrical conductivities.

   B. The van't Hoff factor ($i$) would be expected to be 2 for NaCl, 3 for $MgCl_2$, and 4 for $FeCl_3$.

   C. Using the equation

$$i = \frac{\Delta t}{m \cdot K_b} \qquad \frac{(\text{B.P. of solution } - 100°C)}{0.05 \, \dfrac{\text{mole solute}}{\text{kg}} \cdot 0.512°C \, \dfrac{\text{kg}}{\text{mole solute}}}$$

we find that the van't Hoff factors for these solutions are

| | Calculated | Expected |
|---|---|---|
| NaCl | 1.9 | 2.0 |
| $MgCl_2$ | 2.7 | 3.0 |
| $FeCl_3$ | 3.4 | 4.0 |

   which are in agreement.

   D. The electrical conductivity data support the rationale just provided: The greater the number of particles, which in this case are ions, the higher the B.P.

IV. $C_6H_{12}O_6$

   A. $C_6H_{12}O_6$, glucose, is an organic molecule. It would not be expected to dissociate into ions that would conduct electricity. The reported electrical conductivity for glucose supports this.

B. Because $C_6H_{12}O_6$ does not dissociate, $i$ is expected to be close to 1. The equation in III.C. gives $i$ as exactly 1.

C. The boiling-point-elevation constant of $0.512°C \cdot kg/mole$ would be expected to raise the B.P. $0.0256°C$ for a 0.05 m solution when $n = 1$. The data show that the boiling-point elevation is $0.0255°C$. This agrees with the theory. Therefore, $C_6H_{12}O_6$ does not dissociate. With few or no ions in solution, poor electrical conductivity is expected. This is supported by the evidence in the table.

### The Free Style

This method is the one most commonly used, although in my opinion, it is the method of last resort. Free style often results in aimless, rambling, messy, incomplete answers. This method is simply writing paragraphs to explain the question. If you do adopt this method for an answer (and many questions lend themselves only to this method), you must organize the paragraphs before writing. Also review your list of key terms to see if there are any concepts you want to add to your answers. Note, however, that adding thoughts at a later time is difficult with this approach because they will be out of logical sequence. (Unlike the bullet and outline formats, free style doesn't leave you room to add more ideas where they belong.)

### Essay 4

**If one completely vaporizes a measured amount of a volatile liquid, the molecular weight of the liquid can be determined by measuring the volume, temperature, and pressure of the resulting gas. When one uses this procedure, one uses the ideal gas equation and assumes that the gas behaves ideally. However, if the sample is slightly above the boiling point of the liquid, the gas deviates from ideal behavior. Explain the postulates of the ideal gas equation, and explain why, when measurements are taken just above the boiling point, the calculated molecular weight of a liquid deviates from the true value.**

*Answer*

4. Restatement: Explain ideal gas equation and why MW measurements taken above boiling point deviate.

The ideal gas equation, $PV = nRT$, stems from three relationships known to be true for gases under ordinary conditions:

1. The volume is directly proportional to the amount, $V \sim n$
2. The volume is directly proportional to the absolute temperature, $V \sim T$
3. The volume is inversely proportional to the pressure, $V \sim 1/P$

We obtain $n$, the symbol used for the moles of gas, by dividing the mass of the gas by the molecular weight. In effect, $n = $ mass/molecular weight ($n = m/$MW). Substituting this relationship into the ideal gas law gives

$$PV = \frac{mRT}{\text{MW}}$$

Solving the equation for molecular weight yields

$$\text{MW} = \frac{mRT}{PV}$$

Real gas behavior deviates from the values obtained using the ideal gas equation because the ideal gas equation assumes that (1) the molecules do not occupy space and (2) there is no attractive force between the individual molecules. However, at low temperatures (just above the boiling point of liquid), these factors become significant, and we must use an alternative equation, known as the van der Waals equation, that accounts for them.

At the lower temperatures, a greater attraction exists between the molecules, so the compressibility of the gas is significant. This causes the product of $P \cdot V$ to be smaller than predicted. Because $PV$ is found in the denominator in the foregoing equation, the calculated molecular weight would tend to be higher than the molecular weight actually is.

# MATHEMATICAL OPERATIONS

## SIGNIFICANT FIGURES

In order to receive full credit in Section II, the essay section, you must be able to express your answer with the correct number of significant figures (s.f.). There are slight penalties on the AP chemistry exam for not doing so. The "golden rule" for using significant figures is that *your answer cannot contain more significant figures than the least accurately measured quantity. Do not use conversion factors for determining significant figures.* Review the following rules for determining significant figures. Underlined numbers are significant.

- Any digit that is not zero is significant. $\underline{123}$ = 3 s.f.

- Zeros between significant figures (captive zeros) are significant. $\underline{80601}$ = 5 s.f.; $\underline{10.001}$ = 5 s.f.

- Zeros to the left of the first nonzero digit (leading zeros) are not significant. $0.00\underline{2}$ = 1 s.f.

- If a number is equal to or greater than 1, then all the zeros written to the right of the decimal point (trailing zeros) count as significant figures. $\underline{9.00}$ = 3 s.f. The number 100 has only one significant figure ($\underline{1}00$), but written as 100. (note the decimal point), it has three significant figures. $\underline{400.}$ = 3 s.f.

- For numbers less than 1, only zeros that are at the end of the number and zeros that are between nonzero digits are significant. $0.0\underline{70}$ = 2 s.f.

- For addition or subtraction, the limiting term is the one with the smallest number of decimal places, so count the decimal places. For multiplication and division, the limiting term is the number that has the least number of significant figures, so count the significant figures.

$$11.01 + 6.\mathbf{2} + 8.995 = 26.\mathbf{2} \text{ (one decimal place)}$$

$$32.010 \times \underline{501} = 1.60 \times 10^4 \text{ (three significant figures)}$$

## LOGS AND ANTILOGS

You will use your calculator in Section II to determine logs and antilogs. There are two types of log numbers that you will use on the AP exam: $\log_{10}$, or log, and natural log, or ln. Log base 10 of a number is that exponent to which 10 must be raised to give the original number. Therefore, the log of 10 is 1 because $10^1$ is 10. The log of 100 is 2 because $10^2$ is 100. The log of 0.001 is $-3$, and so on.

There are a few types of problems on the AP exam in which you may have to use a natural logarithm. The symbol for a natural logarithm is $\ln_e$. The relationship between $\log_{10}$ and $\ln_e$ is given by the equation $\ln_e x = 2.303 \log_{10} x$. Two examples are $\ln 2 = 0.693$ and $e^{0.152} = 1.164$.

## SCIENTIFIC NOTATION

Try to use scientific notation when writing your answers. For example, instead of writing 1,345,255, write $1.345255 \times 10^6$. Remember always to write one digit, a decimal point, the rest of the digits (making sure to use only the correct number of significant figures), and then times 10 to the proper power. An answer such as 0.000045 should be written $4.5 \times 10^{-5}$ (2 s.f.). Also, don't forget that when you multiply exponents you add them and that when you divide exponents you subtract them. Your chemistry textbook or math book probably has a section that covers significant figures, logs, antilogs, scientific notation, and the like. If your math background or algebra skills are weak, you must thoroughly review and polish these skills before attempting to do the problems in this book.

# MATHEMATICS SELF-TEST

Try taking this short mathematics self-test. If you understand these math problems and get the answers correct, you're ready to go on. If you miss problems in this area, you need to back up and review those operations with which you are uncomfortable.

*Determine the number of significant figures in the following numbers.*

1. 100

2. 100.01

3. 0.010

4. 1234.100

*Round the following numbers to the number of significant figures indicated and express in scientific notation.*

5. 100.075 rounded to 3 significant figures

6. 140 rounded to 2 significant figures

7. 0.000787 rounded to 2 significant figures

*Perform the following math operations, expressing your answers to the proper number of significant figures.*

8. $(4.5 \times 10^{-3}) + (5.89 \times 10^{-4})$

9. $(5.768 \times 10^9) \times (6.78 \times 10^{-2})$

10. $(5.661 \times 10^{-9})$ divided by $(7.66 \times 10^{-8})$

11. $8.998 + 9.22 + 1.3 \times 10^2 + 0.006$

*Determine:*

12. log of 98.71

13. log of 0.0043

14. ln of 3.99

15. ln of 0.0564

16. log (0.831/0.111)

17. ln $(1.5^2/3.0 \times 10^{-4})$

*Evaluate:*

18. $e^{7.82}$

*Solve for x:*

19. log $(12.0/x) = 3.0$

20. $40.1 = 5.13^x$

### Answers to Mathematics Self-Test

1. 1 significant figure

2. 5 significant figures

3. 2 significant figures

4. 7 significant figures

5. $1.00 \times 10^2$

6. $1.4 \times 10^2$

7. $7.9 \times 10^{-4}$

8. $5.1 \times 10^{-3}$

9. $3.91 \times 10^8$

10. $7.39 \times 10^{-2}$

11. $1.5 \times 10^2$

12. 1.994

13. $-2.4$

14. 1.38

15. $-2.88$

16. 0.874

17. 8.9

18. $2.49 \times 10^3$

19. $x = 0.012$

20. $x = 2.26$

# Part II: Specific Topics

# GRAVIMETRICS

## Key Terms

Words that can be used as topics in essays:

accuracy

atomic theory

density

empirical formula

extensive property

fractional crystallization

heterogeneous

homogeneous

intensive property

isotopes

law of conservation of mass and energy

law of definite proportions
  (law of constant composition)

limiting reactant

mixture

molecular formula

percentage yield

precision

random error

systematic error

theoretical yield

uncertainty

## Key Concepts

Equations and relationships that you need to know:

- $1 \text{ nm} = 1 \times 10^{-9} \text{ m} = 10 \text{ Å}$

  $1 \text{ cm}^3 = 1 \text{ ml}$

  $°F = 1.8 \, (°C) + 32$

  $K = °C + 273.16$

- density $= \dfrac{\text{mass}}{\text{volume}}$

Avogadro's number $= 6.02 \times 10^{23} = 1$ mole

number of moles $= \dfrac{\text{mass}}{\text{molecular weight}}$

molecular weight $=$ density $\times$ molar volume

% yield $= \dfrac{\text{actual yield}}{\text{theoretical yield}} \times 100\%$

% composition $= \dfrac{\text{mass of element in compound}}{\text{mass of compound}} \times 100\%$

% error $= \dfrac{\text{observed value} - \text{expected value}}{\text{expected value}} \times 100\%$

## Measurement Terms

### SI (International System) Multipliers

| Multiple | Prefix | Symbol |
|----------|--------|--------|
| $10^{12}$ | tera | T |
| $10^{9}$ | giga | G |
| $10^{6}$ | mega | M |
| $10^{3}$ | kilo | k |
| $10^{2}$ | hecto | h |
| $10^{1}$ | deka | da |
| $10^{-1}$ | deci | d |
| $10^{-2}$ | centi | c |
| $10^{-3}$ | milli | m |
| $10^{-6}$ | micro | μ |
| $10^{-9}$ | nano | n |
| $10^{-12}$ | pico | p |
| $10^{-15}$ | femto | f |
| $10^{-18}$ | atto | a |

### SI Base Units

| | |
|---|---|
| meter | m |
| kilogram | kg |
| second | s (sec) |
| ampere | A |
| kelvin | K |
| mole | mol |
| candela | cd |

## SI Derived Units

| becquerel | Bq | 1 disintegration/sec |
| coulomb | C | $A \cdot sec$ |
| farad | F | $A \cdot sec/V = A^2 \cdot sec^4 \cdot kg^{-1} \cdot m^{-2}$ |
| gray | Gy | $J/kg$ |
| henry | H | $Wb/A$ |
| hertz | Hz | $sec^{-1}$ (cycle/sec) |
| joule | J | $kg \cdot m^2 \cdot sec^{-2} = 10^7$ ergs |
| lumen | lm | $cd \cdot sr$ |
| lux | lx | $lm/m^2$ |
| newton | N | $kg \cdot m \cdot sec^{-2}$ |
| pascal | Pa | $N/m^2 = kg \cdot m^{-1} \cdot sec^{-2}$ |
| ohm | $\Omega$ | $V/A = kg \cdot m^2 \cdot sec^{-3} \cdot A^{-2}$ |
| siemens | S | $\Omega^{-1} = A \cdot V^{-1} = sec^3 \cdot A^2 \cdot kg^{-1} \cdot m^{-2}$ |
| tesla | T | $Wb/m^2$ |
| volt | V | $J \cdot A^{-1} \cdot sec^{-1} = kg \cdot m^2 \cdot sec^{-3} \cdot A^{-1}$ |
| watt | W | $J/sec = kg \cdot m^2 \cdot sec^{-3}$ |
| weber | Wb | $V \cdot sec$ |

## Non-SI Units

| angstrom | Å | $10^{-8}$ cm |
|---|---|---|
| atmosphere | atm | 101,325 N/m$^2$ or 760 mm Hg or 101.3 kPa or 760 torr |
| bar | bar | $10^5$ N/m$^2$ |
| calorie | cal | 4.184 J |
| dyne | dyn | $10^{-5}$ N $= 1$ g · cm · sec$^{-2}$ $= 2.39 \times 10^{-8}$ cal · cm$^{-1}$ |
| erg | erg | $10^{-7}$ J |
| inch | in | 2.54 cm |
| millimeter of mercury | mm Hg | $13.591 \cdot 980.665 \cdot 10^{-2}$ N/m$^2$ |
| pound | lb | 0.453502 kg |
| torr | torr | 101,325/760 N/m$^2$ |

### Examples: Multiple-Choice Questions

1. **A popular bourbon whiskey is listed as being "92 Proof." The liquor industry defines "Proof" as being twice the weight percentage of alcohol in a blend. Ethanol (drinking alcohol) has the structural formula $CH_3CH_2OH$ (MW = 46 g/mole). If 10. ml of this bourbon whiskey weighs 0.010 kg, how many liters must one have in order to have 50. moles of carbon?**
   (A) 0.80 liters
   (B) 1.0 liters
   (C) 1.5 liters
   (D) 2.0 liters
   (E) 2.5 liters

*Answer: (E)*

*Step 1:* Write down an equals sign (=).

*Step 2:* To the right of the equals sign, write down the units you want the answer to be in. Examination of the problem reveals that you want your answers in "liters of whiskey," so you have

$$= \text{liters of whiskey}$$

*Step 3:* Begin the problem with the item you are limited to. In this case, it is 50. moles of carbon—no more, no less. Place the 50. moles of carbon over 1.

$$\frac{50. \text{ moles of carbon}}{1} = \text{liters of whiskey}$$

*Step 4:* Get rid of the units "moles of carbon" by placing them in the denominator of the next factor. What do you know about moles of carbon? There are 2 moles of carbon in each mole of ethanol.

$$\frac{50. \text{ \sout{moles carbon}}}{1} \times \frac{1 \text{ mole ethanol}}{2 \text{ \sout{moles carbon}}} = \text{liters of whiskey}$$

*Step 5:* Continue in this fashion, getting rid of unwanted units until you are left in the units you desire. At that point, stop and do the calculations.

$$\frac{50. \; \cancel{\text{moles carbon}}}{1} \times \frac{1 \; \cancel{\text{mole ethanol}}}{2 \; \cancel{\text{moles carbon}}} \times \frac{46 \; \cancel{\text{grams ethanol}}}{1 \; \cancel{\text{mole ethanol}}}$$

$$\times \frac{100 \; \cancel{\text{grams whiskey}}}{46 \; \cancel{\text{grams ethanol}}} \times \frac{1 \; \cancel{\text{kg whiskey}}}{1000 \; \cancel{\text{grams whiskey}}}$$

$$\times \frac{10. \; \cancel{\text{ml whiskey}}}{0.010 \; \cancel{\text{kg whiskey}}} \times \frac{1 \; \text{liter whiskey}}{1000 \; \cancel{\text{ml whiskey}}}$$

$$= 2.5 \; \text{liters of whiskey}$$

2. **A sample of a pure compound was found to contain 1.201 grams of carbon, 0.202 grams of hydrogen, and 7.090 grams of chlorine. What is the empirical formula for the compound?**
   (A) $CHCl_3$
   (B) $CH_2Cl$
   (C) $CH_2Cl_2$
   (D) $CH_3Cl$
   (E) $C_2H_2Cl_4$

*Answer: (C)*

First, change the grams of each element to moles. You end up with 0.100 mole of carbon, 0.200 mole of hydrogen, and 0.200 mole of chlorine. This represents a 1 carbon : 2 hydrogen : 2 chlorine molar ratio.

3. **Balance the following equation using the lowest possible whole-number coefficients:**

$$2\,NH_3 + 3\,CuO \rightarrow 3\,Cu + N_2 + 3\,H_2O$$

**The sum of the coefficients is**
(A) 9   (B) 10   (C) 11   (D) 12   (E) 13

*Answer: (D)*

*Step 1:* Begin balancing equations by trying suitable coefficients that will give the same number of atoms of each element on both sides of the equation. Remember to change coefficients, not subscripts.

$$\underline{2}\,\underline{NH_3} \rightarrow \underline{1}\,\underline{N_2}$$

*Step 2:* Look for elements that appear only once on each side of the equation and with equal numbers of atoms on each side. The formulas containing these elements must have the same coefficients.

$$\_\,CuO \rightarrow \_\,Cu$$

*Step 3:* Look for elements that appear only once on each side of the equation but in unequal numbers of atoms. Balance these elements.

$$\underline{2}\,N\underline{H_3} \rightarrow \underline{3}\,\underline{H_2}O$$

*Step 4:* Balance elements that appear in two or more formulas on the same side of the equation.

*Step 5:* Double check your balanced equation and be sure the coefficients are the lowest possible whole numbers.

$$2\,NH_3 + 3\,CuO \rightarrow 3\,Cu + N_2 + 3\,H_2O$$

$$2 + 3 + 3 + 1 + 3 = 12$$

(Be sure to include the unwritten 1 that is in front of $N_2$.)

4. When **0.600** mole of $BaCl_2(aq)$ is mixed with **0.250** mole of $K_3AsO_4$ (aq), what is the maximum number of moles of solid $Ba_3(AsO_4)_2$ that could be formed?
   (A)  **0.125 mole**
   (B)  **0.200 mole**
   (C)  **0.250 mole**
   (D)  **0.375 mole**
   (E)  **0.500 mole**

*Answer: (A)*

Begin by writing a balanced equation:

$$3\ BaCl_2 + 2\ K_3AsO_4 \rightarrow Ba_3(AsO_4)_2 + 6\ KCl$$

Next, realize that this problem is a limited-reactant problem. That is, one of the two reactants will run out first, and when that happens, the reaction will stop. You need to determine which one of the reactants will run out first. To do this, you need to be able to compare them on a 1:1 basis. But their coefficients are different, so you need to relate both reactants to a common product, say $Ba_3(AsO_4)_2$. Set the problem up like this:

$$\frac{0.600\ \text{mole } BaCl_2}{1} \times \frac{1\ \text{mole } Ba_3(AsO_4)_2}{3\ \text{moles } BaCl_2} = 0.200\ \text{mole } Ba_3(AsO_4)_2$$

$$\frac{0.250\ \text{mole } K_3AsO_4}{1} \times \frac{1\ \text{mole } Ba_3(AsO_4)_2}{2\ \text{moles } K_3AsO_4} = 0.125\ \text{mole } Ba_3(AsO_4)_2$$

Given the two amounts of starting materials, you discover that you can make a maximum of 0.125 mole of $Ba_3(AsO_4)_2$, because at that point you will have exhausted your supply of $K_3AsO_4$.

5. **A test tube containing $CaCO_3$ is heated until *all* of the compound decomposes. If the test tube plus calcium carbonate originally weighed 30.08 grams and the loss of mass during the experiment was 4.400 grams, what was the mass of the empty test tube?**
   (A) 20.07 g
   (B) 21.00 g
   (C) 24.50 g
   (D) 25.08 g
   (E) 25.68 g

*Answer: (A)*

Begin by writing a balanced equation. Remember that all Group II carbonates decompose to yield the metallic oxide plus carbon dioxide gas.

$$CaCO_3(s) \rightarrow CaO(s) + CO_2(g)$$

According to your balanced equation, any loss of mass during the experiment would have to have come from the carbon dioxide gas leaving the test tube. 4.400 grams of $CO_2$ gas correspond to 0.1000 mole. Because all of the calcium carbonate decomposed, and the calcium carbonate and carbon dioxide gas are in a 1:1 molar ratio, you must originally have had 0.1000 mole of calcium carbonate, or 10.01 grams. The calcium carbonate and test tube weighed 30.08, so if you get rid of the calcium carbonate, you are left with 20.07 grams for the empty test tube.

6. **32.0 grams of oxygen gas, 32.0 grams of methane gas, and 32.0 grams of sulfur dioxide gas are mixed. What is the mole fraction of the oxygen gas?**
   (A) 0.143  (B) 0.286  (C) 0.333  (D) 0.572  (E) 0.666

*Answer: (B)*

First change all the grams to moles:

$$32.0 \text{ grams of } O_2 = 1.00 \text{ mole}$$
$$32.0 \text{ grams of } CH_4 = 2.00 \text{ moles}$$
$$32.0 \text{ grams of } SO_2 = 0.500 \text{ mole}$$

Mole fraction of oxygen gas: $\dfrac{1 \text{ mole } O_2}{3.50 \text{ total moles}} = 0.286$ mole fraction

7. **Element X is found in two forms: 90.0% is an isotope that has a mass of 20.0, and 10.0% is an isotope that has a mass of 22.0. What is the atomic mass of element X?**
   (A) 20.1  (B) 20.2  (C) 20.8  (D) 21.2  (E) 21.8

*Answer: (B)*

To solve this problem, multiply the percentage of each isotope by its atomic mass and add those products.

$(0.900 \times 20.0) + (0.100 \times 22.0) = 20.2$ atomic mass of element X

8. **What is the formula of a compound formed by combining 50. grams of element X (atomic weight = 100.) and 32 grams of oxygen gas?**
   (A) $XO_2$  (B) $XO_4$  (C) $X_4O$  (D) $X_2O$  (E) $XO$

*Answer: (B)*

According to the information given, you have 0.50 mole of element X (50. g/100. g · mole$^{-1}$ = 0.50 mole). For the oxygen, remember that you will use 16 g/mole for the atomic weight, giving you 2.0 moles of oxygen atoms. A 0.50:2.0 molar ratio is the same as a 1:4 molar ratio, so the answer is $XO_4$.

9. **An oxide is known to have the formula $X_2O_7$ and to contain 76.8% X by mass. Which of the following would you use to determine the atomic mass of X?**

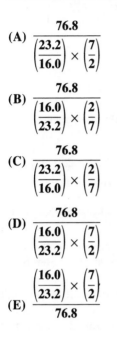

(A) $$\dfrac{76.8}{\left(\dfrac{23.2}{16.0}\right) \times \left(\dfrac{7}{2}\right)}$$

(B) $$\dfrac{76.8}{\left(\dfrac{16.0}{23.2}\right) \times \left(\dfrac{2}{7}\right)}$$

(C) $$\dfrac{76.8}{\left(\dfrac{23.2}{16.0}\right) \times \left(\dfrac{2}{7}\right)}$$

(D) $$\dfrac{76.8}{\left(\dfrac{16.0}{23.2}\right) \times \left(\dfrac{7}{2}\right)}$$

(E) $$\dfrac{\left(\dfrac{16.0}{23.2}\right) \times \left(\dfrac{7}{2}\right)}{76.8}$$

*Answer: (C)*

From the information provided, you know that the oxide $X_2O_7$ contains 76.8% X and 23.2% oxygen by weight. If you had 100.0 g of the oxide, you would have 76.8 g of X and 23.2 g of O (or 23.2/16.0 moles of O atoms). Because for each mole of O in the oxide you have 2/7 mole of X, you have in effect (23.2/16.0) × 2/7 mole of X. Since the units of atomic mass are g/mole, the setup is:

$$\dfrac{76.8}{\left(\dfrac{23.2}{16.0}\right) \times \left(\dfrac{2}{7}\right)}$$

Finding the solution is unnecesssary for selecting an answer; however, here is the solution for your information.

$$\frac{76.8 \text{ g X}}{\left(\dfrac{23.2 \text{ g O}}{16.0 \text{ g O/mole O}}\right) \times \left(\dfrac{2 \text{ mole X}}{7 \text{ mole O}}\right)} = 186 \text{ g/mole}$$

(The element is rhenium.)

10. **A freshman chemist analyzed a sample of copper(II) sulfate pentahydrate for water of hydration by weighing the hydrate, heating it to convert it to anhydrous copper(II) sulfate, and then weighing the anhydride. The % $H_2O$ was determined to be 30%. The theoretical value is 33%. Which of the following choices is definitely NOT the cause of the error?**
    (A) **After the student weighed the hydrate, a piece of rust fell from the tongs into the crucible.**
    (B) **Moisture driven from the hydrate condensed on the inside of the crucible cover before the student weighed the anhydride.**
    (C) **All the weighings were made on a balance that was high by 10%.**
    (D) **The original sample contained some anhydrous copper(II) sulfate.**
    (E) **The original sample was wet.**

*Answer: (E)*

30% $H_2O$ in the hydrate sample represents

$$\frac{\text{mass of hydrate} - \text{mass of anhydride}}{\text{mass of hydrate}} \times 100\%$$

In a problem like this, I like to make up some *easy* fictitious numbers that I can use to fit the scenarios and see how the various changes affect the final outcome. Let's say the mass of the hydrate is 10 g and the mass of the anhydride is 7 g. This would translate as

$$\frac{10 \text{ g} - 7 \text{ g}}{10 \text{ g}} \times 100\% = 30\% \text{ H}_2\text{O}$$

In examining choice (A), the original mass of the hydrate would not change; however, because rust will not evaporate, the final mass of the anhydride would be higher than expected—let's say 8 g. Substituting this value into the formula for % water would give

$$\frac{10 \text{ g} - 8 \text{ g}}{10 \text{ g}} \times 100\% = 20\% \text{ H}_2\text{O}$$

which is less than the theoretical value of 30%. This is in the direction of the student's experimental results, and since we are looking for the choice that is NOT the cause, we can rule out (A) as an answer.

In choice (B), the mass of the hydrate would not change, but the mass of the anhydride would be higher than it should be. Let's estimate the anhydride at 8 g again.

$$\frac{10 \text{ g} - 8 \text{ g}}{10 \text{ g}} \times 100\% = 20\% \text{ H}_2\text{O}$$

In choice (C), because all masses are being measured on a *consistently* wrong balance, the faultiness does not matter in the final answer.

$$\frac{11.0 \text{ g} - 7.7 \text{ g}}{11.0 \text{ g}} \times 100\% = 30.\% \text{ H}_2\text{O}$$

In choice (D), the original mass of the hydrate would remain unchanged. However, the mass of the anhydride would be higher than expected because the sample would lose less water than if it had been a pure hydrate. This fits the scenario of

$$\frac{10 \text{ g} - 8 \text{ g}}{10 \text{ g}} \times 100\% = 20\% \text{ H}_2\text{O}$$

with the error being consistent with the direction of the student's results. Therefore, (D) is not the correct answer.

In choice (E), the original sample is wet. The freshman chemist weighs out 10 g of the hydrate, but more weight is lost in the heating process than expected, making the final mass of the anhydride lower than expected, say 6 g. Using the equation for % $H_2O$ shows

$$\frac{10 \text{ g} - 6 \text{ g}}{10 \text{ g}} \times 100\% = 40\% \text{ H}_2\text{O}$$

which is higher than the theoretical value of 30% and in line with the reasoning that this could NOT have caused the error.

11. **When 100 grams of butane gas ($C_4H_{10}$, MW = 58.14) is burned in excess oxygen gas, the theoretical yield of $H_2O$ is:**

(A) $\dfrac{58.14 \times 18.02}{100 \times 5}$

(B) $\dfrac{5 \times 58.14}{100 \times 18.02}$

(C) $\dfrac{4 \times 18.02}{13/2 \times 100} \times 100\%$

(D) $\dfrac{5 \times 58.14 \times 18.02}{100}$

(E) $\dfrac{100 \times 5 \times 18.02}{58.14}$

*Answer: (E)*

Begin with a balanced equation:

$$C_4H_{10} + 13/2 \, O_2 \rightarrow 4 \, CO_2 + 5 H_2O$$

Next, set up the equation in factor-label fashion:

$$\frac{100 \text{ g } \cancel{C_4H_{10}}}{1} \times \frac{1 \text{ mole } \cancel{C_4H_{10}}}{58.14 \text{ g } \cancel{C_4H_{10}}} \times \frac{5 \text{ moles } \cancel{H_2O}}{1 \text{ mole } \cancel{C_4H_{10}}} \times \frac{18.02 \text{ g H}_2\text{O}}{1 \text{ mole } \cancel{H_2O}} = \text{g H}_2\text{O}$$

12. **Element Q occurs in compounds X, Y, and Z. The mass of element Q in 1 mole of each compound is as follows:**

| Compound | Grams of Q in Compound |
|----------|------------------------|
| X | 38.00 |
| Y | 95.00 |
| Z | 133.00 |

**Element Q is most likely:**
**(A) N   (B) O   (C) F   (D) Ir   (E) Cs**

*Answer: (C)*

All of the numbers are multiples of 19.00 (fluorine). Use the law of multiple proportions.

13. **Which one of the following represents an intensive property?**
    **(A) temperature**
    **(B) mass**
    **(C) volume**
    **(D) length**
    **(E) heat capacity**

*Answer: (A)*

The measured value of an intensive property does NOT depend on how much matter is being considered. The formula for heat capacity (C) is $C = m \cdot s$, where m = mass and s = specific heat.

**14. Which of the following would have an answer with three significant figures?**

(A)  $103.1 + 0.0024 + 0.16$

(B)  $(3.0 \times 10^4)(5.022 \times 10^{-3})/(6.112 \times 10^2)$

(C)  $(4.3 \times 10^5)/(4.225 + 56.0003 - 0.8700)$

(D)  $(1.43 \times 10^3 + 3.1 \times 10^1)/(4.11 \times 10^{-6})$

(E)  $(1.41 \times 10^2 + 1.012 \times 10^4)/(3.2 \times 10^{-1})$

*Answer: (D)*

$(1.43 \times 10^3 + 3.1 \times 10^1) = 14.3 \times 10^2 + 0.31 \times 10^2 = 14.6 \times 10^2$

$$= \frac{14.6 \times 10^2}{\underline{4.11} \times 10^{-6}} = 3 \text{ s.f. } (\underline{3.55} \times 10^8)$$

## Examples: Free-Response Questions

1. A student performed the following experiment in the laboratory: She suspended a clean piece of silver metal in an evacuated test tube. The empty test tube weighed 42.8973 grams. The silver weighed 1.7838 grams. Next, she introduced a stream of chlorine gas into the test tube and allowed it to react with the silver. After a few minutes, a white compound was found to have formed on the silver strip, coating it uniformly. She then opened the apparatus, weighed the coated strip, and found it to weigh 1.9342 grams. Finally, she washed the coated strip with distilled water, removing all of the white compound from the silver strip, and then dried the compound and the strip and reweighed. She discovered that the silver strip weighed 1.3258 grams.

   (a) Show how she would determine
      (1) the number of moles of chlorine gas that reacted
      (2) the number of moles of silver that reacted
   (b) Show how she could determine the simplest formula for the silver chloride.
   (c) Show how her results would have been affected if
      (1) some of the white compound had been washed down the sink before it was dried and reweighed
      (2) the silver strip was not thoroughly dried when it was reweighed

*Answer*

*Step 1:* Do a restatement of the general experiment. In this case, I would draw a sketch of the apparatus before and after the reaction, labeling everything. This will get rid of all the words and enable you to visualize the experiment. Be sure to number your general restatement, even if numbered subparts follow.

1.

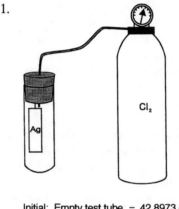

Initial: Empty test tube = 42.8973 g
         Ag strip = 1.7838 g
Final:   Coated strip = 1.9342 g
         Ag strip = 1.3258 g

*Step 2:* Write a balanced chemical equation that describes the reaction.

silver + chlorine gas yields silver chloride.

$$2\,Ag(s) + Cl_2(g) \rightarrow 2\,AgCl(s)$$

*Step 3:* Begin to answer the questions asked. Remember to give a brief restatement for each question, to label each specific question so that the grader knows which question you are answering, and to underline the conclusion(s) where necessary.

1. (a) (1) Restatement: Number of moles of chlorine atoms that reacted.

mass of chlorine that reacted
= (mass of silver strip + compound)
                                        − mass of original silver strip

1.9342 g − 1.7838 g = 0.1504 g of chlorine atoms

moles of chlorine atoms that reacted
= mass of chlorine atoms/atomic mass of chlorine

*(Do not use $Cl_2(g)$ for chlorine, because you will eventually be using the moles of chlorine to get to a molar ratio of silver atoms to chlorine atoms.)*

0.1504 g/35.45 g · mole$^{-1}$
                        = **0.004243 mole of chlorine atoms**

(a) (2) Restatement: Moles of silver that reacted.

moles of silver atoms
$$= \frac{\text{(mass of original silver strip − mass of dry strip after washing)}}{\text{atomic mass of silver}}$$

1.7838 g − 1.3258 g = 0.4580 g

0.4580 g/107.87 g · mole$^{-1}$ = **0.004246 mole of silver atoms**

(b) Restatement: Empirical formula for silver chloride.

empirical formula
                = moles of silver atoms/moles of chlorine atoms

$$\frac{0.004246 \text{ mole of silver}}{0.004242 \text{ mole of chlorine}} = 1.001 \rightarrow \textbf{AgCl}$$

(c) (1) Restatement: Effect on the empirical formula if some of the white product got washed down the sink before being weighed.

The white product was silver chloride. Had she lost some before she weighed it, the mass of silver chloride would have been less than what it should have been. This would have made the number of grams of chlorine appear too low, which in turn would have made the number of moles of chlorine appear too low. Thus, in the ratio of moles of silver to moles of chlorine, the denominator would have been lower than expected and **the ratio would have been *larger*.** Because the mass of the compound does not enter into the calculations for the moles of silver that reacted, the moles of silver would not have been affected.

(c) (2) Restatement: Effect on the empirical formula if the silver strip had not been dried thoroughly after being washed free of the silver chloride.

Because the strip has been washed free of the compound (silver chloride), you assume that any silver missing from the strip went into the making of the silver chloride. If the strip had been wet when you weighed it, you would have been led to think that the strip was heavier than expected, and therefore that less silver had gone into the making of the silver chloride. Thinking that less silver had been involved in the reaction, you would have calculated fewer moles of silver. The calculated **ratio of moles of silver to moles of chlorine would have been *less than expected*.**

2. **Three compounds, D, E, and F, all contain element G. The percent (by weight) of element G in each of the compounds was determined by analysis. The experimental data are presented in the following chart.**

| Compound | % by Weight of Element G | Molecular Weight |
|----------|--------------------------|------------------|
| D | 53.9% | 131.7 |
| E | 64.2% | 165.9 |
| F | 47.7% | 74.5 |

(a) **Determine the mass of element G contained in 1.00 mole of each of compounds D, E, and F.**

(b) **What is the most likely value for the atomic weight of element G?**

(c) **Compound F contains carbon, hydrogen, and element G. When 2.19 g of compound F is completely burned in oxygen gas, 3.88 g of carbon dioxide gas and 0.80 g of water are produced. What is the most likely formula for compound F?**

*Answer*

2. Given: Compounds D, E, and F with % (by weight of element G) and their respective MW's

(a) Restatement: Calculate the mass of element G in 1.00 mole of compounds D, E, and F.

$$0.539 \times 131.7 \text{ g/mole} = \textbf{71.0 g G/mole D}$$
$$0.642 \times 165.9 \text{ g/mole} = \textbf{107 g G/mole E}$$
$$0.477 \times 74.5 \text{ g/mole} = \textbf{35.5 g G/mole F}$$

(b) Restatement: Most likely atomic weight of G.

According to the law of multiple proportions, the ratios of the mass of element G to the masses of compounds D, E, and F must be small, whole numbers. The largest common denominator of 71.0, 106.5, and 35.5 is 35.5, so our best estimate is that the **atomic weight of G is 35.5** (chlorine).

(c) Restatement: Compound $F = C_xH_yG_z$ or $C_xH_yCl_z$?

$$C_xH_yCl_z + O_2(g) \rightarrow CO_2(g) + H_2O(\ell) + Cl_2(g)$$

$$2.19 \text{ g} + \text{ ? g} \rightarrow 3.88 \text{ g} + 0.80 \text{ g} + \text{ ? g } Cl_2(g)$$

moles of carbon = moles of $CO_2$

$$= \frac{3.88 \text{ g } CO_2}{44.01 \text{ g} \cdot \text{mole}^{-1}} = 0.0882$$

moles of hydrogen = $2 \times$ moles of $H_2O$

$$= 2 \times \frac{0.80 \text{ g } H_2O}{18.02 \text{ g} \cdot \text{mole}^{-1}} = 0.088$$

(2.19 grams of F)(1 mole F/74.5 g F) = 0.0294 mole of compound F

This means that each mole of F contains 3 moles of C (0.0882/0.0294) and 3 moles of H (0.088), or 39 grams of CH. This leaves $74.5 - 39 = 36$ grams, corresponding to 1 mole of element G (Cl). Therefore, the empirical formula is **$C_3H_3Cl$.**

# THERMOCHEMISTRY

## Key Terms

Words that can be used as topics in essays:

adiabatic

calorimeter

endothermic

enthalpy

entropy

exothermic

first law of thermodynamics

Gibbs free energy

heat

heat of dilution

heat of formation

heat of fusion

heat of hydration

heat of reaction

heat of solution

Hess's law

internal energy

kinetic energy

law of conservation of energy

potential energy

second law of thermodynamics

specific heat

standard state

state property (function)

surroundings

system (closed, isolated, open)

temperature

thermodynamics

third law of thermodynamics

work

## Key Concepts

Equations and relationships that you need to know:

- Endothermic reaction has $+\Delta H$;  $H_{products} > H_{reactants}$

  Exothermic reaction has $-\Delta H$;  $H_{products} < H_{reactants}$

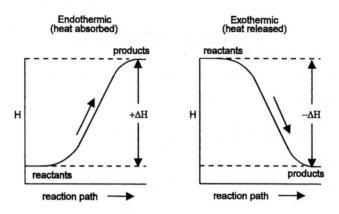

$$\Delta H = \Delta E + w = \Delta E + (\Delta n)RT = \Delta E + P\Delta V$$

- $\Delta E = q + w = q + P\Delta V = q_v$

  $\Delta E = E_{final} - E_{initial}$

- $w = -P_{external} \cdot \Delta V = \Delta n_{gas} RT$

  where $n$ = gaseous moles of product − gaseous moles of reactants. For gas expansion, $\Delta V > 0$, so $-P\Delta V$ is negative. For gas compression, $\Delta V < 0$, so $-P\Delta V$ is a positive quantity.

$$w = 2.30 \, RT \log \frac{V_f}{V_i} \text{ (constant temperature)}$$

|         | Done *on* a system | Done *by* a system |
|---------|--------------------|--------------------|
| Work, $w$ | $+w$ | $-w$ |
| Heat, $q$ | $+q$ (endothermic) | $-q$ (exothermic) |

- "bomb" calorimeter

  $\boxed{\Delta E = q_v}$ (valid with constant volume: "bomb" calorimeter)

  $q_{\text{reaction}} = -(q_{\text{water}} + q_{\text{bomb}})$

  $q_{\text{bomb}} = C \cdot \Delta t$
  where $C$ = calorimeter constant (heat capacity) in J/°C.

- "coffee cup" calorimeter

  $\boxed{\Delta H = q_p}$ (valid with constant pressure: "coffee cup" calorimeter)

  $q = m \cdot c \cdot \Delta t$

  $Cp = \dfrac{\Delta H}{\Delta t}$

  $\Delta H_{\text{reaction}} = -q_{\text{water}}$

  specific heat of water $= \dfrac{4.18 \text{ J}}{\text{g} \cdot \text{°C}} = \dfrac{1 \text{ cal}}{\text{g} \cdot \text{°C}}$

  $\Delta H° = \Sigma H°_{f\,\text{products}} - \Sigma H°_{f\,\text{reactants}} = q_p$
  where $q_p$ = heat flow, constant $p$

  $-\Delta H°_f - \frac{1}{2}\Delta H°\text{diss}$ (for diatomic gaseous molecules)

  1 calorie = 4.184 Joules
  101 Joules = 1 liter · atm
  24.14 calories = 1 liter · atm

- law of Dulong and Petit
  molar mass · specific heat $\approx$ 25 J/mole · °C

- first law of thermodynamics

  $\Delta E = q + w = q_p - P\Delta V = \Delta H - P\Delta V$

  In any process, the total change in energy of the system, $\Delta E$, is equal to the sum of the heat absorbed, $q$, and the work, $w$, done on the system.

- second law of thermodynamics

$\Delta S_{\text{univ}} = \Delta S_{\text{sys}} + \Delta S_{\text{surr}} > 0$    spontaneous

$\Delta S_{\text{univ}} = \Delta S_{\text{sys}} + \Delta S_{\text{surr}} < 0$    nonspontaneous

$\Delta S_{\text{univ}} = \Delta S_{\text{sys}} + \Delta S_{\text{surr}} = 0$    equilibrium

The entropy of the universe increases in a spontaneous process and remains unchanged in an equilibrium process.

- third law of thermodynamics

$S^\circ = q_p/T$

$\Delta S^\circ = \Sigma S^\circ_{\text{products}} - \Sigma S^\circ_{\text{reactants}}$

The entropy of a perfect crystalline substance is zero at absolute zero.

- Hess's law: If reaction (1) has $\Delta H_1$ and reaction (2) has $\Delta H_2$ and reaction (1) + reaction (2) = reaction (3), then

$$\Delta H_3 = \Delta H_1 + \Delta H_2$$

- Bond breaking: potential energy (enthalpy) of bond is increased; "strong" bonds → "weak" bonds; $\Delta H > 0$.

Bond forming: potential energy (enthalpy) of bond is decreased; bond distance is decreased; "weak" bonds → "strong" bonds; $\Delta H < 0$.

$\Delta H = \Sigma$ bond energy (reactants) $- \Sigma$ bond energy (products) = total energy input $-$ total energy released

- given: $aA + bB = cC + dD$

$\Delta S_{\text{rxn (or sys)}} = [cS^\circ(C) + dS^\circ(D)] - [aS^\circ(A) + bS^\circ(B)]$

$\Delta S_{\text{surr}} = \dfrac{-\Delta H}{T}$ which derives to $\boxed{\Delta G = \Delta H - T\Delta S}$

$\Delta G^\circ = \Sigma \Delta G^\circ_{f\,\text{products}} - \Sigma \Delta G^\circ_{f\,\text{reactants}}$

$\Delta G^\circ = -RT \ln K = -2.303\,RT \log K = -n\mathscr{F}E^\circ$

$\Delta G = \Delta G^\circ + RT \ln Q = \Delta G^\circ + 2.303\,RT \log Q$

## Examples: Multiple-Choice Questions

1. **Given the following information:**

   **Reaction (1):** $H_2(g) + 1/2\ O_2(g) \rightarrow H_2O(\ell)$   $\Delta H° = -286$ kJ

   **Reaction (2):** $CO_2(g) \rightarrow C(s) + O_2(g)$   $\Delta H° = 394$ kJ

   **Reaction (3):** $2\ CO_2(g) + H_2O(\ell) \rightarrow$

   $$C_2H_2(g) + 5/2\ O_2(g) \quad \Delta H° = 1300 \text{ kJ}$$

   **Find $\Delta H°$ for the reaction $C_2H_2(g) \rightarrow 2\ C(s) + H_2(g)$.**

   (A)  $-226$ kJ
   (B)  $-113$ kJ
   (C)   113 kJ
   (D)   226 kJ
   (E)   452 kJ

*Answer: (A)*

Recognize that this is a Hess's law problem, which basically requires that you rearrange the three reactions listed if necessary (remembering to reverse the sign of $\Delta H°$ if you reverse the reaction) and then add up the reactions and the $\Delta H°$'s for the answer.

Looking at the first reaction, you notice that $H_2(g)$ is on the wrong side. This requires that you reverse the reaction, thus changing the sign of $\Delta H°$. In the second reaction, C is on the correct side of the equation, so the second equation should be left as is. In the third reaction, $C_2H_2(g)$ is on the wrong side of the equation, so the reaction and the sign of $\Delta H°$ must be reversed. At this point the set-up should look like

$H_2O(\ell) \rightarrow H_2(g) + 1/2\ O_2(g)$ $\quad\quad\quad\quad$ $\Delta H° = +286$ kJ

$CO_2(g) \rightarrow C(s) + O_2(g)$ $\quad\quad\quad\quad\quad\quad$ $\Delta H° = +394$ kJ

$C_2H_2(g) + 5/2\ O_2(g) \rightarrow 2\ CO_2(g) + H_2O(\ell)$ $\quad$ $\Delta H° = -1300$ kJ

Before you add up the three reactions, note that there is no $CO_2(g)$ in the final reaction. The 2 $CO_2(g)$ in the third reaction must be able to cancel with two $CO_2(g)$'s in the second reaction. In order to get 2 $CO_2(g)$ in the second reaction, multiply everything in the second equation by 2, which yields

$$\begin{array}{ll} \cancel{H_2O(\ell)} \rightarrow H_2(g) + \cancel{1/2\,O_2(g)} & \Delta H° = +286 \text{ kJ} \\ \cancel{2\,CO_2(g)} \rightarrow 2\,C(s) + \cancel{2\,O_2(g)} & \Delta H° = +788 \text{ kJ} \\ \underline{C_2H_2(g) + \cancel{5/2\,O_2(g)} \rightarrow \cancel{2\,CO_2(g)} + \cancel{H_2O(\ell)}} & \underline{\Delta H° = -1300 \text{ kJ}} \\ C_2H_2(g) \rightarrow H_2(g) + 2\,C(s) & \Delta H° = -226 \text{ kJ} \end{array}$$

2. **A piece of metal weighing 500. grams is put into a boiling water bath. After 10 minutes, the metal is immediately placed in 250. grams of water at 40.°C. The maximum temperature that the system reaches is 50.°C. What is the specific heat of the metal? (The specific heat of water is 1.00 cal/g · °C.)**
   (A) **0.010 cal/g · °C**
   (B) **0.050 cal/g · °C**
   (C) **0.10 cal/g · °C**
   (D) **0.20 cal/g · °C**
   (E) **0.50 cal/g · °C**

*Answer: (C)*

Begin this problem by realizing that the heat gained by the water is equal to the heat lost by the metal.

heat lost or gained = specific heat of the substance
$$\times \text{ mass of the substance} \times \Delta t$$

Substituting the numbers into this concept gives

$$\text{heat gained by water} = \text{heat lost by metal}$$

$$(1.00 \text{ cal/g} \cdot °C) \times (250. \text{ g } H_2O) \times (50.°C - 40.°C)$$

$$= -(x \text{ cal/g} \cdot °C) \times (500. \text{ g metal})(50.°C - 100.°C)$$

$$2500 = 25{,}000\,x$$

$$x = 0.10 \text{ cal/g} \cdot °C$$

3. Given the following heat of reaction and the bond energies listed in the accompanying table, calculate the energy of the C=O bond. All numerical values are in kilocalories per mole, and all substances are in the gas phase.

$$CH_3CHO + H_2 \rightarrow CH_3CH_2OH \qquad \Delta H° = -17 \text{ kcal/mole}$$

| Bond | O—H | C—H | C—C | C—O | H—H |
|---|---|---|---|---|---|
| Bond Energy (kcal/mole) | 111 | 99 | 83 | 84 | 104 |

- (A) 79 kcal
- (B) 157 kcal
- (C) 173 kcal
- (D) 190 kcal
- (E) 277 kcal

*Answer: (C)*

Begin this problem by drawing a structural diagram of the reaction.

$$
\begin{array}{ccc}
\text{H} & & \text{H} \quad \text{H} \\
| & & | \quad\; | \\
\text{H—C—C=O} + \text{H—H} & \rightarrow & \text{H—C—C—O—H} \\
| \;\; | & & | \quad\; | \\
\text{H} \;\; \text{H} & & \text{H} \quad \text{H}
\end{array}
$$

There are three steps you need to take to do this problem:

*Step 1:* Decide which bonds need to be broken on the reactant side of the reaction. Add up all the bond energies for the bonds that are broken. Call this subtotal $\Delta H_1$. Assign $\Delta H_1$ a positive value because energy is required when bonds are broken. In the example given, a C=O and a H—H bond need to be broken. This becomes $x$ kcal/mole + 104 kcal/mole, or $\Delta H_1 = 104 + x$ kcal/mole.

*Step 2:* Decide which bonds need to be formed on the product side of the reaction. Add up all of the bond energies that are formed. Call this subtotal $\Delta H_2$. Assign $\Delta H_2$ a negative value because energy is released when bonds are formed. In the example given, a C—H, a C—O, and a O—H bond need to be formed. This becomes 99 kcal/mole + 84 kcal/mole + 111 kcal/mole, or 294 kcal/mole. Remember to assign a negative sign, which makes $\Delta H_2 = -294$ kcal/mole.

*Step 3:* Apply Hess's law: $\Delta H° = \Delta H_1 + \Delta H_2$. You know that $\Delta H°$ is $-17$ kcal/mole, so Hess's law becomes

$-17$ kcal/mole $= 104$ kcal/mole $+ x$ kcal/mole $- 294$ kcal/mole

$x = 173$ kcal/mole

which represents the bond energy of the C$=$O bond.

**4. Given the following heats of formation:**

| Substance | $\Delta H_f°$ |
|-----------|---------------|
| acetic acid | $-120$ kcal/mole |
| carbon dioxide | $-95$ kcal/mole |
| water | $-60$ kcal/mole |

**Find $\Delta H°$ of combustion for acetic acid ($CH_3COOH$).**

(A)  $-430$ kcal/mole
(B)  $-190$ kcal/mole
(C)   $-45$ kcal/mole
(D)    45 kcal/mole
(E)   190 kcal/mole

*Answer: (B)*

Begin this problem by realizing that $\Delta H°$ of combustion for acetic acid represents the amount of heat released when acetic acid burns in oxygen gas. The products are carbon dioxide and water. According to the following balanced equation,

$$CH_3COOH(\ell) + 2\,O_2(g) \rightarrow 2\,CO_2(g) + 2\,H_2O(\ell)$$

Because $\Delta H^\circ = \Sigma H_f^\circ$ products $- \Sigma H_f^\circ$ reactants, you can substitute at this point to give

$\Delta H^\circ = 2(-95 \text{ kcal/mole}) + 2(-60 \text{ kcal/mole}) - (-120 \text{ kcal/mole})$

$\Delta H^\circ = -190 \text{ kcal/mole}$

5. **For $H_2C{=}CH_2(g) + H_2(g) \rightarrow H_3C{-}CH_3(g)$, predict the enthalpy given the following bond dissociation energies:**

**H—C, 413 kJ/mole      H—H, 436 kJ/mole**

**C=C, 614 kJ/mole      C—C, 348 kJ/mole**

(A)  $-656 \text{ kJ/mole}$
(B)  $-343 \text{ kJ/mole}$
(C)  $-289 \text{ kJ/mole}$
(D)  $-124 \text{ kJ/mole}$
(E)  $-102 \text{ kJ/mole}$

*Answer: (D)*

Begin this problem by drawing a structural diagram:

H   H            H   H
|   |            |   |
H—C=C—H  +  H—H  →  H—C—C—H
                        |   |
                        H   H

There are three steps you need to take to do this problem.

*Step 1:* Decide which bonds need to be broken on the reactant side of the reaction. Add up all the bond energies for the bonds that are broken. Call this subtotal $\Delta H_1$, and assign it a positive value because when energy is required, bonds are broken. In the example given, a C=C and a H—H bond need to be broken. This becomes 614 kJ/mole + 436 kJ/mole = $\Delta H_1$ = 1050 kJ/mole.

*Step 2:* Decide which bonds need to be formed on the product side of the reaction. Add up all the bond energies for the bonds that are formed. Call this subtotal $\Delta H_2$. Assign $\Delta H_2$ a negative value because when energy is released, bonds are formed. In the example given, two C—H bonds and a C—C bond need to be formed. This becomes $2 \times 413$ kJ/mole + 348 kJ/mole, or 1174 kJ/mole. Remember to assign a negative sign, which makes $\Delta H_2 = -1174$ kJ/mole.

*Step 3:* Apply Hess's law: $\Delta H° = \Delta H_1 + \Delta H_2$
This becomes 1050 kJ/mole + ($-1174$ kJ/mole) = $-124$ kJ/mole.

6. **According to the law of Dulong and Petit, the best prediction for the specific heat of technetium (Tc), MM = 100., is**
   (A) **0.10 J/g · °C**
   (B) **0.25 J/g · °C**
   (C) **0.50 J/g · °C**
   (D) **0.75 J/g · °C**
   (E) **1.0 J/g · °C**

*Answer: (B)*

The law of Dulong and Petit states that

$$\text{molar mass} \times \text{specific heat} \approx 25 \text{ J/mole} \cdot °C$$

You know that technetium has an atomic mass of 100., and substituting this into the law of Dulong and Petit gives you

$$100. \text{ g/mole} \times x \text{ J/g} \cdot °C \approx 25 \text{ J/mole} \cdot °C$$

$$x \approx 0.25 \text{ J/g} \cdot °C$$

7. **How much heat is necessary to convert 10.0 grams of ice at $-10.0°C$ to steam at 150°C? The specific heat capacity of ice is 0.500 cal/g · °C. The heat of fusion of ice is 76.4 cal/g. The specific heat capacity of water is 1.00 cal/g · °C. The heat of vaporization of water is 539 cal/g. The specific heat capacity of steam is 0.482 cal/g · °C.**
   (A) **2500 cal**
   (B) **4433 cal**
   (C) **7445 cal**
   (D) **8255 cal**
   (E) **9555 cal**

*Answer: (C)*

First, the ice must be heated to its melting point, 0.0°C.

$$(\text{mass}) \times \begin{pmatrix} \text{specific} \\ \text{heat} \\ \text{capacity} \end{pmatrix} \times (\Delta t)$$

$$\frac{10.0 \text{ g ice}}{1} \times \frac{0.500 \text{ cal}}{\text{g} \cdot °\text{C}} \times \frac{10.0°\text{C}}{1} = 50.0 \text{ cal}$$

Next, the ice must be melted.

$$(\text{mass}) \times (\Delta H_{\text{fus}})$$

$$\frac{10.0 \text{ g ice}}{1} \times \frac{76.4 \text{ cal}}{\text{g}} = 764 \text{ cal}$$

Next, the water must be heated to its boiling point, 100.0°C.

$$\frac{10.0 \text{ g water}}{1} \times \frac{1.00 \text{ cal}}{\text{g} \cdot °\text{C}} \times \frac{100.0°\text{C}}{1} = 1.00 \times 10^3 \text{ cal}$$

Next, the water must be vaporized.

$$\frac{10.0 \text{ g water}}{1} \times \frac{539 \text{ cal}}{\text{g}} = 5390 \text{ cal}$$

Next, the steam must be heated to 150.0°C

$$\frac{10.0 \text{ g steam}}{1} \times \frac{0.482 \text{ cal}}{\text{g} \cdot °\text{C}} \times \frac{50.0°\text{C}}{1} = 241 \text{ cal}$$

The last step is to add up all quantities of heat required.

50.0 cal + 764 cal + 1000 cal + 5390 cal + 241 cal = 7445 calories

8. Given these two standard enthalpies of formation:

   Reaction (1)    $S(s) + O_2(g) \rightleftarrows SO_2(g)$        $\Delta H^\circ = -295$ kJ/mole

   Reaction (2)    $S(s) + 3/2\, O_2(g) \rightleftarrows SO_3(g)$        $\Delta H^\circ = -395$ kJ/mole

   What is the reaction heat for $2\, SO_2(g) + O_2(g) \rightleftarrows 2\, SO_3(g)$ under the same conditions?

   (A)  $-1380$ kJ/mole
   (B)  $-690.$ kJ/mole
   (C)  $-295$ kJ/mole
   (D)  $-200.$ kJ/mole
   (E)  $-100.$ kJ/mole

*Answer: (D)*

Examine the first reaction and realize that $SO_2(g)$ needs to be on the reactant side. Reverse the equation and change the sign of $\Delta H^\circ$. When you examine the second reaction, you notice that $SO_3(g)$ is on the correct side, so there is no need to reverse this equation. At this point, your two reactions can be added together.

$$\begin{aligned} SO_2(g) &\rightarrow S(s) + O_2(g) & \Delta H^\circ = \phantom{-}295 \text{ kJ/mole} \\ S(s) + 3/2\, O_2(g) &\rightarrow SO_3(g) & \Delta H^\circ = -395 \text{ kJ/mole} \\ \hline SO_2(g) + 1/2\, O_2(g) &\rightarrow SO_3(g) & \Delta H^\circ = -100. \text{ kJ/mole} \end{aligned}$$

But before concluding that this is your answer, note that the question asks for $\Delta H^\circ$ in terms of 2 moles of $SO_2(g)$. Doubling the $\Delta H^\circ$ gives the answer, $-200.$ kJ/mole.

9. **In expanding from 3.00 to 6.00 liters at a constant pressure of 2.00 atmospheres, a gas absorbs 100.0 calories. (24.14 calories = 1 liter · atm) The change in energy, $\Delta E$, for the gas is**
   (A)  − 600. calories
   (B)  − 100. calories
   (C)   − 44.8 calories
   (D)    44.8 calories
   (E)    100. calories

*Answer: (C)*

The first law of thermodynamics states that $\Delta E = q + w$. Since $w = P_{ext} \cdot \Delta V$, the equation can be stated as

$$\Delta E = \Delta H - P_{ext} \cdot \Delta V$$

$\Delta E = 100.0$ calories $- (2.00$ atmospheres $\cdot 3$ liters $\cdot 24.14$ cal/$l \cdot$ atm$)$
   $= -44.8$ calories

10. **A gas which initially occupies a volume of 6.00 liters at 4.00 atm is allowed to expand to a volume of 14.00 liters at a pressure of 1.00 atm. Calculate the value of work, $w$, done by the gas on the surroundings.**
   (A)  − 8.00 l · atm
   (B)  − 7.00 l · atm
   (C)  6.00 l · atm
   (D)  7.00 l · atm
   (E)  8.00 l · atm

*Answer: (A)*

$$w = -P\Delta V = -(1.00 \text{ atm})(8.00 \text{ liters})$$
$$= -8.00 \text{ l} \cdot \text{atm}$$

Because the gas was expanding, $w$ is negative (work was being done by the system).

11. The molar heat of sublimation for molecular iodine is 62.30 kJ/mole at 25°C and 1.00 atm. Calculate the $\Delta H$ for the reaction

$$I_2(s) \to I_2(g) \quad R = 8.314 \text{ J/mole} \cdot \text{K}$$

(A) $\dfrac{62.30}{8.314 \cdot 298}$

(B) $62.30 - (8.314)(298)$

(C) $62.30 + (8.314)(298)$

(D) $62.30(1000) + 1 \cdot (8.314)(298)$

(E) none of the above are correct

*Answer: (D)*

$\Delta n$ = moles of gaseous product + moles of gaseous reactants
$= 1 - 0 = 1$

Use the equation $\Delta H = \Delta E + \Delta n \cdot RT$

$$= \frac{62.30 \text{ kJ}}{\text{mole}} \times \frac{1000 \text{ J}}{1 \text{ kJ}} + [1 \cdot (8.314 \text{ J/mole} \cdot \text{K}) \cdot (298\text{K})]$$

## Examples: Free-Response Questions

1. **To produce molten iron aboard ships, the Navy uses the thermite reaction, which consists of mixing iron(III) oxide (rust) with powdered aluminum, igniting it, and producing aluminum oxide as a by-product. $\Delta H_f^\circ$ for aluminum oxide is $-1669.8$ kJ/mole, and that for iron(III) oxide is $-822.2$ kJ/mole.**
   (a) **Write a balanced equation for the reaction.**
   (b) **Calculate $\Delta H$ for the reaction.**
   (c) **The specific heat of aluminum oxide is 0.79 J/g · °C, and that of iron is 0.48 J/g · °C. If one were to start the reaction at room temperature, how hot would the aluminum oxide *and* the iron become?**
   (d) **If the temperature needed to melt iron is 1535°C, and the heat of fusion for iron is 270 joules/g, confirm through calculations that the reaction will indeed produce molten iron.**

*Answer*

1. (a) Restatement: Balanced equation.

$$2\ Al(s) + Fe_2O_3(s) \rightarrow Al_2O_3(s) + 2\ Fe(s)$$

   (b) Restatement: Calculation of $\Delta H$.

$$\Delta H = \Sigma \Delta H_f^\circ \text{products} - \Sigma \Delta H_f^\circ \text{reactants}$$

$$\Delta H = [\Delta H_f Al_2O_3(s) + 2\ \Delta H_f Fe(s)] - [2\ \Delta H_f Al(s) + \Delta H_f\ Fe_2O_3(s)]$$

$$\Delta H = [-1669.8 + 2(0)] - [2(0) + (-822.2)]$$
*Remember that $\Delta H_f$ for elements is 0.*

$$\Delta H = -847.6\text{ kJ}$$

(c) Restatement: How hot will the products become?

Given: Specific heat of aluminum oxide = 0.79 J/g · °C

Given: Specific heat of iron = 0.48 J/g · °C

Going back to the balanced reaction (answer a), you note that 1 mole of $Al_2O_3$ is being produced for every 2 moles of iron—they are not being produced in a ratio of 1 gram to 1 gram. For each of the two products, determine how much energy (in joules) is required for a 1°C rise in temperature.

For $Al_2O_3$:  $\dfrac{1 \text{ mole } Al_2O_3}{1} \times \dfrac{101.96 \text{ g } Al_2O_3}{1 \text{ mole } Al_2O_3} \times \dfrac{0.79 \text{ J}}{\text{g} \cdot °C} = 81 \text{ J/°C}$

For Fe:  $\dfrac{2 \text{ moles Fe}}{1} \times \dfrac{55.85 \text{ g Fe}}{1 \text{ mole Fe}} \times \dfrac{0.48 \text{ J}}{\text{g} \cdot °C} = 54 \text{ J/°C}$

Together, the products are absorbing 81 J/°C + 54 J/°C = 135 joules for every 1°C rise in temperature. Because the reaction is producing 847.6 kJ of energy (you know this from your answer to part b), the change in temperature, from the initial conditions of the reactants (presumably at room temperature) to those of the hot products, is found by dividing the heat of reaction by the energy absorbed per degree Celsius (J divided by J/°C = °C). Thus

$$\dfrac{847,600 \text{ J}}{135 \text{ J/°C}} = \textbf{6280°C change in temperature}$$

(d) Restatement: Confirmation that the heat produced from the thermite reaction is sufficient to melt iron.

Given: $H_{fus}$ Fe = 270 J/g

Because $\Delta H_{fus}$ represents the amount of energy *absorbed* in melting iron, you must subtract this component from the $\Delta H$ you obtained in part (b). And because $\Delta H$ reflects the amount of heat produced when 2 moles of iron are produced, $\Delta H_{fus}$ for the reaction is

$$\frac{2 \text{ \sout{moles of Fe}}}{1} \times \frac{55.85 \text{ \sout{g Fe}}}{1 \text{ \sout{mole Fe}}} \times \frac{270 \text{ J}}{1 \text{ \sout{g Fe}}} = 30{,}200 \text{ J}$$

The 30,200 J of energy was *absorbed* in melting iron, so you subtract it from the $\Delta H$ value obtained in part (b) to find how much energy was actually *released* in the reaction.

$$847{,}600 \text{ J} - 30{,}200 \text{ J} = 817{,}400 \text{ J}$$

Finally, from part (c), you know that the amount of energy *released* divided by the energy absorbed per degree Celsius (J divided by J/°C = °C) equals the *change* in temperature. Thus you have

$$\frac{817{,}400 \text{ J}}{135 \text{ J/°C}} = \mathbf{6050°C}$$

which is above the melting point of iron, 1535°C.

2. **You pack six aluminum cans of cola in a cooler filled with ice. Each aluminum can (empty) weighs 50.0 grams. When filled, each can contains 355 ml of cola. The density of the cola is 1.23 g/ml. The specific heat of aluminum is 0.902 J/g · °C, and that of the cola is 4.00 J/g · °C.**
   (a) **If the cola is initially at 30°C and you wish to cool it to 10°C, how much heat must be absorbed by the ice?**
   (b) **What is the minimum amount of ice (at 0°C) need to cool the cola? $\Delta H_{fus}$ for ice is 6.00 kJ/mole.**

*Answer*

2. Given: 6 aluminum cans (empty) at 50.0 g each
   each can = 355 ml cola
   density of cola = 1.23 g/ml
   specific heat of aluminum = 0.902 J/g · °C
   specific heat of cola = 4.00 J/g · °C
   $t_i = 30°C$
   $t_f = 10°C$

   (a) Restatement: Amount of heat absorbed by ice.

   quantity of heat released by six pack

   $$= \text{heat released by cans + cola}$$

   $$q_{\text{six-pack}} = q_{\text{cans}} + q_{\text{cola}}$$

   $$q = \text{mass} \times \text{specific heat} \times \Delta t$$

   $$q_{\text{cans}} = \frac{6 \text{ cans}}{1} \times \frac{50.0 \text{ g Al}}{1 \text{ can}} \times \frac{0.902 \text{ J}}{\text{g} \cdot °C} \times \frac{(10°C - 30°C)}{1}$$

   $$= -5412.00 \text{ J}$$

   $$q_{\text{cola}} = \frac{6 \text{ cans}}{1} \times \frac{355 \text{ ml cola}}{1 \text{ can}} \times \frac{1.23 \text{ g cola}}{1 \text{ ml cola}}$$

   $$\times \frac{4.00 \text{ J}}{\text{g} \cdot °C} \times \frac{(10°C - 30°C)}{1}$$

   $$= -2.10 \times 10^5 \text{ J}$$

   $$q_{\text{six-pack}} = -5412 \text{ J} + (-2.10 \times 10^5 \text{ J})$$

   $$= -2.15 \times 10^5 \text{ J, or } -215 \text{ kJ}$$

   Therefore, the amount of heat absorbed by the ice is **215 kJ.**

(b) Restatement: Minumum amount of ice required to accomplish the necessary cooling.

amount of heat absorbed by ice
$$= \text{amount of heat released by six-pack}$$

$$q_{\text{ice}} = -q_{\text{six-pack}}$$

$$q_{\text{ice}} = \text{mass ice} \times \Delta H_{\text{fus}}$$

$$215 \text{ kJ} = \frac{x \text{ g ice}}{1} \times \frac{1 \text{ mole ice}}{18.02 \text{ g ice}} \times \frac{6.00 \text{ kJ}}{1 \text{ mole ice}}$$

$$x = \textbf{646 g ice}$$

# THE GAS LAWS

## Key Terms

Words that can be used as topics in essays:

absolute zero
Avogadro's law
Boyle's law
Charles's law
combined gas law
Dalton's law
diffusion
effusion
Gay-Lussac's law
Graham's law of effusion
ideal gas

ideal gas law
kinetic theory
molar volume
mole fraction
partial pressure
real gas
root-mean-square velocity
STP
translational energy
van der Waals equation

## Key Concepts

Equations and relationships that you need to know:

- 1 atm = 760 mm Hg = 760 torr = 101.3 kPa = 14.7 lb/in$^2$

  K = °C + 273.15

- Avogadro's law: $V_1 n_2 = V_2 n_1$
  Boyle's law: $P_1 V_1 = P_2 V_2$
  Charles's law: $V_1 T_2 = V_2 T_1$

  combined gas law: $\dfrac{P_1 V_1}{T_1} = \dfrac{P_2 V_2}{T_2}$

  Dalton's law of partial pressures: $P_{\text{total}} = P_1 + P_2 + P_3 + \ldots$

  derivation: $P_i = \dfrac{n_i}{n_{total}} \times P_{total}$

$$\text{density} = \frac{g}{V} = \frac{P \times \text{MW}}{R \cdot T}$$

Gay-Lussac's law: $P_1 T_2 = P_2 T_1$

ideal gas law: $PV = nRT$

$R = 0.0821$ liter $\cdot$ atm/mole $\cdot$ K

$\quad = 8.31$ liter $\cdot$ kPa/mole $\cdot$ K

$\quad = 8.31$ J/mole $\cdot$ K

$\quad = 8.31 \, V \cdot C$/mole $\cdot$ K

$\quad = 8.31 \times 10^{-7}$ g $\cdot$ cm$^2$/sec$^2 \cdot$ mole $\cdot$ K

$\quad$ (for calculating the average speed of molecules)

$\quad = 6.24 \times 10^4$ L $\cdot$ mm Hg/mole $\cdot$ K

$\quad = 1.99$ cal/mole $\cdot$ K

$$\text{molecular weight} = \text{MW} = \frac{g \cdot R \cdot T}{P \cdot V}$$

van der Waal's (real gases):   $(P + a/V^2)(V - b) = R \cdot T$

$$\text{or}$$

$$(P + n^2 a/V^2)(V - nb) = n \cdot R \cdot T$$

Here $a$ corrects for force of attraction between gas molecules, and $b$ corrects for particle volume.

- Graham's law of effusion:

$$\frac{r_1}{r_2} = \frac{\sqrt{d_2}}{\sqrt{d_1}} = \frac{\sqrt{\text{MW}_2}}{\sqrt{\text{MW}_1}} = \frac{t_2}{t_1} = \frac{u_1}{u_2}$$

where

$\quad\quad r = $ rate of effusion
$\quad\quad d = $ density
$\quad \text{MW} = $ molecular weight
$\quad\quad t = $ time
$\quad\quad u = $ average speed

- **Kinetic Molecular Theory**

  1. Gases are composed of tiny, invisible molecules that are widely separated from one another in empty space.

  2. The molecules are in constant, continuous, random, and straight-line motion.

  3. The molecules collide with one another, but the collisions are perfectly elastic (no net loss of energy).

  4. The pressure of a gas is the result of collisions between the gas molecules and the walls of the container.

  5. The average kinetic energy of all the molecules collectively is directly proportional to the absolute temperature of the gas. Equal number of molecules of any gas have the same average kinetic energy at the same temperature.

- $E_t = \dfrac{m \cdot u^2}{2} = cT$

  $c = \dfrac{3R}{2N_A}$

  $u^2 = \dfrac{3 \cdot R \cdot T}{m \cdot N_A} = \dfrac{3 \cdot R \cdot T}{MW}$

  where

    $E_t$ = average kinetic energy of translation
    $m$ = mass (of particle)
    $u$ = velocity (average speed)
    $c$ = constant
    $N_A$ = Avogadro's number
    $R = 8.31 \times 10^{-7}\, g \cdot cm^2/sec^2 \cdot mole \cdot K$
    $T$ = temperature in K

## Examples: Multiple-Choice Questions

1. **Which of the following would express the approximate density of carbon dioxide gas at 0°C and 2.00 atm pressure (in grams per liter)?**
   (A) 2 g/l
   (B) 4 g/l
   (C) 6 g/l
   (D) 8 g/l
   (E) none of the above

*Answer: (B)*

First, calculate the volume the $CO_2$ gas would occupy at 2.00 atm using the relationship

$$\frac{P_1 V_1}{T_1} = \frac{P_2 V_2}{T_2}$$

Since the temperature is remaining constant, we can use $P_1 V_1 = P_2 V_2$, where initial conditions are at STP and final conditions are at 0°C and 2.00 atm.

$$(1.00 \text{ atm})(22.4 \text{ liters}) = (2.00 \text{ atm})(V_2)$$
$$V_2 = 11.2 \text{ liters}$$

Since the amount of gas has not changed from the initial STP conditions (1 mole or 44.01 grams), the density of the gas at 2.00 atm and 0°C would be

$$\frac{44.01 \text{ grams}}{11.2 \text{ liters}} = \sim 4 \text{ g/l}$$

Another approach to this problem would be to use the ideal gas law, $PV = nRT$.

$$\text{density} = \frac{g}{V} = \frac{P \cdot MW}{RT}$$

$$= \frac{2.00 \text{ atm} \cdot 44.01 \text{ g} \cdot \text{mole}^{-1}}{0.08211 \cdot \text{atm} \cdot \text{mole}^{-1} \cdot K^{-1} \cdot 273 \text{ K}}$$

$$= \sim 4 \text{ g/l}$$

2. **The combustion of carbon monoxide yields carbon dioxide. The volume of oxygen gas needed to produce 22 grams of carbon dioxide at STP is**
   (A) **4.0 liters**
   (B) **5.6 liters**
   (C) **11 liters**
   (D) **22 liters**
   (E) **32 liters**

*Answer: (B)*

Begin by writing down a balanced equation.

$$2CO(g) + O_2(g) \rightarrow 2\,CO_2(g)$$

Next, use the factor-label method to solve the problem.

$$\frac{22\,\text{g}\,\cancel{CO_2}}{1} \times \frac{1\,\text{mole}\,\cancel{CO_2}}{44\,\text{g}\,\cancel{CO_2}} \times \frac{1\,\text{mole}\,\cancel{O_2}}{2\,\text{moles}\,\cancel{CO_2}} \times \frac{22.4\,\text{l}\,O_2}{1\,\text{mole}\,\cancel{O_2}} = 5.6\,\text{l}\,O_2$$

Hint: Cancel the 22 and the 44 first, leaving 1/4 times 22.4 = 5.6 l.

3. **If the average velocity of a methane molecule, $CH_4$ (MW = 16), is $5.00 \times 10^4$ cm/sec at 0°C, what is the average velocity of helium molecules at the same temperature and pressure conditions?**
   (A) $2.50 \times 10^4$ **cm/sec**
   (B) $5.00 \times 10^4$ **cm/sec**
   (C) $1.00 \times 10^5$ **cm/sec**
   (D) $2.00 \times 10^5$ **cm/sec**
   (E) $5.00 \times 10^5$ **cm/sec**

*Answer: (C)*

Graham's law of effusion:

$$\frac{u_1}{u_2} = \frac{\sqrt{MW_2}}{\sqrt{MW_1}}$$

$$\frac{5.00 \times 10^4}{x} = \frac{\sqrt{4}}{\sqrt{16}}$$

$$x = 1.00 \times 10^5 \text{ cm/sec}$$

4. **When 2.00 grams of a certain volatile liquid is heated, the volume of the resulting vapor is 821 ml at a temperature of 127°C at standard pressure. The molecular weight of this substance is**
   (A)   20.0 g/mole
   (B)   40.0 g/mole
   (C)   80.0 g/mole
   (D) 120. g/mole
   (E) 160. g/mole

*Answer: (C)*

Begin this problem by listing the known facts.

$$m = 2.00 \text{ g} \qquad V = 0.821 \text{ liter} \qquad T = 4.00 \times 10^2 \text{ K}$$

$$P = 1.00 \text{ atm} \qquad \text{MW} = ?$$

You will need to use the ideal gas law to solve the problem: $PV = nRT$. Because moles can be calculated by dividing the mass of the sample by its molecular weight, the ideal gas law becomes

$$PV = \frac{m}{\text{MW}} R \cdot T$$

Solving for MW yields

$$\text{MW} = \frac{m \cdot R \cdot T}{P \cdot V} = \frac{(2.00 \text{ g})(0.0821 \text{ liter} \cdot \text{atm})(400 \text{ K})}{(1.00 \text{ atm})(0.821 \text{ liter}) \cdot \text{mole} \cdot \text{K}} = 80.0 \text{ g/mole}$$

5.  **A sample of zinc metal reacts completely with excess hydrochloric acid according to the following equation:**

$$Zn(s) + 2HCl(aq) \rightarrow ZnCl_2(aq) + H_2(g)$$

**8.00 liters of hydrogen gas at 720. mm Hg is collected over water at 40.°C (vapor pressure of water at 40.°C = 55 mm Hg). How much zinc was consumed by the reaction?**

(A) $\dfrac{(720/760) \cdot 8.00}{(0.0821) \cdot 313}$

(B) $\dfrac{(760/720) \cdot 313}{(0.0821) \cdot 2}$

(C) $\dfrac{(665/760) \cdot 8.00 \cdot (65.39)}{(0.0821) \cdot 313}$

(D) $\dfrac{(665/760) \cdot 8.00}{(65.39) \cdot (0.0821) \cdot 313}$

(E) $\dfrac{8.00 \cdot 313 \cdot 65.39}{(665/760) \cdot (0.0821)}$

*Answer: (C)*

Begin by listing the information that is known.

$V$ = 8.00 liters $H_2$

$P$ = 720. mm Hg − 55 mm Hg = 665 mm Hg
(corrected for vapor pressure)

$T$ = 40°C + 273 = 313K

Using the ideal gas law, $PV = nRT$, and realizing that one can determine grams from moles, the equation becomes

$$n_{H_2} = \frac{PV}{RT} = \frac{(665/760 \text{ atm}) \cdot 8.00 \text{ l } H_2}{(0.0821 \text{ l} \cdot \text{atm}/\text{mole} \cdot \text{K}) \cdot 313\text{K}}$$

Since for every mole of hydrogen produced, one mole of zinc is consumed, the last step would be to convert these moles to grams by multiplying by the molar mass of zinc.

$$\frac{\text{moles } H_2}{1} \cdot \frac{1 \text{ mole Zn}}{1 \text{ mole } H_2} \cdot \frac{65.39 \text{ g Zn}}{1 \text{ mole Zn}} = \frac{(665/760) \cdot 8.00 \cdot 65.39}{(0.0821) \cdot 313}$$

6. **What is the partial pressure of helium when 8.0 grams of helium and 16 grams of oxygen are in a container with a total pressure of 5.00 atm?**
   (A) **0.25 atm**
   (B) **1.00 atm**
   (C) **1.50 atm**
   (D) **2.00 atm**
   (E) **4.00 atm**

*Answer: (E)*

Use the formula

$$P_1 = \frac{n_1}{n_{\text{total}}} P_{\text{total}}$$

derived from Dalton's law of partial pressures. Find the number of moles of the two gases first.

$$\frac{8.0 \text{ g He}}{1} \times \frac{1 \text{ mole He}}{4.0 \text{ g He}} = 2.0 \text{ moles He}$$

$$\frac{16 \text{ g O}_2}{1} \times \frac{1 \text{ mole O}_2}{32 \text{ g O}_2} = 0.50 \text{ mole O}_2$$

$$n_{\text{total}} = 2.0 \text{ moles} + 0.50 \text{ mole} = 2.5 \text{ moles}$$

$$P_{\text{He}} = \frac{2.0 \text{ moles}}{2.5 \text{ moles}} \times 5.00 \text{ atm} = 4.00 \text{ atm}$$

7. **For a substance that remains a gas under the conditions listed, deviation from the ideal gas law would be most pronounced at**
   (A)  −100°C and 5.0 atm
   (B)  −100°C and 1.0 atm
   (C)  0°C and 1.0 atm
   (D)  100°C and 1.0 atm
   (E)  100°C and 5.0 atm

*Answer: (A)*

The van der Waals constant *a* corrects for the attractive forces between gas molecules. The constant *b* corrects for particle volume. The attractive forces between gas molecules become pronounced when the molecules are closer together. Conditions which favor this are low temperatures (−100°C) and high pressures (5.0 atm).

8. **100 grams of $O_2(g)$ and 100 grams of He($g$) are in separate containers of equal volume. Both gases are at 100°C. Which one of the following statements is true?**
   (A) **Both gases would have the same pressure.**
   (B) **The average kinetic energy of the $O_2$ molecules is greater than that of the He molecules.**
   (C) **The average kinetic energy of the He molecules is greater than that of the $O_2$ molecules.**
   (D) **There are equal numbers of He molecules and $O_2$ molecules.**
   (E) **The pressure of the He($g$) would be greater than that of the $O_2(g)$.**

*Answer: (E)*

Oxygen gas weighs 32 grams per mole, whereas helium gas weighs only 4 grams per mole. One can see that there are roughly 3 moles of oxygen molecules and 25 moles of helium molecules. Gas pressure is proportional to the number of molecules and temperature, and inversely proportional to the size of the container. Since there are more helium molecules, you would expect a higher pressure in the helium container (with all other variables being held constant). As long as the temperatures of the two containers are the same, the average kinetic energies of the two gases are the same.

**9. Which one of the manometers below represents a gas pressure of 750 mm Hg? (Atmospheric pressure is 760 mm Hg.)**

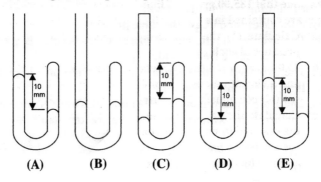

(A)    (B)    (C)    (D)    (E)

*Answer: (D)*

Manometer (D), the correct answer, shows the air pressure to be 10 mm Hg greater than that of the gas. Manometer (A) shows the gas pressure to be 10 mm Hg greater than air pressure. Manometer (B) shows the gas pressure to be equal to that of the air pressure. Manometer (C) is a closed manometer showing that the pressure of the gas is 10 mm Hg greater than the unknown pressure on the left side of the manometer. Manometer (E) is also closed and shows that the gas on the right side (770 mm Hg) is exerting a pressure 10 mm Hg greater than the gas on the left side.

## Examples: Free-Response Questions

1. Assume that 185.00 grams of fluorine gas and 4.0 moles of xenon gas are contained in a flask at 0°C and 2.5 atm of pressure.
   (a) Calculate (1) the volume of the flask and (2) the partial pressure of each gas.
   (b) 23.00 grams of lithium metal is introduced into the flask, and a violent reaction occurs in which one of the reactants is entirely consumed. What weight of lithium fluoride is formed?
   (c) Calculate the partial pressures of any gas(es) present after the reaction in part (b) is complete and the temperature has been brought back to 0°C. (The volumes of solid reactants and products may be ignored.)

*Answer*

1. Given: 185.00 $F_2(g)$     4.0 moles $Xe(g)$     $T = 273K$
              $P = 2.5$ atm

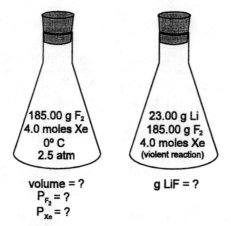

volume = ?
$P_{F_2}$ = ?
$P_{Xe}$ = ?

g LiF = ?

(a) (1) Restatement: Volume of flask.

$PV = nRT$

$n$ = total moles = moles $F_2$ + moles xenon

$$\text{moles } F_2 = \frac{185.00 \text{ g } F_2}{1} \times \frac{1 \text{ mole } F_2}{38.00 \text{ g } F_2} = 4.868 \text{ moles } F_2$$

total moles of gas = 4.868 + 4.0 = 8.9 moles

Solve for the volume.

$$V = \frac{nRT}{P} = \frac{8.9 \text{ moles} \cdot (0.0821 \text{ liter} \cdot \text{atm}) \cdot 273 \text{ K}}{\text{mole} \cdot \text{K} \cdot 2.5 \text{ atm}}$$

$$= \mathbf{8.0 \times 10^1 \text{ liters}}$$

(a) (2) Restatement: Find partial pressure of each gas.

$P_{\text{total}} = P_{\text{fluorine}} + P_{\text{xenon}}$

$$P_{\text{fluorine}} = \frac{n_{\text{fluorine}} \cdot R \cdot T}{V}$$

$$= \frac{4.868 \text{ moles} \cdot 0.0821 \text{ liter} \cdot \text{atm} \cdot 273 \text{ K}}{\text{mole} \cdot \text{K} \cdot 8.0 \times 10^1 \text{ liters}}$$

$$= \mathbf{1.4 \text{ atm}}$$

$$P_{\text{xenon}} = \frac{n_{\text{xenon}} \cdot R \cdot T}{V}$$

$$= \frac{4.0 \text{ moles} \cdot 0.0821 \text{ liter} \cdot \text{atm} \cdot 273 \text{ K}}{\text{mole} \cdot \text{K} \cdot 8.0 \times 10^1 \text{ liters}}$$

$$= \mathbf{1.1 \text{ atm}}$$

(b) Restatement: 23.00 g Li added to flask. Weight of LiF formed?

Xe is inert (no reaction with lithium).
The balanced equation for the reaction is thus
$F_2(g) + 2Li(s) \rightarrow 2 LiF(s)$.

$$\frac{23.00 \text{ g Li}}{1} \times \frac{1 \text{ mole Li}}{6.94 \text{ g Li}} = 3.31 \text{ mole Li}$$

Therefore, lithium is the limiting reagent. So 3.31 moles of Li is used up along with 3.31/2 or 1.66 moles of $F_2$. This leaves 3.21 moles (4.868 − 1.66) of $F_2$.

$$\frac{3.31 \text{ moles Li}}{1} \times \frac{2 \text{ moles LiF}}{2 \text{ moles Li}} \times \frac{25.94 \text{ g LiF}}{1 \text{ mole LiF}} = \textbf{86.0 g LiF}$$

(c) Restatement: Partial pressures of gases present after reaction, 0°C

Xenon is inert (no reaction): **1.1 atm pressure**

$$P_{\text{fluorine}} = \frac{n_{\text{fluorine}} \cdot R \cdot T}{V}$$

$$= \frac{3.21 \text{ moles} \cdot 0.0821 \text{ liter} \cdot \text{atm} \cdot 273 \text{ K}}{\text{mole} \cdot \text{K} \cdot 8.0 \times 10^1 \text{ liters}}$$

$$= \textbf{0.90 atm}$$

2. **Three students, Mason, Amir, and Kamyar, measured an empty Erlenmeyer flask and a tight-fitting stopper and found the mass to be 62.371 g. The students then carefully measured out 4.4 ml of a volatile liquid, poured the liquid into the flask, and heated the flask containing the liquid in a 101.1°C boiling water bath. As soon as all the liquid had vaporized, the students covered the flask with the stopper and set it aside to cool. Then, after a few minutes, they very quickly removed and replaced the stopper and reweighed the flask. The mass of the flask, stopper, and condensed vapor was 63.088 g. At the conclusion of the experiment, the students rinsed out the flask, filled it with water to the top, replaced the tight-fitting stopper (being sure there were no air bubbles), and obtained a volume of 261.9 ml. The barometric air pressure that day was 733 mm Hg.**
   (a) **Calculate the pressure of the vapor inside the flask (in atm) after the vapor had cooled and the students opened the flask momentarily.**
   (b) **What was the mass of the vapor in the flask?**
   (c) **Calculate the mass of 1 mole of the vapor.**
   (d) **Explain how each of the following errors in the laboratory procedure would affect the calculation of the molecular mass.**
      (1) **The volatile liquid contained nonvolatile impurities.**
      (2) **The students removed the flask from the water bath before all of the liquid had vaporized.**
      (3) **There was a hole in the stopper.**
      (4) **There were a few drops of water left on the flask from the water bath when the final mass was taken.**

*Answer*

*Begin this problem by numbering the problem and listing the critical information, getting rid of superfluous words, and clarifying the situation in your mind.*

2.  Given: 62.371 g = Erlenmeyer flask + stopper
    4.388 ml of volatile liquid
    101.1°C boiling water bath = 374.1 K
    63.088 g = flask, stopper, condensed vapor
    261.87 ml = volume of stoppered flask
    733 mm Hg = barometric pressure

*Then, number each section; restate the question in as few words as possible; list the necessary information; write down any generic formulas; substitute the data from the problem into the generic formulas; do the math; and underline or box your answer.*

(a)  Restatement: Pressure inside of flask after vapor cooled and the flask was opened momentarily.

$$\frac{733 \; \text{mm Hg}}{1} \times \frac{1 \; \text{atm}}{760 \; \text{mm Hg}} = \textbf{0.964 atm}$$

*The students opened the flask and thus made the pressure inside the flask equal to the pressure outside it.*

(b)  Restatement: Mass of vapor inside the flask.

$$63.088 \; \text{g} - 62.371 \; \text{g} = \textbf{0.717 g}$$

(c)  Restatement: Mass of 1 mole of vapor.

$$PV = nRT \rightarrow PV = \frac{g \cdot R \cdot T}{\text{MW}}$$

$$\text{MW} = \frac{g \cdot R \cdot T}{P \cdot V}$$

$$= \frac{(0.717 \; \text{g}) \cdot (0.0821 \; \text{liter} \cdot \text{atm}) \cdot (374.1 \; \text{K})}{\text{mole} \cdot \text{K} \; (0.964 \; \text{atm}) \cdot (0.2619 \; \text{liter})}$$

$$= \textbf{87.2 g/mole}$$

(d) Restatement: How could each of these mistakes affect the molecular mass of the liquid?

(1) The volatile liquid contained nonvolatile impurities.

The molecular mass would be **too high** because the nonvolatile impurities would contribute additional mass. The contribution to volume would be negligible.

(2) The students removed the flask from the water bath before all the liquid had vaporized.

The mass of the condensed vapor would be too high. The excess mass would be due to both the vapor and the mass of liquid that had not vaporized. Examine the equation for determining the molecular weight.

$$\text{MW} = \frac{g \cdot R \cdot T}{P \cdot V}$$

The value for g would be too high, so the calculated MW would also be **too high.**

(3) There was a hole in the stopper.

The mass of the vapor would be too small, because some of the vapor would have escaped through the hole in the stopper before condensing on the flask. The variable $g$ would be smaller than expected, resulting in a molecular mass **lower than expected.**

(4) A few drops of water were left on the flask from the water bath when the final mass was taken.

The mass of the condensate would be too large, because it would include both the mass of the condensate and the mass of the water left on the flask. The variable $g$ would be larger than expected, resulting in a molecular mass **higher than expected.**

# ELECTRONIC STRUCTURE OF ATOMS

## Key Terms

Words that can be used as topics in essays:

amplitude, $\psi$
atomic radii
atomic spectrum
Aufbau principle
Balmer series, $n_2 = 2$
Bohr model
continuous spectrum
de Broglie relation
degenerate orbital
diamagnetic
effective nuclear charge, $Z_{\text{eff}}$
electromagnetic radiation
electron affinity
electron configuration
electronegativity
electron spin
emission spectra
excited state
frequency, $\nu$
ground state
Heisenberg uncertainty principle
Hund's rule
ionic radii
ionization energy

isoelectronic
line spectrum
Lyman series, $n_2 = 1$
nodal surface
orbital
orbital diagram
paramagnetic
Paschen series, $n_2 = 3$
Pauli exclusion principle
penetration effect
photon
probability distribution
quantization
quantum mechanics
quantum numbers
shielding
Schrödinger equation
valence electrons
wave function
wavelength, $\lambda$
wave mechanical model
wave-particle duality
    of nature

## Key Concepts

Equations and relationships that you need to know:

- **Postulates of the Quantum Theory**

    1. Atoms and molecules can exist only in discrete states, characterized by definite amounts of energy. When an atom or molecule changes state, it absorbs or emits just enough energy to bring it to another state.

    2. When atoms or molecules absorb or emit light in moving from one energy state to another, the wavelength of the light is related to the energies of the two states as follows:

    $$E_{\text{high}} - E_{\text{low}} = \frac{h \cdot c}{\lambda}$$

    3. The allowed energy states of atoms and molecules are described by quantum numbers.

- $h$ = Planck's constant = $6.626 \times 10^{-34} \dfrac{\text{J} \cdot \text{s}}{\text{particle}}$

    $$= 6.626 \times 10^{-27} \text{ erg} \cdot \text{sec}$$

    $c$ = speed of light = $2.998 \times 10^{10}$ cm/sec

    $$\Delta E = \frac{1.196 \times 10^5 \text{ kJ} \cdot \text{nm}}{\lambda \cdot \text{mole}}$$

    $$E = \frac{-1312 \text{ kJ}}{n^2 \cdot \text{mole}} = h \cdot \nu = \frac{2.18 \times 10^{-11} \text{ erg}}{n^2} = mc^2$$

    $$= \left(\frac{Z_{\text{eff}}}{n^2}\right) 1312 \text{ kJ/mole}$$

    $Z_{\text{eff}} = Z - \sigma$
    where $Z_{\text{eff}}$ = effective nuclear charge, $Z$ = actual nuclear charge, and $\sigma$ = shielding or screening constant

Rydberg-Ritz equation: $E_n = -R_H \left( \dfrac{1}{n^2} \right)$

$$\frac{1}{\lambda} = R_H \left( \frac{1}{n_i^2} - \frac{1}{n_f^2} \right) = \Delta E = h\nu$$

$n_i$ and $n_f$ are quantum numbers
$R_H = 2.18 \times 10^{-18}\,\text{J} = 109{,}737\,\text{cm}^{-1}$

$$m \cdot v \cdot r = \frac{n \cdot h}{2\pi}$$

$$E_b - E_a = \frac{z^2 e^2}{2a_0} \left[ \frac{1}{n_a^2} - \frac{1}{n_b^2} \right]$$

where $n$ = quantum energy level
$\quad E$ = energy (at states $a$ and $b$)
$\quad$ e = charge on electron
$\quad a_0$ = Bohr radius
$\quad z$ = atomic radius

$\quad n$ = principal energy level
$\quad l$ = angular momentum = sublevel ($s, p, d,$ and $f$)
$\quad m_l$ = magnetic quantum number = orientation of orbital
$\quad m_s$ = electron spin quantum number

- **Predicted Electron Configuration**

$1s^2\,2s^2\,2p^6\,3s^2\,3p^6\,4s^2\,3d^{10}\,4p^6\,5s^2\,4d^{10}\,5p^6\,6s^2\,4f^{14}\,5d^{10}\,6p^6$
$7s^2\,5f^{14}\,6d^{10}$

*Common Exceptions*

| | |
|---|---|
| chromium | $4s^1 3d^5$ |
| copper | $4s^1 3d^{10}$ |
| molybdenum | $5s^1 4d^{10}$ |
| silver | $5s^1 4d^{10}$ |
| gold | $6s^1 4f^{14} 5d^{10}$ |

- **Important Colors**

| | | | |
|---|---|---|---|
| $Li^+$ | red | flame test | |
| $Na^+$ | yellow | flame test | |
| $K^+$ | violet | flame test | Group IA |
| $Rb^+$ | purple | flame test | |
| $Cs^+$ | blue | flame test | |

| | | | |
|---|---|---|---|
| $Ca^{2+}$ | red | flame test | |
| $Sr^{2+}$ | crimson | flame test | Group IIA |
| $Ba^{2+}$ | green | flame test | |

- **Transitional Metal Cations (in aqueous solution)**

| | | | |
|---|---|---|---|
| $Ag^+$ | colorless | $Fe^{3+}$ | pale yellow |
| $Cd^+$ | colorless | $Hg^{2+}$ | colorless |
| $Co^{2+}$ | pink | $Mn^{2+}$ | pale pink |
| $Cr^{3+}$ | purple | $Ni^{2+}$ | green |
| $Cu^{2+}$ | blue | $Zn^{2+}$ | colorless |
| $Fe^{2+}$ | pale green | | |

- **Polyatomic Anions (in aqueous solution)**

| | | | |
|---|---|---|---|
| $CrO_4^{2-}$ | yellow | $Cr_2O_7^{2-}$ | orange |

## Examples: Multiple-Choice Questions

1. **Which of the following setups would be used to calculate the wavelength (cm) of a photon emitted by a hydrogen atom when the electron moves from the $n = 5$ state to the $n = 2$ state? (The Rydberg constant is $R_H = 2.18 \times 10^{-18}$ J. Planck's constant is $h = 6.63 \times 10^{-34}$ J · sec. The speed of light $= 3.00 \times 10^{10}$ cm/sec.)**

(A) $(2.18 \times 10^{-18}) \left( \dfrac{1}{5^2} - \dfrac{1}{2^2} \right) (6.63 \times 10^{-34})$

(B) $\dfrac{(6.63 \times 10^{-34})(3.00 \times 10^{10})}{(2.18 \times 10^{-18}) \left( \dfrac{1}{5^2} - \dfrac{1}{2^2} \right)}$

(C) $\dfrac{(2.18 \times 10^{-18})(3.00 \times 10^{10})}{(6.63 \times 10^{-34}) \left( \dfrac{1}{5^2} - \dfrac{1}{2^2} \right)}$

(D) $\dfrac{(2.18 \times 10^{-18})/(3.00 \times 10^{10})}{(6.63 \times 10^{-34}) \left/ \left( \dfrac{1}{5^2} - \dfrac{1}{2^2} \right) \right.}$

(E) $\dfrac{(2.18 \times 10^{-18})(3.00 \times 10^{10})}{(6.63 \times 10^{-34}) \left/ \left( \dfrac{1}{5^2} - \dfrac{1}{2^2} \right) \right.}$

*Answer: (B)*

The following relationships are needed to solve this problem:

$$\Delta E = R_H \left( \frac{1}{n_{i^2}} - \frac{1}{n_{f^2}} \right) \text{ and } \lambda = \frac{h \cdot c}{\Delta E}$$

Combining these equations to solve for $\lambda$ gives the equation

$$\lambda = \frac{h \cdot c}{R_H \left( \dfrac{1}{n_{i^2}} - \dfrac{1}{n_{f^2}} \right)} = \frac{(6.63 \times 10^{-34} \,\cancel{J} \cdot \cancel{sec})(3.00 \times 10^{10} \text{ cm}/\cancel{sec})}{(2.18 \times 10^{-18} \,\cancel{J}) \left( \dfrac{1}{5^2} - \dfrac{1}{2^2} \right)}$$

2. A $Co^{+3}$ ion has _____ unpaired electron(s) and is _____ .
   (A) 1, diamagnetic
   (B) 3, paramagnetic
   (C) 3, diamagnetic
   (D) 4, paramagnetic
   (E) 10, paramagnetic

*Answer: (D)*

The electron configuration for the $Co^{+3}$ ion is $1s^2 2s^2 2p^6 3s^2 3p^6 3d^6$. If you missed this, review electron configurations of transitional metals. The $Co^{+3}$ ion would have a total of 24 electrons: 10 pairs of electrons and four unpaired electrons in the $3d$ orbits. Atoms in which one or more electrons are unpaired are paramagnetic.

3. Which of the following series of elements is listed in order of increasing atomic radius?
   (A) Na, Mg, Al, Si
   (B) C, N O, F
   (C) O, S, Se, Te
   (D) I, Br, Cl, F
   (E) K, Kr, O, Au

*Answer: (C)*

Atomic radius increases as one moves down a column (or group).

4. A characteristic that is unique to the alkali metals is
   (A) their metallic character
   (B) the increase in atomic radius with increasing atomic number
   (C) the decrease in ionization energy with increasing atomic number
   (D) the noble gas electron configuration of the singly charged positive ion
   (E) None of these answer choices is correct.

*Answer: (D)*

The word *unique* in this question means that *only* the alkali metals possess this particular characteristic. Of the choices listed, (D) is the only property that is unique to the alkali metals.

5. **Which of the following elements most readily show the photoelectric effect?**
   (A) **Noble gases**
   (B) **Alkali metals**
   (C) **Halogen elements**
   (D) **Transition metals**
   (E) **The chalcogen family**

*Answer: (B)*

The photoelectric effect is the emission of electrons from the surface of a metal when light shines on it. Electrons are emitted, however, only when the frequency of that light is greater than a certain threshold value characteristic of the particular metal. The alkali metals, with only one electron in their valence shells, have the lowest threshold values.

6. **The lithium ion and the hydride ion are isoelectronic. Which of the following statements is true of these two chemical species in the ground state?**
   (A) **$Li^+$ is a better reducing agent than $H^-$.**
   (B) **The $H^-$ ion is several times larger than the $Li^+$ ion.**
   (C) **It requires more energy to remove an electron from $H^-$ than from $Li^+$.**
   (D) **The chemical properties of the two ions must be the same because they have the same electronic structure.**
   (E) **None of these is a true statement.**

*Answer: (B)*

Both the lithium ion, $Li^+$, and the hydride ion, $H^-$, have the configuration $1s^2$. Both species have 2 electrons, but the lithium ion has 3 protons, which cause a greater "pull" on the 2 electrons than the 1 proton found in the hydride ion.

7. **Which of the following configurations represents a neutral transition element?**
   (A) $1s^2\, 2s^2\, 2p^2$
   (B) $1s^2\, 2s^2\, 2p^6\, 3s^2\, 3p^4$
   (C) $1s^2\, 2s^2\, 2p^6\, 3s^2$
   (D) $1s^2\, 2s^2\, 2p^6\, 3s^2\, 3p^6\, 3d^8\, 4s^2$
   (E) $1s^2\, 2s^2\, 2p^6\, 3s^2\, 3p^6\, 3d^{10}\, 4s^2\, 4p^6$

*Answer: (D)*

The transition elements are filling the $d$ orbitals. When completely filled, the $d$ orbitals hold a maximum of 10 electrons.

8. **The four quantum numbers ($n$, $l$, $m_l$, and $m_s$) that describe the valence electron in the cesium atom are**
   (A) $6, 0, -1, +1/2$
   (B) $6, 1, 1, +1/2$
   (C) $6, 0, 0, +1/2$
   (D) $6, 1, 0, +1/2$
   (E) $6, 0, 1, -1/2$

*Answer: (C)*

The valence electron for the cesium atom is in the $6s$ orbital. In assigning quantum numbers, $n$ = principal energy level = 6. The quantum number $l$ represents the angular momentum (type of orbital) with $s$ orbitals = 0, $p$ orbitals = 1, $d$ orbitals = 2, and so forth. In this case, $l = 0$. The quantum number $m_l$ is known as the magnetic quantum number and describes the orientation of the orbital in space. For $s$ orbitals (as in this case), $m_l$ always equals 0. For $p$ orbitals, $m_l$ can take on the values of $-1$, 0, and $+1$. For $d$ orbitals, $m_l$ can take on the values $-2$, $-1$, 0, $+1$, and $+2$. The quantum number $m_s$ is known as the electron spin quantum number and can take only two values, $+1/2$ and $-1/2$, depending on the spin of the electron.

9. **When subjected to the flame test, a solution that contains K$^+$ ions produces the color**
   - (A) **yellow**
   - (B) **violet**
   - (C) **crimson**
   - (D) **green**
   - (E) **orange**

*Answer: (B)*

Refer to Key Concepts for colors of flame tests.

10. **Which of the following results indicates exothermic change in atoms?**
    - (A) **The production of line emission spectra**
    - (B) **The appearance of dark lines in absorption spectra**
    - (C) **The formation of ions from a metal in the gaseous state**
    - (D) **The production of isotopic species of CO$^+$ and CO$_2^+$ when CO$_2$ is placed in a mass spectrometer**
    - (E) **The absence of all spectral lines in the region of excitation**

*Answer: (A)*

When atoms absorb energy, electrons move from ground states to excited levels. When the electrons move back to their ground state, they release energy (exothermic) at particular wavelengths (or frequencies).

11. **An energy value of $3.313 \times 10^{-12}$ ergs is needed to break a chemical bond. What is the wavelength of energy needed to break the bond? (The speed of light = $3.00 \times 10^{10}$ cm/sec; Planck's constant = $6.626 \times 10^{-27}$ erg · sec.)**
    (A) $5.00 \times 10^{-4}$ cm
    (B) $1.00 \times 10^{-5}$ cm
    (C) $2.00 \times 10^{-5}$ cm
    (D) $6.00 \times 10^{-5}$ cm
    (E) $1.20 \times 10^{-5}$ cm

*Answer: (D)*

You need to know two relationships to do this problem. First,

$$V = \frac{E}{h} = \frac{3.313 \times 10^{-12} \text{ erg}}{6.626 \times 10^{-27} \text{ erg} \cdot \text{sec}} = 5.000 \times 10^{14} \text{ sec}^{-1}$$

The second relationship you need to know is

$$\lambda = \frac{c}{\nu} = \frac{3.00 \times 10^{10} \text{ cm} \cdot \text{sec}}{\text{sec} \cdot 5.000 \times 10^{14}} = 6.00 \times 10^{-5} \text{ cm}$$

An alternative approach would be to use the relationship

$$\lambda = \frac{h \cdot c}{E} = \frac{6.626 \times 10^{-27} \text{ erg} \cdot \text{sec} \cdot 3.00 \times 10^{10} \text{ cm} \cdot \text{sec}^{-1}}{3.313 \times 10^{-12} \text{ erg}}$$

12. **A characteristic of the structure of metallic atoms is that**
    (A) **they tend to share their electrons with other atoms**
    (B) **their atoms are smaller and more compact than those of nonmetallic elements**
    (C) **their outermost orbital of electrons is nearly complete, and they attract electrons from other atoms**
    (D) **the small numbers of electrons in their outermost orbital are weakly held and easily lost**
    (E) **they have heavier nuclei than nonmetallic atoms**

*Answer: (D)*

Metals lose their electrons readily to become positively charged ions with charges of +1, +2, or +3.

## Examples: Free-Response Questions

1. **The electon configuration of an element determines its chemical properties. For the elements sodium, magnesium, sulfur, chlorine, and argon, provide evidence that illustrates this statement and show how the evidence supports the statement.**

*Answer*

1. Restatement: Electron configuration and chemical properties for Na, Mg, S, Cl, and Ar.

   *This question lends itself to the outline format.*

   I. Sodium, Na

       A. Electron configuration $1s^2\, 2s^2\, 2p^6\, 3s^1$
       B. Lewis diagram **Na** ·
       C. Alkali metal
       D. Chemical properties
           1. Loses valence electron easily
           2. Very reactive
           3. Low ionization energy
           4. Reacts with nonmetals to form ionic solid
           5. When reacting with nonmetal, metal acts as a reducing agent

   II. Magnesium, Mg

       A. Electron configuration $1s^2\, 2s^2\, 2p^6\, 3s^2$
       B. Lewis diagram **Mg** :
       C. Alkaline earth metal
       D. Chemical properties
           1. Forms only divalent compounds that are stable and have high heats of formation
           2. Very reactive only at high temperatures
           3. Powerful reducing agent when heated
           4. Reacts with most acids
           5. Burns rapidly in air ($O_2$)

III. Sulfur, S

    A. Electron configuration $1s^2\,2s^2\,2p^6\,3s^2\,3p^4$

    B. Lewis diagram

$$: \overset{\cdot}{\underset{\cdot}{S}} :$$

    C. Nonmetal

    D. Chemical properties

       1. Combines with almost all elements except gold, iodine, platinum, and inert gases

       2. Burns in air to give sulfur dioxide

       3. Stable at room temperature

       4. Oxidizing agent

IV. Chlorine, Cl

    A. Electron configuration $1s^2\,2s^2\,2p^6\,3s^2\,3p^5$

    B. Lewis diagram

$$: \overset{\cdot\,\cdot}{\underset{\cdot}{Cl}} :$$

    C. Nonmetal

    D. Chemical properties

       1. Diatomic in natural state: $Cl_2$

       2. Strong oxidizing agent

V. Argon, Ar

    A. Electron configuration $1s^2\,2s^2\,2p^6\,3s^2\,3p^6$

    B. Lewis diagram

$$: \overset{\cdot\,\cdot}{\underset{\cdot\,\cdot}{Ar}} :$$

    C. Nonmetal

    D. Chemical properties

       1. Inert, will not react with any element

2. (a) **Write the ground-state electron configuration for a phosphorus atom.**

   (b) **Write the four quantum numbers that describe all the valence electrons in the phosphorus atom.**

   (c) **Explain whether a phosphorus atom, in its ground state, is paramagnetic or diamagnetic.**

   (d) **Phosphorus can be found in such diverse compounds as $PCl_3$, $PCl_5$, $PCl_4^+$, $PCl_6^-$, and $P_4$. How can phosphorus, in its ground state, bond in so many different arrangements? Be specific in terms of hybridization, type of bonding, and geometry.**

*Answer*

2. (a) Restatement: Electron configuration of P.

$$1s^2 \, 2s^2 \, 2p^6 \, 3s^2 \, 3p^3$$

   (b) Restatement: Quantum numbers for valence electrons in P.

   *Here's a good place to use the chart format.*

| Electron Number | $n$ | $l$ | $m_l$ | $m_s$ |
|---|---|---|---|---|
| 11 | 3 | 0 | 0 | +1/2 |
| 12 | 3 | 0 | 0 | −1/2 |
| 13 | 3 | 1 | 1 | +1/2 |
| 14 | 3 | 1 | 0 | +1/2 |
| 15 | 3 | 1 | −1 | +1/2 |

   (c) Restatement: P paramagnetic or diamagnetic? Explain.

   Phosphorus is **paramagnetic,** because a paramagnetic atom is defined as having magnetic properties caused by unpaired electrons. The unpaired electrons are found in the $3p$ orbitals, each of which is half-filled.

(d) Restatement: Explain how $PCl_3$, $PCl_5$, $PCl_4^+$, $PCl_6^-$, and $P_4$ exist in nature.

*Here's another question where the chart format is appropriate.*

|  | $PCl_3$ | $PCl_5$ | $PCl_4^+$ | $PCl_6^-$ | $P_4$ |
|---|---|---|---|---|---|
| Type of bond | covalent | covalent | covalent | covalent | covalent |
| Lewis structure | | | | | |
| Geometry | pyramidal | triangular bipyramidal | tetrahedral | octahedral | tetrahedral |
| Hybridization | $sp^3$ | $sp^3d$ | $sp^3$ | $sp^3d^2$ | $sp^3$ |

# COVALENT BONDING

Words that can be used as topics in essays:

antibonds
atomic radius
bond energy
bond length
bond order
bond polarity
coordinate covalent bond
  or dative bond
delocalization
delocalized pi bonding
diagonal relationships
diamagnetism
dipole moment
electron affinity
electronegativity
expanded octet theory
formal charge
hybridization
hydrogen bonding

interatomic forces
intermolecular forces
Lewis structures
localized electron
  model (LE model)
lone pair
molecular orbital theory
molecular structure (geometry)
network covalent solid
octet rule
paramagnetism
pi bonds
polar covalent bond
polarity
resonance
sigma bonds
valence bond model
valence shell electron pair repulsion
  model (VSEPR model)

## Key Concepts

Equations and relationships that you need to know:

- bond order

$$= \frac{\text{number of bonding electrons} - \text{number of antibonding electrons}}{2}$$

101

## • Geometry and Hybridization Patterns

| Number of Atoms Bonded to Central Atom X | Number of Unshared Pairs on X | Hybridization | Geometry | Example* |
|:---:|:---:|:---:|:---:|:---:|
| 2 | 0 | $sp$ | linear | $\underline{C}O_2$ |
| 2 | 1 | $sp^2$ | bent | $\underline{S}O_2$ |
| 2 | 2 | $sp^3$ | bent | $H_2\underline{O}$ |
| 2 | 3 | $sp^3d$ | linear | $\underline{Xe}F_2$ |
| 3 | 0 | $sp^2$ | trigonal planar | $\underline{B}Cl_3$ |
| 3 | 1 | $sp^3$ | trigonal pyramidal | $\underline{N}H_3$ |
| 3 | 2 | $sp^3d$ | T-shaped | $\underline{Cl}F_3$ |
| 4 | 0 | $sp^3$ | tetrahedral | $\underline{C}H_4$ |
| 4 | 1 | $sp^3d$ | distorted tetrahedral | $\underline{S}Cl_4$ |
| 4 | 2 | $sp^3d^2$ | square planar | $\underline{Xe}F_4$ |
| 5 | 0 | $sp^3d$ | triangular bipyramidal | $\underline{P}Cl_5$ |
| 5 | 1 | $sp^3d^2$ | square pyramidal | $\underline{Cl}F_5$ |
| 6 | 0 | $sp^3d^2$ | octahedral | $\underline{S}F_6$ |

*Underlined atom is central atom, X.

- **Character of Bonds**

| Electronegativity Difference | Type of Bond | Example |
|---|---|---|
| $0 \rightarrow 0.2$ | nonpolar covalent | $Br_2$, HI, $CH_4$ |
| $0.2 \rightarrow 1.7$ | polar covalent | NO, LiH |
| 1.7 or greater | ionic | LiBr, CuF |

- formal charge =

$$\begin{pmatrix} \text{total number of} \\ \text{valence electrons} \\ \text{in the free atom} \end{pmatrix} - \begin{pmatrix} \text{total number of} \\ \text{nonbonding} \\ \text{electrons} \end{pmatrix} - 1/2 \begin{pmatrix} \text{total number} \\ \text{of bonding} \\ \text{electrons} \end{pmatrix}$$

single bond = 1 sigma bond
double bond = 1 sigma bond, 1 pi bond
triple bond = 1 sigma bond, 2 pi bonds

Homonuclear diatomic molecules of second-period elements $B_2$, $C_2$, and $N_2$:

$$\sigma 1s < \sigma *1s < \sigma 2s < \sigma *2s < \pi_{2p_y} = \pi_{2p_z} < \sigma_{2p_x} < \pi *_{2p_y}$$
$$= \pi *_{2p_z} < \sigma *_{2p_x}$$

For $O_2$ and $F_2$:

$$\sigma 1s < \sigma *1s < \sigma 2s < \sigma *2s < \sigma_{2p_x} < \pi_{2p_y} = \pi_{2p_z} < \pi *_{2p_y}$$
$$= \pi *_{2p_z} < \sigma *_{2p_x}$$

## Examples: Multiple-Choice Questions

**For Examples 1–5 use the following choices:**

(A) **Trigonal planar**
(B) **Tetrahedral**
(C) **Pyramidal**
(D) **Bent**
(E) **Linear**

### 1. What is the geometry of $S_2Cl_2$?

*Answer: (D)*

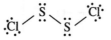

### 2. What is the geometry of OPN?

*Answer: (E)*

$$\ddot{O}{=}P{=}\ddot{N}$$

### 3. What is the geometry of $SeO_4^{2-}$?

*Answer: (B)*

**4. What is the geometry of $SiO_3^{2-}$?**

*Answer: (A)*

**5. What is the geometry of the hydronium ion, $H_3O^+$?**

*Answer: (C)*

**6. Which one of the following is a nonpolar molecule with one or more polar bonds?**
   (A) H—Br
   (B) Cl—Be—Cl
   (C) H—H
   (D) H—O—H
   (E) K—Cl

*Answer: (B)*

(A) H—B̈r:

(B) C̈l=Be=C̈l

(C) H—H

(D) ⠀⠀Ö⠀⠀
⠀⠀HH

(E) Compound is ionic, $K^+ : \ddot{\underset{..}{Cl}} :^-$

The Cl atom is more electronegative than the Be atom, resulting in a polar bond. However, because the molecule is linear and the two ends are identical, the overall molecule is nonpolar.

7. **How many total sigma bonds are in the benzene molecule, $C_6H_6$?**
   (A) 6   (B) 9   (C) 12   (D) 14   (E) 18

*Answer: (C)*

All single bonds are sigma ($\sigma$) in nature. Double bonds contain one sigma bond and one pi ($\pi$) bond. Triple bonds contain one sigma bond and two pi bonds.

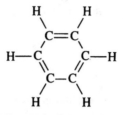

In the benzene molecule, there are 9 single bonds ($9\sigma$) and 3 double bonds ($3\sigma$ and $3\pi$) for a total of 12 sigma bonds.

8. **Which one of the following does NOT exhibit resonance?**
   (A) $SO_2$   (B) $SO_3$   (C) $CH_3Br$   (D) $CO_3^{2-}$   (E) $NO_3^-$

*Answer: (C)*

There are no alternative ways of positioning electrons around the $CH_3Br$ molecule. If you missed this question, refer to your textbook on the concept of resonance.

9. **What type of hybridization would you expect to find in BCl₃?**
   (A)  *sp*
   (B)  *sp²*
   (C)  *sp³*
   (D)  *sp³d²*
   (E)  No hybridization occurs in this molecule.

*Answer: (B)*

10. **The electronegativity of carbon is 2.5, whereas that of oxygen is 3.5. What type of bond would you expect to find in carbon monoxide?**
    (A)  Nonpolar covalent
    (B)  Polar covalent
    (C)  Covalent network
    (D)  Ionic
    (E)  Delta

*Answer: (B)*

Electronegativity differences less than 1.7 are classified as covalent. *Unequal* differences in *sharing* electrons are known as polar covalent.

**11. Which one of the following contains a coordinate covalent bond?**
(A) $N_2H_5^+$   (B) $BaCl_2$   (C) HCl   (D) $H_2O$   (E) NaCl

*Answer: (A)*

A coordinate covalent bond, also known as a dative bond, is a bond in which both electrons are furnished by one atom.

**12. What is the formal number of pairs of unshared valence electrons in the $NO_2^+$ ion?**
(A) 0   (B) 2   (C) 4   (D) 8   (E) 10

*Answer: (C)*

$$\left[ \ddot{O}\!=\!N\!=\!\ddot{O} \right]^+$$

**13. The bond energy of Br—Br is 192 kJ/mole, and that of Cl—Cl is 243 kJ/mole. What is the energy of the Cl—Br bond?**
(A)   54.5 kJ/mole
(B)   109 kJ/mole
(C)   218 kJ/mole
(D)   435 kJ/mole
(E)   870 kJ/mole

*Answer: (C)*

If the polarity of the bond A—B is about the same as those of the nonpolar bonds A—A and B—B, then the bond energy of A—B can be taken as the average of the bond energies of A—A and B—B.

**Examples: Free-Response Questions**

1. Given $ClO_2^-$, $ClO_4^-$, $Cl_2O$, $ClO_3^-$, and $ClO_2$.
   (a) Draw Lewis structures for all species.
   (b) Predict the bond angle for all species.
   (c) Predict the geometry for all species.
   (d) Predict the hybridization of the chlorine in all species.
   (e) Identify any of the species that might dimerize.
   (f) Identify any species that might be polar.

*Answer*

*This problem is best done in the chart format. Note how the column heads record what is given and how the first entries in the rows serve as a restatement of what is wanted.*

| 1. | $ClO_2^-$ | $ClO_4^-$ | $Cl_2O$ | $ClO_3^-$ | $ClO_2$ |
|---|---|---|---|---|---|
| (a) Lewis structure | $\left[:\ddot{O}{\sim}^{\overset{..}{Cl}}{\sim}\ddot{O}:\right]^-$ | $\left[:\ddot{O}-\overset{:\ddot{O}:}{\underset{:\ddot{O}:}{Cl}}-\ddot{O}:\right]^-$ | $:\ddot{Cl}{\sim}^{\overset{..}{O}}{\sim}\ddot{Cl}:$ | $\left[:\ddot{O}{\sim}^{\overset{..}{Cl}}{\underset{:\ddot{O}:}{\sim}}\ddot{O}:\right]^-$ | $:\ddot{O}{\sim}^{\overset{.}{Cl}}{\sim}\ddot{O}:$ |
| (b) Bond angles | less than 180° | 109.5° | less than 180° | less than 109.5° | less than 180° |
| (c) Geometry | bent | tetrahedral | bent | pyramidal | bent |
| (d) Hybridization | $sp^3$ | $sp^3$ | $sp^3$ | $sp^3$ | $sp^3$ |
| (e) Dimerization | no | no | no | no | yes—unpaired electron will give  $\overset{:\ddot{O}}{\underset{:\ddot{O}}{}}Cl-Cl\overset{\ddot{O}:}{\underset{\ddot{O}:}{}}$ |
| (f) Polarity | polar | nonpolar | polar | polar | polar |

2. As one moves down the halogen column, one notices that the boiling point increases. However, when examining the alkali metal family, one discovers that the melting point decreases as one moves down the column.
   (a) Account for the increase in boiling point of the halogens as one moves down the column.
   (b) Account for the decrease in melting point of the alkali metals as one moves down the column.
   (c) Rank Cs, Li, KCl, $I_2$, and $F_2$ in order of decreasing melting point, and explain your reasoning.

*Answer*

*This answer might best be done in the bullet format.*

2. (a) Restatement: Explain increase in B.P. of halogens as one moves down column.

   - Halogens are nonmetals.
   - Halogens are diatomic.
   - Bonding found within halogen molecule is covalent—formed as a result of sharing of electrons.
   - Forces found between halogen molecules are van der Waals forces, which are due to temporarily induced dipoles caused by polarization of electron clouds.
   - Moving down the column, one would expect greater nuclear charge.
   - Moving down the column, one would expect larger electron clouds due to higher energy levels being filled as well as greater atomic numbers and hence a greater number of electrons.
   - Moving down halogen family, shielding effect and greater distance from nucleus would cause easier polarization of electron cloud.
   - Therefore, greater polarization of electron cloud would cause greater attractive force (van der Waals force), resulting in higher boiling points.
   - Furthermore, one must consider the effect of the molecular weight on the B.P. As the individual molecules become more and more massive, they need higher and higher temperatures to give them enough kinetic energy and velocity to escape from the surface and "boil."

(b) Restatement: Explain decrease in melting point of alkali metals as one moves down column.

- Alkali metal family are all metals.
- Metals have low electronegativity.
- Metals have low ionization energies.
- Metals exist in definite crystal arrangement—cations surrounded by "sea of electrons."
- As one moves down the alkali metal column, nuclear charge increases.
- As one moves down the alkali metal column, the electron cloud would be expected to get larger due to higher energy levels being filled.
- As one moves down the alkali metal family, the charge density would be expected to decrease due to significantly larger volume and more shielding.
- As one moves down the alkali metal family, one would expect the attractive forces holding the crystal structure together to decrease due to this last factor.
- Boiling point and melting point would be expected to be comparable because they both are functions of the strength of intermolecular attractive forces.

(c) Restatement: Rank Cs, Li, KCl, $I_2$, and $F_2$ in order of decreasing melting point. Explain.

- #1 KCl—highest melting point. Ionic bond present—formed by the transfer of electrons.
- #2 Li—alkali metal. Metallic bonds present (cations, mobile electrons). Low-density metal.
- #3 $I_2$—solid at room temperature. Covalent bond present. Nonpolar.
- #4 Cs—liquid at near room temperature. Metallic bonds present; however, due to low charge density as explained above, attractive forces are very weak.
- #5 $F_2$—gas at room temperature. Covalent bonds present. One would expect a smaller electron cloud than in $I_2$ due to reasons stated above.

# IONIC BONDING

## Key Terms

Words that can be used as topics in essays:

anions
atomic orbital model
bond energy
cation
chelates
complex ion
coordination number
Coulomb's law
crystal-field model
crystal-field splitting energy
dissociation constant, $K_d$
electronegativity
free radical
high-spin complex

inert complex
ionic radius
isoelectronic
labile complex
lattice energy
ligand
low-spin complex
noble-gas structure
orbital diagram
polarity
polydentate ligand
spectrochemical series
valence electron

## Key Concepts

Equations and relationships that you need to know:

- % ionic character = $\dfrac{\text{measured dipole moment of } X^+Y^-}{\text{calculated dipole moment of } X^+Y^-} \cdot 100\%$

  net dipole moment = charge × distance

Coulomb's law: $E = 2.31 \times 10^{-19} J \cdot nm\left(\dfrac{Q_1Q_2}{r}\right)$

lattice energy $= k\left(\dfrac{Q_1Q_2}{r}\right)$    $k = $ constant

- **Ligand Nomenclature**

| | | | |
|---|---|---|---|
| $Br^-$ | bromo | $I^-$ | iodo |
| $C_2O_4^{2-}$ | oxalato | $NH_3$ | amine |
| $CH_3NH_2$ | methylamine | $NO$ | nitrosyl |
| $Cl^-$ | chloro | $O^{2-}$ | oxo |
| $CN^-$ | cyano | $OH^-$ | hydroxo |
| $CO$ | carbonyl | $SO_4^{2-}$ | sulfato |
| $CO_3^{2-}$ | carbonato | en | ethylenediamine |
| $F^-$ | fluoro | EDTA | ethylenediamine- |
| $H_2O$ | aquo | | tetraaceto |

- **Coordination Numbers for Common Metal Ions**

| | | | | | |
|---|---|---|---|---|---|
| $Ag^+$ | 2 | $Co^{2+}$ | 4, 6 | $Au^{3+}$ | 4 |
| $Cu^+$ | 2, 4 | $Cu^{2+}$ | 4, 6 | $Co^{3+}$ | 6 |
| $Au^+$ | 2, 4 | $Fe^{2+}$ | 6 | $Cr^{3+}$ | 6 |
| | | $Mn^{2+}$ | 4, 6 | $Se^{3+}$ | 6 |
| | | $Ni^{2+}$ | 4, 6 | | |
| | | $Zn^{2+}$ | 4, 6 | | |

- **Simple Cubic, Body-Centered, and Face-Centered Cubic Cells**

Simple cubic cell          Body-centered          Face-centered
                              cubic cell              cubic cell

## • Common Polyatomic Ions

### +1

| ammonium | $NH_4^+$ |
|----------|----------|

### −1

| acetate | $C_2H_3O_2^-$ | hydrogen sulfate | |
| amide | $NH_2^-$ |   or bisulfate | $HSO_4^-$ |
| azide | $N_3^-$ | hydrogen sulfite | |
| hydrazide | $N_2H_3^-$ |   or bisulfite | $HSO_3^-$ |
| benzoate | $C_7H_5O_2^-$ | hydrosulfide | |
| bitartrate | $HC_4H_4O_6^-$ |   or bisulfide | $HS^-$ |
| bromate | $BrO_3^-$ | hydroxide | $OH^-$ |
| perchlorate | $ClO_4^-$ | iodate | $IO_3^-$ |
| chlorate | $ClO_3^-$ | triiodide | $I_3^-$ |
| chlorite | $ClO_2^-$ | nitrate | $NO_3^-$ |
| hypochlorite | $ClO^-$ | nitrite | $NO_2^-$ |
| cyanate | $OCN^-$ | permanganate | $MnO_4^-$ |
| cyanide | $CN^-$ | monobasic phosphate | |
| hydrogen | |   or dihydrogen | |
|   carbonate | |    phosphate | $H_2PO_4^-$ |
|   or bicarbonate | $HCO_3^-$ | thiocyanate | $SCN^-$ |

### −2

| carbonate | $CO_3^{2-}$ | oxalate | $C_2O_4^{2-}$ |
| chromate | $CrO_4^{2-}$ | peroxide | $O_2^{2-}$ |
| dichromate | $Cr_2O_7^{2-}$ | phthalate | $C_8H_4O_4^{2-}$ |
| dibasic phosphate | | metasilicate | $SiO_3^{2-}$ |
|   or hydrogen | | sulfate | $SO_4^{2-}$ |
|   phosphate | $HPO_4^{2-}$ | sulfite | $SO_3^{2-}$ |
| disulfate | | thiosulfate | $S_2O_3^{2-}$ |
|   or pyrosulfate | $S_2O_7^{2-}$ | tartrate | $C_4H_4O_6^{2-}$ |
| manganate | $MnO_3^{2-}$ | tetraborate | $B_4O_7^{2-}$ |

### −3

| aluminate | $AlO_3^{3-}$ | ferricyanide | $Fe(CN)_6^{3-}$ |
| arsenate | $AsO_4^{3-}$ | phosphate | |
| arsenite | $AsO_3^{3-}$ |   or tribasic | |
| borate | $BO_3^{3-}$ |    phosphate | $PO_4^{3-}$ |
| citrate | $C_6H_5O_7^{3-}$ | phosphite | $PO_3^{3-}$ |

### −4

| ferrocyanide | $Fe(CN)_6^{4-}$ | silicate (ortho) | $SiO_4^{4-}$ |

## • Common Oxidation States of the Elements

| Element | States | | Element | States |
|---|---|---|---|---|
| Actinium | +3 | | Molybdenum | **+6**, +4, +3 |
| Aluminum | +3 | | Neodymium | +3 |
| Americium | +6, +5, +4, **+3** | | Neon | |
| Antimony | +5, **+3**, −3 | | Neptunium | +6, **+5**, +4, +3 |
| Argon | | | Nickel | **+2** |
| Arsenic | +5, **+3**, −3 | | Niobium | **+5**, +4 |
| Astatine | **−1** | | Nitrogen | **+5**, +4, +3, +2, +1, **−3** |
| Barium | **+2** | | Osmium | **+8**, +4 |
| Berkelium | +4, **+3** | | Oxygen | +2, −½, −1, **−2** |
| Beryllium | **+2** | | Palladium | +4, **+2** |
| Bismuth | +5, **+3** | | Phosphorus | **+5**, +3, −3 |
| Boron | **+3** | | Platinum | **+4**, +2 |
| Bromine | +5, +3, +1, **−1** | | Plutonium | +6, +5, **+4**, +3 |
| Cadmium | **+2** | | Polonium | +2 |
| Calcium | **+2** | | Potassium | **+1** |
| Californium | +3 | | Praseodymium | **+3**, +4 |
| Carbon | **+4**, +2, −4 | | Promethium | +3 |
| Cerium | **+3**, +4 | | Protactinium | **+5**, +4 |
| Cesium | **+1** | | Radium | **+2** |
| Chlorine | +7, +6, +5, +4, +3, +1, **−1** | | Radon | |
| Chromium | **+6**, +5, +4, **+3**, +2 | | Rhenium | **+7**, +6, +4 |
| Cobalt | **+3, +2** | | Rhodium | +4, **+3**, +2 |
| Copper | **+2**, +1 | | Rubidium | **+1** |
| Curium | **+3** | | Ruthenium | +8, +6, +4, **+3** |
| Dysprosium | **+3** | | Samarium | **+3**, +2 |
| Erbium | **+3** | | Scandium | **+3** |
| Europium | **+3**, +2 | | Selenium | **+6**, +4, **−2** |
| Fluorine | **−1** | | Silicon | **+4**, −4 |
| Francium | **+1** | | Silver | **+1** |
| Gadolinium | **+3** | | Sodium | **+1** |
| Gallium | **+3** | | Strontium | **+2** |
| Germanium | **+4**, −4 | | Sulfur | **+6**, +4, +2, **−2** |
| Gold | **+3**, +1 | | Tantalum | **+5** |
| Hafnium | **+4** | | Technetium | **+7**, +6, +4 |
| Helium | | | Tellurium | **+6**, +4, **−2** |
| Holmium | **+3** | | Terbium | **+3**, +4 |
| Hydrogen | **+1, −1** | | Thallium | **+3**, +1 |
| Indium | **+3** | | Thorium | **+4** |
| Iodine | +7, +5, +1, **−1** | | Thulium | **+3**, +2 |
| Iridium | **+4**, +3 | | Tin | **+4, +2** |
| Iron | **+3, +2** | | Titanium | **+4**, +3, +2 |
| Krypton | +4, +2 | | Tungsten | **+6**, +4 |
| Lanthanum | **+3** | | Uranium | **+6**, +5, +4, +3 |
| Lead | **+4, +2** | | Vanadium | **+5, +4**, +3, +2 |
| Lithium | **+1** | | Xenon | +6, +4, +2 |
| Lutetium | **+3** | | Yitrium | **+3** |
| Magnesium | **+2** | | Ytterbium | **+3**, +2 |
| Manganese | **+7**, +6, **+4**, +3, **+2** | | Zinc | **+2** |
| Mercury | **+2**, +1 | | Zirconium | **+4** |

*(The most common or stable oxidation states are in bold.)*

### Examples: Multiple-Choice Questions

*Note to the student:* The AP chemistry exam does not emphasize complex ions or coordination compounds. There is nothing on the AP exam that involves the concepts of crystal-field theory, low versus high spin, valence bond theory, and other related areas. If you understand the questions presented here, then you are basically "safe" in this area of the exam. Most high school AP chemistry programs do not focus much on this area of chemistry because of time constraints.

1. **Which of the following is the electron configuration for $Ni^{2+}$?**
   (A) $1s^2\ 2s^2\ 2p^6\ 3s^2\ 3p^6\ 4s^2\ 3d^6$
   (B) $1s^2\ 2s^2\ 2p^6\ 3s^2\ 3p^6\ 4s^2\ 3d^{10}$
   (C) $1s^2\ 2s^2\ 2p^6\ 3s^2\ 3p^6\ 3d^8$
   (D) $1s^2\ 2s^2\ 2p^6\ 3s^2\ 3p^6\ 4s^2\ 3d^8$
   (E) $1s^2\ 2s^2\ 2p^6\ 3s^2\ 3p^6\ 4s^2\ 3d^4$

*Answer: (C)*

In forming ions, the transition metals lose their valence (outermost) shell electrons first, followed by their outer *d* electrons. *Note:* In order for transitional metal ions to be colored, the *d* orbitals must be *partially* filled. In this case, the solution containing the $Ni^{2+}$ ion would be colored (green).

2. **As the atomic number of the elements increases down a column,**
   (A) **the atomic radius decreases**
   (B) **the atomic mass decreases**
   (C) **the elements become less metallic**
   (D) **ionization energy decreases**
   (E) **the number of electrons in the outermost energy level increases**

*Answer: (D)*

Because the distance between the electrons and the nucleus is increasing, the electrons are becoming further away from the nucleus, making it easier to remove them by overcoming the electrostatic force attracting them to the nucleus. Also, there are more electrons in the way, increasing interference (the electron shielding effect).

3. **What is the oxidation number of platinum in $PtCl_6{}^{2-}$?**
   (A) $-4$   (B) $-2$   (C) $-1$   (D) $+4$   (E) $+6$

*Answer: (D)*

Because chlorine is a halogen, it has an oxidation number of $-1$. And because there are 6 chlorines, there is a total charge of $-6$ for the chlorines. The overall charge is $-2$, so algebraically, $x + (-6) = -2$. Solving this yields $x = +4$. Thus, the charge (or oxidation number) of platinum is $+4$.

4. **What type of bond would you expect in CsI?**
   (A) **Ionic**
   (B) **Covalent**
   (C) **Hydrogen**
   (D) **Metallic**
   (E) **van der Waals**

*Answer: (A)*

Generally, expect an ionic bond whenever you have a metal (Cs) bonded to a nonmetal (I). If you have a table of electronegativities to refer to, the electronegativity difference is greater than 1.7 for ionic compounds.

5. **Arrange the following ions in order of increasing ionic radius: $Mg^{2+}$, $F^-$, and $O^{2-}$.**
   (A) $O^{2-}$, $F^-$, $Mg^{2+}$
   (B) $Mg^{2+}$, $O^{2-}$, $F^-$
   (C) $Mg^{2+}$, $F^-$, $O^{2-}$
   (D) $O^{2-}$, $Mg^{2+}$, $F^-$
   (E) $F^-$, $O^{2-}$, $Mg^{2+}$

*Answer: (C)*

Note that all the ions have 10 electrons; that is, they are all isoelectronic with neon. Because they all have the same number of electrons, the only factor that will determine their size will be the nuclear charge—the greater the nuclear charge, the smaller the radius. Therefore, magnesium, with a nuclear charge of $+2$, has the smallest radius among these ions.

**6. Which of the following is the correct Lewis structure for the ionic compound $Ca(ClO_2)_2$?**

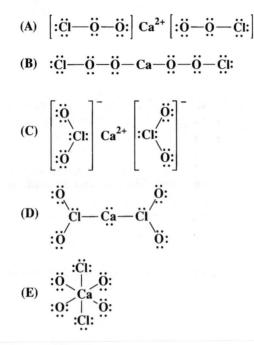

*Answer: (C)*

7. **The compound expected when chlorine reacts with aluminum is**
   (A) $Al_2Cl_3$
   (B) $Al_3Cl_2$
   (C) $AlCl_3$
   (D) $Al_3Cl$
   (E) $AlCl_2$

*Answer: (C)*

The compound is ionic—a metal (Al) bonded to a nonmetal (Cl). All ionic compounds are solids at room temperature and pressure. Aluminum has 13 electrons. As an ion, it will lose 3 electrons to become isoelectronic with neon. Thus the aluminum ion will have the electronic configuration $1s^2 2s^2 2p^6$. Chlorine as a free element is diatomic ($Cl_2$); however, as an ion, it will gain one electron to become isoelectronic with argon. The electronic configuration of the chloride ion is $1s^2 2s^2 2p^6 3s^2 3p^6$. The compound thus formed, aluminum chloride, has the formula $AlCl_3$.

8. **What ions would you find in solution if potassium perchlorate was dissolved in water?**
   (A) $KCl, O_2$
   (B) $K^+, Cl^-, O^{-2}$
   (C) $KCl, O^{-2}$
   (D) $K^+, ClO_4^-$
   (E) $K^+, Cl^-, O^{-2}$

*Answer: (D)*

Refer to page 117. Potassium is a metal, and the polyatomic anion, $ClO_4^-$, is a nonmetal; therefore, the compound is an ionic solid at room temperature. When the compound is dissolved in water, the ionic bond between the cation, $K^+$, and the polyatomic anion, $ClO_4^-$, is broken due to the polarity of the water molecule, resulting in the two aqueous ions, $K^+$ and $ClO_4^-$.

**9. Which one of the following is correct?**
   (A)  $KClO_3$          potassium perchlorate
   (B)  $CuO$          copper oxide
   (C)  $Al_3(SO_3)_2$          aluminum sulfate
   (D)  $MgPO_4$          magnesium phosphate
   (E)  $Na_2Cr_2O_7$          sodium dichromate

*Answer: (E)*

   In choice (A), $KClO_3$ is potassium chlorate, not perchlorate. In choice (B), $CuO$ is copper (II) oxide, to distinguish it from copper (I) oxide, $Cu_2O$. In choice (C), the formula for aluminum sulfate is $Al_2(SO_4)_3$. In (D), the formula for magnesium phosphate is $Mg_3(PO_4)_2$. If you missed these, review inorganic nomenclature and refer to page 117 of this book to become familiar with common ions and their charges.

## Examples: Free-Response Questions

1. The first three ionization energies ($I_1$, $I_2$, and $I_3$) for beryllium and neon are given in the following table:

| (kJ/mole) | $I_1$ | $I_2$ | $I_3$ |
|-----------|-------|-------|--------|
| Be | 900 | 1757 | 14,840 |
| Ne | 2080 | 3963 | 6276 |

(a) Write the complete electron configuration for beryllium and for neon.

(b) Explain any trends or significant discrepancies found in the ionization energies for beryllium and neon.

(c) If chlorine gas is passed into separate containers of heated beryllium and heated neon, explain what compounds, if any, might be formed, and explain your answer in terms of the electron configurations of these two elements.

(d) An unknown element, X, has the following three ionization energies:

| (kJ/mole) | $I_1$ | $I_2$ | $I_3$ |
|-----------|-------|-------|--------|
| X | 419 | 3069 | 4600 |

On the basis of the ionization energies given, what is most likely to be the compound produced when chlorine reacts with element X?

*Answer*

*The outline format might work well in part (b).*

1. Given: First three ionization energies of Be and Ne.

(a) Restatement: Electron configuration of Be and Ne.

$$\text{Be: } 1s^2\, 2s^2$$
$$\text{Ne: } 1s^2\, 2s^2\, 2p^6$$

(b) Restatement: Significant trends/discrepancies in the first three ionization energies of Be and Ne.

   I. Note that in the case of both beryllium and neon, ionization energies increase as one moves from $I_1$ to $I_2$ to $I_3$.

  II. The general trend is for ionization energy to increase as one moves from left to right across the periodic table and to decrease as one moves down; this is the inverse of the trend one finds in examining the atomic radius.

  III. Note further than beryllium and neon are in the second period.

  IV. Beryllium

   A. There is generally not enough energy available in chemical reactions to remove inner electrons, as noted by the significantly higher third ionization energy.

   B. The $Be^{2+}$ ion is a very stable species with a noble-gas configuration, so removing the third outermost electron from beryllium requires significantly greater energy.

   V. Neon

   A. Neon is an inert element with a full complement of 8 electrons in its valence shell.

   B. It is significantly more difficult to remove neon's most loosely held electron ($I_1$) than that of beryllium's $I_1$. This trend is also noted when examining $I_2$'s and $I_3$'s. Neon also has a greater nuclear charge than beryllium, which, if all factors are held constant, would result in a smaller atomic radius.

(c) Restatement: $Cl_2(g)$ passed into separate containers of Be and Ne. What compounds formed? Explanation.

The only compound formed would be **$BeCl_2$**. The Be atom readily loses 2 electrons to form the stable $Be^{2+}$ ion. The third ionization energy is too high to form $Be^{3+}$. The electron affinity of neon is very low because it has a stable octet of electrons in its valence shell and the ionization energies of neon are too high.

(d) Restatement: Given the first three ionization energies of element X what compounds is it most likely to form with $Cl_2$?

The first ionization energy ($I_1$) of element X is relatively low when compared to $I_2$ and $I_3$. This means that X is probably a member of the Group I alkali metals. Thus, the formation of $X^{2+}$ and $X^{3+}$ would be difficult to achieve. Therefore, the formula is most likely to be **XCl**.

**2. Bromine reacts with a metal (M) as follows:**

$$M(s) + Br_2(g) \rightarrow MBr_2(s)$$

**Explain how the heat of the reaction is affected by**
**(a) The ionization energy for the metal M**
**(b) The size of the atomic radius for the ion $M^{2+}$**

*Answer*

*This question is probably best answered in the outline format, because you will try to show a logical progression of concepts leading to two overall conclusions. Using the chart format would become too complicated. This question should take about ten minutes to answer.*

2. Restatement: How are ionization energy and atomic radius affected by the heat of reaction for

$$M(s) + Br_2(g) \rightarrow MBr_2(s)$$

  I. Ionization energy

    A. Definition—the amount of energy that a gaseous atom must absorb so that the outermost electron can be completely separated from the atom.

    B. The lower the ionization energy, the more metallic the element.

    C. With all other factors held constant, energy is required to form the $M^{2+}$ ion (endothermic)

    D. With larger ionization energies, the magnitude of the enthalpy decreases accordingly.

II. Atomic radius

    A. Definition—half the distance of closest approach between two nuclei in the ordinary form of an element.

    B. Positive ions are smaller than the metal atoms from which they are formed.

    C. Lattice energy—energy released when an ionic (metal M + nonmetal Br) solid forms from its ions.

    D. The change that occurs from $M(s) \rightarrow M^{2+}$, which exists as the cation in the ionic solid $MBr_2$, results in a decrease in the radius.

    E. In the calculation of lattice energy,

$$\text{L.E.} = \frac{Q_1Q_2}{r}$$

the lattice energy is inversely proportional to the radius, $r$.

    F. Because atomic distances ($r$) are decreasing in the reaction, lattice energy is increasing ($-\Delta H$), which has the effect of increasing the overall heat of reaction.

    G. $Q_1$ and $Q_2$ being opposite in sign further confirms the fact that bringing cations and anions together is an exothermic process.

# LIQUIDS AND SOLIDS

## Key Terms

Words that can be used as topics in essays:

adhesion
alloys
amorphous solids
band model
boiling point
capillary action
closest packing
cohesion
condensation
coordination number
critical point
critical pressure
critical temperature
crystalline solid
cubic close packing
deposition
dipole–dipole attraction
dipole-induced dipole
dipole force
dispersion force
dynamic equilibrium
electron sea model
freezing
heating curve
heat of vaporization
hexagonal close packing
hydrogen bond
induced dipole

intermolecular forces
intramolecular forces
ion-dipole forces
lattice
London dispersion forces
melting
melting point
network solid
normal boiling point
normal melting point
phase diagram
polarization
sublimation
supercooled
superheated
surface tension
triple point
types of structural units
   ions
   macromolecules
   metals
   molecules
unit cell
van der Waals forces
vaporization
vapor pressure
viscosity
x-ray diffraction

## Key Concepts

Equations and relationships that you need to know:

- $\Delta H_{\text{vaporization}} = H_{\text{vapor}} - H_{\text{liquid}}$

  $\Delta H_{\text{fusion}} = H_{\text{liquid}} - H_{\text{solid}}$

  $\Delta H_{\text{sublimation}} = H_{\text{fusion}} - H_{\text{vaporization}}$

- Raoult's law: $P_1 = X_1 P_1^\circ$

    where

    > $P_1$ = vapor pressure of solvent over the solution
    > $X_1$ = mole fraction of solvent
    > $P_1^\circ$ = vapor pressure of pure solvent

- Clausius–Clapeyron equation:

$$\ln (P_{\text{vap}}) = - \frac{\Delta H_{\text{vap}}}{R} \left( \frac{1}{T} \right) + C$$

    where $C$ is a constant that is characteristic of a liquid

$$\log \frac{P_2}{P_1} = \frac{\Delta H_{\text{vap}}}{2.303R} \left( \frac{T_2 - T_1}{T_2 T_1} \right)$$

$$\ln \frac{P_1}{P_2} = \frac{\Delta H_{\text{vap}}}{R} \left( \frac{1}{T_2} - \frac{1}{T_1} \right)$$

- Intermolecular forces
  - I. van der Waals
    - a. dipole-dipole        $HBr$—$H_2S$
    - b. dipole-induced dipole        $NH_3$—$C_6H_6$
    - c. dispersion        $He$—$He$
  - II. Ion-induced dipole        $NO_3^-$—$I_2$
  - III. Hydrogen bond        $H_2O$—$H_2O$

## Examples: Multiple-Choice Questions

For examples 1–5, use the following choices:

(A) Hydrogen bonding
(B) Metallic bonding
(C) Ionic bonding
(D) Dipole forces
(E) van der Waals forces (London dispersion forces)

1. **What accounts for the intermolecular forces between $CCl_4$ molecules?**

*Answer: (E)*

Because $CCl_4$ is a nonpolar molecule, the only force present is dispersion forces.

2. **What explains why the boiling point of acetic acid, $CH_3COOH$, is greater than the boiling point of acetone, $CH_3COCH_3$?**

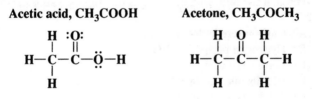

*Answer: (A)*

Note that for acetic acid there is a hydrogen attached to an oxygen atom (a prerequisite for H bonding) but that in acetone there is no H atom connected to an F, O, or N atom.

3. **What holds solid sodium together?**

*Answer: (B)*

Sodium is a metal. Metals are held together in a crystal lattice, which is a network of cations surrounded by a "sea" of mobile electrons.

### 4. What holds solid ICl together?

*Answer: (D)*

ICl is a polar molecule. Polar molecules have a net dipole—that is, a center of positive charge separated from a center of negative charge. Adjacent polar molecules line up so that the negative end of the dipole on one molecule is as close as possible to the positive end of its neighbor. Under these conditions, there is an electrostatic attraction between adjacent molecules. They key word here is *solid,* because if the question just asked for the force holding ICl (the molecule) together, the answer would be covalent bonding.

### 5. What holds calcium chloride together?

*Answer: (C)*

The metallic cations $(Ca^{2+})$ are electrostatically attracted to the nonmetallic anions $(Cl^-)$.

### 6. Which of the following liquids has the highest vapor pressure at 25°C?
   (A)  Carbon tetrachloride, $CCl_4$
   (B)  Hydrogen peroxide, $H_2O_2$
   (C)  Water, $H_2O$
   (D)  Dichloromethane, $CH_2Cl_2$
   (E)  Trichloromethane, $CHCl_3$

*Anwer: (D)*

You can rule out answer (B), hydrogen peroxide, and answer (C), water, because the very strong hydrogen bonds between their molecules lower the vapor pressure (the ease at which the liquid evaporates). Although answer (A), carbon tetrachloride, the only nonpolar molecule in the list, has only dispersion forces present between molecules, answer (D), dichloromethane, has the lowest molecular weight.

7. Which of the following statements is true of the critical temperature of a pure substance?
   (A) The critical temperature is the temperature above which the liquid phase of a pure substance can exist.
   (B) The critical temperature is the temperature above which the liquid phase of a pure substance cannot exist.
   (C) The critical temperature is the temperature below which the liquid phase of a pure substance cannot exist.
   (D) The critical temperature is the temperature at which all three phases can coexist.
   (E) The critical temperature is the temperature at which the pure substance reaches, but cannot go beyond, the critical pressure.

*Answer: (B)*

This is the definition of critical temperature.

8. **A certain metal crystallizes in a face-centered cube measuring $4.00 \times 10^2$ picometers on each edge. What is the radius of the atom? (1 picometer (pm) = $1 \times 10^{-12}$ meter)**
   (A) 141 pm
   (B) 173 pm
   (C) 200. pm
   (D) 282 pm
   (E) 565 pm

*Answer: (A)*

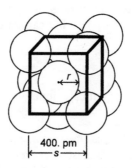

The formula which relates the radius of an atom ($r$) to the length of the side ($s$) of the unit cell for a face-centered cubic cell is $4r = s\sqrt{2}$.

$$r = \frac{400.\ \text{pm} \sqrt{2}}{4} = 100.(1.414) = 141 \text{ pm}$$

9. **The molecules butane and 2-methylpropane are structural isomers. Which of the following characteristics would be the same for both isomers, assuming constant temperature where necessary?**
   (A) **Boiling point**
   (B) **Vapor pressure**
   (C) **Melting point**
   (D) **Solubility**
   (E) **Gas density**

*Answer: (E)*

Choices (A), (B), (C), and (D) involve the strength of intermolecular forces. Because the two compounds differ in structure, there would be intermolecular differences between the two compounds. However, because both isomers have the same molecular mass, they would have the same gas density.

10. **Which of the following choices represents intermolecular forces listed in order from strongest to weakest?**
   (A) **dipole attractions, dispersion forces, hydrogen bonds**
   (B) **hydrogen bonds, dispersion forces, dipole attractions**
   (C) **dipole attractions, hydrogen bonds, dispersion forces**
   (D) **hydrogen bonds, dipole attractions, dispersion forces**
   (E) **dispersion forces, hydrogen bonds, dipole attractions**

*Answer: (D)*

Hydrogen bonds are the strongest of the intermolecular forces listed; dispersion forces are the weakest.

11. **Arrange the following in order of increasing boiling point: $NaCl$, $CO_2$, $CH_3OH$, $CH_3Cl$.**
    (A) $CH_3Cl$, $CO_2$, $CH_3OH$, $NaCl$
    (B) $CO_2$, $CH_3Cl$, $CH_3OH$, $NaCl$
    (C) $CO_2$, $CH_3OH$, $CH_3Cl$, $NaCl$
    (D) $NaCl$, $CH_3OH$, $CH_3Cl$, $CO_2$
    (E) $CH_3OH$, $CO_2$, $CH_3Cl$, $NaCl$

*Answer: (B)*

$CO_2$—nonpolar, dispersion forces only
$CH_3Cl$—polar molecule
$CH_3OH$—polar molecule, hydrogen bonds
$NaCl$—ionic compound

12. **An imaginary metal crystallizes in a cubic lattice. The unit cell edge length is 100. picometers (1 picometer = $1 \times 10^{-12}$ meter). The density of this metal is 200. $g/cm^3$. The atomic mass of the metal is 60.2 $g/mol$. How many of these metal atoms are there within a unit cell?**
    (A) 1.00    (B) 2.00    (C) 4.00    (D) 6.00    (E) 12.0

*Answer: (B)*

First calculate the mass of one cell, 100. pm on an edge:

$$\frac{200.\ g}{1 cm^3} \times \left(\frac{100\ cm}{1\ m}\right)^3 \times \left(\frac{1\ m}{10^{12}\ pm}\right)^3 \times \left(\frac{100.\ pm}{1\ cell}\right)^3 = 2.00 \times 10^{-22}\ g/cell$$

Next, calculate the mass of one metal atom:

$$\frac{60.2\ g}{1\ mole} \times \frac{1\ mole}{6.02 \times 10^{23}\ atoms} = 10.0 \times 10^{-23} = 1.00 \times 10^{-22}\ g/atom$$

Finally, calculate the number of metal atoms in one cell:

$$\frac{2.00 \times 10^{-22}\ g \cdot cell^{-1}}{1.00 \times 10^{-22}\ g \cdot atom^{-1}} = 2.00\ atoms/cell$$

### Examples: Free-Response Questions

1. **Explain each of the following in terms of (1) inter- and intra-atomic or molecular forces and (2) structure.**
   (a) **ICl has a boiling point of 97°C, whereas NaCl has a boiling point of 1400°C.**
   (b) **KI(s) is very soluble in water, whereas $I_2(s)$ has a solubility of only 0.03 gram per 100 grams of water.**
   (c) **Solid Ag conducts an electric current, whereas solid $AgNO_3$ does not.**
   (d) **$PCl_3$ has a measurable dipole moment, whereas $PCl_5$ does not.**

*Answer*

*The bullet format will work well here.*

1. Restatement: Explain each of the following:

   (a) ICl has a significantly lower B.P. than NaCl.

   - ICl is a covalently bonded, molecular solid; NaCl is an ionic solid.
   - There are dipole forces between ICl molecules but electrostatic forces between $Na^+$ and $Cl^-$ ions.
   - Dipole forces in ICl are much weaker than the ionic bonds in NaCl.
   - I and Cl are similar in electronegativity—generates only partial $\delta^+$ and $\delta^-$ around molecule.
   - Na and Cl differ greatly in electronegativity—greater electrostatic force.
   - When heated slightly, ICl boils because energy supplied (heat) overcomes weak dipole forces.

(b) KI is water soluble; $I_2$ is not.

- KI is an ionic solid, held together by ionic bonds.
- $I_2$ is a molecular solid, held together by covalent bonds.
- KI dissociates into $K^+$ and $I^-$ ions.
- $I_2$ slightly dissolves in water, maintaining its covalent bond.
- Solubility rule: Like dissolves like. $H_2O$ is polar; KI is polar; $I_2$ is not polar.

(c) Ag conducts; $AgNO_3$ does not.

- Ag is a metal.
- $AgNO_3$ is an ionic solid.
- Ag structure consists of $Ag^+$ cations surrounded by mobile or "free" electrons.
- $AgNO_3$ structure consists of $Ag^+$ cations electrostatically attracted to $NO_3^-$ polyatomic anions—no free or mobile electrons.

(d) $PCl_3$ has a dipole; $PCl_5$ does not.

- $PCl_3$ Lewis diagram:

- $PCl_3$—note the lone pair of unshared electrons.
- $PCl_3$ is pyramidal, and all pyramidal structures are polar.

- $PCl_5$ Lewis diagram:

- $PCl_5$—no unshared electrons on P
- $PCl_5$ is trigonal bipyramidal and thus perfectly symmetrical, so there is no polarity; all dipoles cancel.

2. Solids can be classified into four categories: ionic, metallic, covalent network, and molecular. For each of the four categories, identify the basic structural unit; describe the nature of the force both within the unit and between units; cite the basic properties of each type of solid; give two examples of each type of solid; and describe a laboratory means of identifying each type of solid.

*Answer*

*This question lends itself to the chart format. Here the column headings express what is given, and the first entry in each row serves as a restatement of what is wanted. Know the chart on the following page!*

|  | Ionic | Metallic | Covalent Network | Molecular |
|---|---|---|---|---|
| Structural Unit | ions | cations surrounded by mobile "sea" of electrons | atoms | polar or nonpolar molecules |
| Force Within Unit (Intra) | covalent bond within polyatomic ion | — | covalent bond | covalent bond |
| Force Between Units (Inter) | ionic bond electrostatic attraction | metallic bond | — | dipole-dipole dispersion (London) H bonds dipole-induced dipole |
| Basic Properties | high M.P. conducts in water solution or molten state soluble in water (variable) hard, brittle poor conductor of heat | variable M.P. conducts malleable ductile not soluble variable hardness good conductor of heat | very high M.P. does not conduct not soluble very hard poor conductor of heat except diamonds | nonpolar—low M.P.; polar—higher M.P. does not conduct nonpolar—insoluble in water; polar—some degree of solubility soft poor conductor of heat |
| Examples | NaCl CaCl$_2$ | Cu Au Fe | SiO$_2$ C (diamond) | H$_2$O—polar I$_2$—nonpolar CO$_2$ |
| Lab Test | conducts only when molten | conducts always | extremely hard; nonconductor | low M.P.; nonconductor |

# SOLUTIONS

## Key Terms

Words that can be used as topics in essays:

boiling-point elevation
colligative properties
colloids
electrolyte
fractional crystallization
fractional distillation
freezing-point depression
heat of solution
Henry's law
ideal solution
ion pairing
isotonic solutions
mass percent
molality
molarity
mole fraction
net ionic equation

nonelectrolyte
normality
osmosis
osmotic pressure
Raoult's law
saturated
solubility
solute
solution
solvent
supersaturated
Tyndall effect
unsaturated
vapor pressure
van't Hoff factor
volatility

## Key Concepts

Equations and relationships that you need to know:

- **Solubility Rules**

| Group | | Solubility | Exceptions |
|---|---|---|---|
| nitrates | $NO_3^-$ | all soluble | none |
| chlorates | $ClO_3^-$ | all soluble | none |
| perchlor- ates | $ClO_4^-$ | all soluble | $KClO_4$* |
| acetates | $C_2H_3O_2^-$ | all soluble | $AgC_2H_3O_2$* |
| alkali metal compounds | Li, Na, K, Rb, Cs | all soluble | all alkali metal hydroxides |
| ammonium compounds | $NH_4^+$ | all soluble | none |
| chlorides | $Cl^-$ | all soluble | those that contain $Ag^+$, |
| bromides | $Br^-$ | all soluble | $Hg_2^{2+}$, $Pb^{2+}$, and $PbCl_2$* |
| iodides | $I^-$ | all soluble | |
| sulfates | $SO_4^{2-}$ | most are soluble | $SrSO_4$, $BaSO_4$, $PbSO_4$, $HgSO_4$, $Hg_2SO_4$, $CaSO_4$*, $Ag_2SO_4$* |
| carbonates | $CO_3^{2-}$ | Group I, $(NH_4)_2CO_3$ | all others |
| phosphates | $PO_4^{3-}$ | Group I, $(NH_4)_3PO_4$ | all others |
| sulfites | $SO_3^{2-}$ | Group I, $(NH_4)_2SO_3$ | all others |
| hydroxides | $OH^-$ | Group I, $Sr(OH)_2$, $Ba(OH)_2$ | all others, $Ca(OH)_2$* |
| sulfides | $S^{2-}$ | Group I, $(NH_4)_2S$ | all others |
| oxides | $O^{2-}$ | CaO, SrO, BaO | all others |

*slightly soluble

- mass percent solute $= \dfrac{\text{mass solute}}{\text{total mass solution}} \times 100\%$

  $\text{molality} = \dfrac{\text{moles solute}}{\text{kg solvent}}$

  $\text{molarity} = \dfrac{\text{moles solute}}{\text{liter solution}}$

  In dilute aqueous solutions, molarity = molality.

  $$M_1V_1 = M_2V_2$$

- extent of solubility

    1. nature of solute-solvent interactions
    2. temperature
    3. pressure of gaseous solute

- Henry's law: $C = kP$

    where

    $P =$ partial pressure of gas solute over the solution (atm)
    $C =$ concentration of dissolved gas (mole/liter)
    $k =$ Henry's constant (dependent on temperature, mole/L · atm)

- Raoult's law: $P_1 = X_1 P_1^\circ$

    where

    $P_1 =$ vapor pressure of solvent over the solution
    $P_1^\circ =$ vapor pressure of pure solvent at same temperature
    $X_1 =$ mole fraction of solvent

- $\pi = \dfrac{nRT}{V} = iMRT$

    where

    $\pi$ = osmotic pressure (atm)

    $i$ = van't Hoff factor; should be 1 for all nonelectrolytes

    $= \dfrac{\text{actual number of particles in solution after dissociation}}{\text{number of formula units initially dissolved in solution}}$

    $\text{MW} = \dfrac{gRT}{\pi V}$

- $\Delta T_b = i \cdot k_b \cdot m$       for water, $k_b = 0.52°\text{C/m}$

    $\Delta T_f = i \cdot k_f \cdot m$       for water, $k_f = 1.86°\text{C/m}$

## Examples: Multiple-Choice Questions

1. **A 10.0% sucrose solution has a density of 2.00 g/ml. What is the weight of sucrose dissolved in 1.00 liter of this solution?**
   (A) $1.00 \times 10^2$ g
   (B) $2.00 \times 10^2$ g
   (C) $5.00 \times 10^2$ g
   (D) $1.00 \times 10^3$ g
   (E) $1.00 \times 10^4$ g

*Answer: (B)*

This problem can be easily solved using the factor-label method:

$$\frac{1.00 \text{ liter solution}}{1} \times \frac{1000 \text{ ml solution}}{1 \text{ liter solution}}$$

$$\times \frac{2.00 \text{ g solution}}{1 \text{ ml solution}} \times \frac{10.0 \text{ g sucrose}}{100.0 \text{ g solution}} = 2.00 \times 10^2 \text{ g sucrose}$$

2. **How many milliliters of a 50.0% (by weight) $HNO_3$ solution, with a density of 2.00 grams per milliliter, are required to make 500. ml of a 2.00 M $HNO_3$ solution?**
   (A) 50.0 ml
   (B) 63.0 ml
   (C) 100. ml
   (D) 200. ml
   (E) 250. ml

*Answer: (B)*

This problem can be easily solved using the factor-label method:

$$\frac{500. \text{ ml (2.00 M sol'n)}}{1} \times \frac{1 \text{ liter (2.00 M sol'n)}}{1000 \text{ ml (2.00 M sol'n)}} \times \frac{2.00 \text{ moles } HNO_3}{1 \text{ liter (2.00 M sol'n)}}$$

$$\times \frac{63.0 \text{ g } HNO_3}{1 \text{ mole } HNO_3} \times \frac{100. \text{ g } 50.0\% \text{ sol'n}}{50.0 \text{ g } HNO_3} \times \frac{1 \text{ ml } 50.0\% \text{ sol'n}}{2.00 \text{ g } 50.0\% \text{ sol'n}}$$

$$= 63.0 \text{ ml of a } 50.0\% \text{ sol'n}$$

3. **What is the normality of a solution that contains 9.80 g of $H_2SO_4$ in 200. ml of solution?**
   (A) **0.500 N**  (B) **1.00 N**  (C) **1.50 N**  (D) **2.00 N**  (E) **2.50 N**

*Answer: (B)*

This problem can be solved using the factor-label method:

$$\frac{9.80 \text{ g } H_2SO_4}{200. \text{ ml sol'n}} \times \frac{1000. \text{ ml sol'n}}{1 \text{ liter sol'n}} \times \frac{1 \text{ mole } H_2SO_4}{98.1 \text{ g } H_2SO_4}$$

$$\times \frac{2 \text{ g-eq } H_2SO_4}{1 \text{ mole } H_2SO_4} = 1.00 \text{ g-eq/liter} = 1.00 \text{ N}$$

4. **Calculate the number of gram-equivalents of solute in 0.500 liter of a 3.00 N solution.**
   (A) **1.00 g-eq**
   (B) **1.50 g-eq**
   (C) **2.00 g-eq**
   (D) **3.00 g-eq**
   (E) **6.00 g-eq**

*Answer: (B)*

This problem can be solved using the factor-label method:

$$\frac{0.500 \text{ liter sol'n}}{1} \times \frac{3.00 \text{ g-eq}}{1 \text{ liter sol'n}} = 1.50 \text{ g-eq}$$

5. **What is the percentage (by mass) of NaCl (FW = 58.50) in a 10.0-molal solution?**

(A) $\dfrac{10.0 \times 58.50}{1585}$

(B) $\dfrac{10.0 \times 58.50}{1000.00}$

(C) $\dfrac{2 \times 58.50 \times 10.0}{1000.00}$

(D) $\dfrac{10.0 \times 58.50}{100.00}$

(E) $\dfrac{100 \times 58.50}{1000.00}$

*Answer: (A)*

This problem can be solved using the factor-label method:

$$\frac{10.0 \text{ moles NaCl}}{1000. \text{ g H}_2\text{O}} \times \frac{58.50 \text{ g NaCl}}{1 \text{ mole NaCl}} = \frac{585 \text{ g NaCl}}{1000. \text{ g H}_2\text{O}}$$

The question is asking for the parts of NaCl per *total* solution (solute + solvent).

$$\frac{585 \text{ g NaCl}}{1000. \text{ g H}_2\text{O} + 585 \text{ g NaCl}}$$

6. **When 5.92 grams of a nonvolatile, nonionizing compound is dissolved in 186 grams of water, the freezing point (at normal pressure) of the resulting solution is $-0.592°C$. What is the molecular weight of the compound?**
   (A) 10.0 g/mole
   (B) 100. g/mole
   (C) 110. g/mole
   (D) 200. g/mole
   (E) 210. g/mole

*Answer: (B)*

This problem can be solved using the factor-label method:

$$\frac{0.592°\cancel{C}}{1} \times \frac{1 \text{ mole solute}}{1.86°\cancel{C} \cdot \cancel{\text{kg H}_2\text{O}}} \times \frac{186 \cancel{\text{ g H}_2\text{O}}}{5.92 \text{ g solute}}$$

$$\times \frac{1 \cancel{\text{ kg H}_2\text{O}}}{1000 \cancel{\text{ g H}_2\text{O}}} = 0.0100 \text{ mole/g} = 100. \text{ g/mole}$$

7. **Calculate the number of grams of glycerol, $C_3H_5(OH)_3$ (MW = 92.1 g/mole), that must be dissolved in 520. grams of water to raise the boiling point to 102.00°C.**
   (A) 5.65 g   (B) 92.0 g   (C) 184 g   (D) 194 g   (E) 204 g

*Answer: (C)*

This problem can be solved using the factor-label method:

$$\frac{520. \cancel{\text{ g H}_2\text{O}}}{1} \times \frac{1 \cancel{\text{ kg H}_2\text{O}}}{1000 \cancel{\text{ g H}_2\text{O}}} \times \frac{1 \cancel{\text{ mole C}_3\text{H}_5\text{(OH)}_3}}{0.52°\cancel{C} \cdot \cancel{\text{kg H}_2\text{O}}}$$

$$\times \frac{92.1 \text{ g C}_3\text{H}_5\text{(OH)}_3}{1 \cancel{\text{ mole C}_3\text{H}_5\text{(OH)}_3}} \times \frac{2.00°\cancel{C}}{1} = 184 \text{ g C}_3\text{H}_5\text{(OH)}_3$$

8. **In order to determine the molecular weight of a particular protein, 0.010 g of the protein was dissolved in water to make 2.93 ml of solution. The osmotic pressure was determined to be 0.821 torr at 20.0°C. What is the molecular weight of the protein?**
   (A) **$3.8 \times 10^3$ g/mole**
   (B) **$7.6 \times 10^3$ g/mole**
   (C) **$3.8 \times 10^4$ g/mole**
   (D) **$7.6 \times 10^4$ g/mole**
   (E) **None of the above**

*Answer: (D)*

Begin with the equation

$$MW = \frac{gRT}{\pi V}$$

$$= \frac{0.010 \text{ g}}{1} \times \frac{0.0821 \text{ liter} \cdot \text{atm}}{\text{mole} \cdot \text{K}} \times \frac{293 \text{ K}}{1} \times \frac{1}{0.821 \text{ torr}}$$

$$\times \frac{1}{2.93 \text{ ml}} \times \frac{760 \text{ torr}}{1 \text{ atm}} \times \frac{1000 \text{ ml}}{1 \text{ liter}}$$

$$= 7.6 \times 10^4 \text{ g/mole}$$

**9. A solution of $NH_3$ dissolved in water is 10.0 m. What is the mole fraction of water in the solution?**

(A) $\dfrac{1.00}{1.18}$   (B) $\dfrac{1.00}{2.18}$   (C) $\dfrac{0.18}{1.00}$   (D) $\dfrac{0.18}{10.0}$   (E) $1.18$

*Answer: (A)*

This problem can be solved using the factor-label method:

$$\frac{10.0 \text{ moles } NH_3}{1 \text{ kg } H_2O} \times \frac{1 \text{ kg } H_2O}{1000 \text{ g } H_2O} \times \frac{18.02 \text{ g } H_2O}{1 \text{ mole } H_2O} = \frac{0.180 \text{ mole } NH_3}{1.00 \text{ mole } H_2O}$$

total number of moles $= 0.180$ mole $NH_3 + 1.00$ mole $H_2O$
$$= 1.18 \text{ moles sol'n}$$

$$\text{mole fraction of water} = \frac{1.00 \text{ mole } H_2O}{1.18 \text{ mole sol'n}}$$

10. **At 37°C and 1.00 atm of pressure, nitrogen dissolves in the blood at a solubility of $6.0 \times 10^{-4}$ M. If a diver breathes compressed air where nitrogen gas constitutes 80.% of the gas mixture, and the total pressure at this depth is 3.0 atm, what is the concentration of nitrogen in her blood?**
   (A) $1.4 \times 10^{-4}$ M
   (B) $6.0 \times 10^{-4}$ M
   (C) $1.0 \times 10^{-3}$ M
   (D) $1.4 \times 10^{-3}$ M
   (E) $6.0 \times 10^{-3}$ M

*Answer: (D)*

Determine $k$ by using $C = kP$ (Henry's law).

$$k = \frac{\text{concentration } N_2}{\text{pressure } N_2} = \frac{6.0 \times 10^{-4} \text{ M}}{1.00 \text{ atm}} = 6.0 \times 10^{-4} \text{ M} \cdot \text{atm}^{-1}$$

To solve the problem

$$P = 0.80 \times 3.0 \text{ atm} = 2.4 \text{ atm}$$

$$C = kP = \frac{6.0 \times 10^{-4} \text{ moles}}{\text{liter} \cdot \text{atm}} \times \frac{2.4 \text{ atm}}{1} = 1.4 \times 10^{-3} \text{ M}$$

11. **The vapor pressure of an ideal solution is 450. mm Hg. If the vapor pressure of the pure solvent is 1000. mm Hg, what is the mole fraction of the nonvolatile solute?**

   **(A)  0.450**
   **(B)  0.500**
   **(C)  0.550**
   **(D)  0.950**
   **(E)  None of the above**

*Answer: (C)*

$$P_1 = X_1 P_1{}^\circ$$

$$X_1 = \frac{P_1}{P_1{}^\circ} = \frac{450. \text{ mm Hg}}{1000. \text{ mm Hg}} = 0.450$$

The mole fraction of the solute is

$$1.000 - X_1 = 1.000 - 0.450 = 0.550$$

## Examples: Free-Response Questions

1. **An unknown hydrocarbon is burned in the presence of oxygen in order to determine its empirical formula. Another sample of the hydrocarbon is subjected to colligative property tests in order to determine its molecular mass.**
   (a) **Calculate the empirical formula of the hydrocarbon, if upon combustion at STP, 9.01 grams of liquid $H_2O$ and 11.2 liters of $CO_2$ gas are produced.**
   (b) **Determine the mass of the oxygen gas that is used.**
   (c) **The hydrocarbon dissolves readily in $CCl_4$. A solution prepared by mixing 135 grams of $CCl_4$ and 4.36 grams of the hydrocarbon has a boiling point of 78.7°C. The molal boiling-point-elevation constant of $CCl_4$ is 5.02°C/molal, and its normal boiling point is 76.8°C. Calculate the molecular weight of the hydrocarbon.**
   (d) **Determine the molecular formula of the hydrocarbon.**

*Answer*

1. Given: Unknown hydrocarbon is combusted in $O_2$ and subjected to colligative tests.

   (a) Given: 9.01 g $H_2O$ + 11.2 liters $CO_2$ produced.

   Restatement: Find empirical formula of hydrocarbon.

   $$\frac{9.01 \text{ g } H_2O}{18.02 \text{ g/mole}} = 0.500 \text{ mole } H_2O$$

   $$\frac{0.500 \text{ mole } H_2O}{1} \times \frac{2 \text{ moles H}}{1 \text{ mole } H_2O} = 1.00 \text{ mole H}$$

   $$\frac{11.2 \text{ liters } CO_2}{22.4 \text{ liters/mole}} = 0.500 \text{ mole } CO_2$$

   $$\frac{0.500 \text{ mole } CO_2}{1} \times \frac{1 \text{ mole C}}{1 \text{ mole } CO_2} = 0.500 \text{ mole C}$$

   empirical formula = $C_{0.5}H_1 \rightarrow$ **$CH_2$**

(b) Restatement: Calculate mass of $O_2$ required for complete combustion.

$$2\,CH_2(g) + 3O_2(g) \rightarrow 2\,CO_2(g) + 2\,H_2O(\ell)$$

$$\frac{0.500\ \cancel{mole\ H_2O}}{1} \times \frac{3\ \cancel{moles\ O_2}}{2\ \cancel{moles\ H_2O}} \times \frac{32.00\ g\ O_2}{1\ \cancel{mole\ O_2}} = \mathbf{24.0\ g\ O_2}$$

(c) Given:

- The unknown hydrocarbon dissolves in $CCl_4$.
- 135 grams of $CCl_4$ + 4.36 grams of hydrocarbon.
- B.P. of $CCl_4$ = 76.8°C
- New B.P. = 78.7°C
- $K_b$ = 5.02°C/m

Restatement: Calculate MW of hydrocarbon.

$$\Delta T = K_b m$$

$$\Delta T = \frac{(K_b)(g/MW)}{kg\ solvent}$$

$$MW = \frac{(K_b)(grams\ solute)}{(\Delta T)(kg\ solvent)}$$

$$MW = \frac{(5.02°\cancel{C} \cdot \cancel{kg\ solvent}/moles\ solute)(4.36\ g)}{(78.7°\cancel{C} - 76.8°\cancel{C})(0.135\ \cancel{kg\ solvent})} = \mathbf{85.2\ g/mole}$$

(d) Restatement: Determine molecular formula of hydrocarbon.

$$\frac{85\ \cancel{g/mole}\ (molecular\ mass)}{14.03\ \cancel{g/mole}\ (empircal\ mass)} = 6.1$$

Thus, the molecular mass is 6 times greater than the empirical mass.

**molecular formula = $C_6H_{12}$**

2. **An experiment is to be performed to determine the formula mass of a solute ($KNO_3$) through boiling-point elevation.**
   (a) **What data are needed to calculate the formula mass of the solute? Create appropriate data that can be used in part (c).**
   (b) **What procedures are needed to obtain these data?**
   (c) **List the calculations necessary to determine the formula mass; use your data to calculate the formula mass.**
   (d) **Calculate the % error in your determination of the formula mass of $KNO_3$.**

*Answer*

2. (a) Restatement: Data needed to determine FM through B.P. elevation.

   - Boiling point of water: 100.0°C
   - Boiling point of $KNO_3$ solution: 102.2°C
   - Changes in temperature between water and $KNO_3$ solution: 2.2°C
   - Grams of solute: 10.0 g
   - Grams of solvent: 50.0 g

   (b) Restatement: Procedures needed.

   - Measure 50.0 grams of distilled water into a 125-ml Erlenmeyer flask.
   - Heat the water to the boiling point, and record the temperature of the water to the nearest 0.5°C.
   - Do not let thermometer touch sides or bottom of flask.
   - Be sure temperature is constant when reading.
   - Prepare a solution of 10.0 grams of $KNO_3$ in 50.0 grams of distilled water. May have to add more water to the Erlenmeyer due to loss of evaporation.
   - Determine B.P. of this solution.

(c) Restatement: Calculations necessary.

- Change in boiling point

    change in B.P. = B.P. of solution − B.P. of solvent

    $$= 102.2°C − 100.0°C = 2.2°C$$

- Mole fraction of solute

    $$\frac{\text{change in boiling-point temperature}}{n(0.52°C)} \times \frac{1 \text{ mole}}{1 \text{ kg}}$$

    $$= \text{mole fraction of solute}$$

    where $n = 2$ because two moles of ions are formed for each mole of $KNO_3$ used.

    $$\frac{2.2°C}{2(0.52°C)} \times \frac{1 \text{ mole}}{1 \text{ kg}} = 2.1 \text{ moles/kg}$$

- Formula mass of $KNO_3$ from the mole fraction

    $$\frac{\text{grams of solute}}{\text{grams of solvent}} \times \frac{1.0 \times 10^3 \text{ g water}}{\text{mole fraction}}$$

    $$\frac{10.0 \text{ g } KNO_3}{50.0 \text{ g } H_2O} \times \frac{1.0 \times 10^3 \text{ g } H_2O}{2.1 \text{ moles } KNO_3} = \textbf{95 g/mole}$$

(d) Restatement: Calculate the % error.

$KNO_3$ formula mass (theoretical) = 101 g/mole

$KNO_3$ formula mass (from data) = 95 g/mole

$$\% \text{ error} = \frac{\substack{\text{difference between theoretical} \\ \text{and experimental values}}}{\text{theoretical value}} \times 100$$

$$\% \text{ error} = \frac{101 − 95}{101} \times 100 = \textbf{6\%}$$

# KINETICS

## Key Terms

Words that can be used as topics in essays:

activated complex
activation energy
adsorption
Arrhenius equation
catalyst (heterogeneous
    or homogeneous)
chain reaction
collision model
elementary reaction
    (step)
enzyme
first order
half-life

integrated rate law
kinetics
molecular orientations
molecular steps (uni, bi, ter)
order of reaction
overall order
rate constant
rate-determining step
rate expression
rate of reaction
reaction mechanism
second order
steric factor

## Key Concepts

Equations and relationships that you need to know:

- 

| Reaction Order | 0 | 1 | 2 |
|---|---|---|---|
| Rate Law | $k$ | $k[A]$ | $k[A]^2$ |
| Integrated Rate Law | $[A] = kt + [A]_0$ | $\ln [A] = -kt + \ln [A]_0$ | $\dfrac{1}{[A]} = kt + \dfrac{1}{[A]_0}$ |
| Relationship Between Concentration and Time | $[A]_0 - [A] = kt$ | $\log_{10} \dfrac{[A]_0}{[A]} = \dfrac{kt}{2.30}$ | $\dfrac{1}{[A]} - \dfrac{1}{[A]_0} = kt$ |
| Half-life | $\dfrac{[A]_0}{2k}$ | $\dfrac{0.693}{k}$ | $\dfrac{1}{k[A]_0}$ |
| Linear Plot | $[A]$ vs. $t$ | $\log_{10} [A]$ vs. $t$ | $\dfrac{1}{[A]}$ vs. $t$ |
| Slope | $-k$ | $-k$ | $k$ |

- Zero order: $m = 0$, rate is independent of the concentration of the reactant. Doubling the concentration of the reactant does not affect the rate.

  First order: $m = 1$, rate is directly proportional to the concentration of the reactant. Doubling the concentration of the reactant doubles the rate.

  Second order: $m = 2$, rate is proportional to the square of the concentration of the reactant. Doubling the concentration of the reactant increases the rate by a factor of 4.

- $\text{rate} = \dfrac{\Delta \text{ concentration}}{\Delta \text{ time}}$

- Arrhenius equation

$k = Ae^{-E_a/RT}$

> where
>
> > $k$ = rate constant
> > $A$ = Arrhenius constant
> > $e$ = base of natural logarithm
> > $E_a$ = activation energy
> >
> > $R$ = universal gas constant
> >
> > $T$ = temperature (K)

$$\ln k = -\frac{E_a}{RT} + \ln A \qquad \ln \frac{k_1}{k_2} = \frac{E_a}{R}\left(\frac{T_1 - T_2}{T_1 T_2}\right)$$

$$\log k = \log A - \frac{E_a}{2.30RT}$$

$$\text{slope} = \frac{-E_a}{2.30R}$$

$$\log \frac{k_2}{k_1} = \frac{E_a}{2.30R} \cdot \frac{(T_2 - T_1)}{(T_2 T_1)}$$

- $\Delta E = \Sigma E_{\text{products}} - \Sigma E_{\text{reactants}}$

- collision theory: rate = $f \cdot Z$

> where
>
> > $Z$ = total number of collisions
> > $f$ = fractions of total number of collisions that occur
> >     at sufficiently high energy for reaction

$Z = Z_0[A]^n[B]^m$

> where
>
> > $Z_0$ = collision frequency when all reactants are at unit
> >      concentration

- $\Delta H = E_a - E_a'$

  where

  > $E_a$ = forward reaction activation energy
  > $E_a'$ = reverse reaction activation energy

## Examples: Multiple-Choice Questions

1. Acetaldehyde, $CH_3CHO$, decomposes into methane gas and carbon monoxide gas. This is a second-order reaction. The rate of decomposition at 140°C is 0.10 mole/liter · sec when the concentration of acetaldehyde is 0.10 mole/liter. What is the rate of the reaction when the concentration of acetaldehyde is 0.50 mole/liter?
   (A) 0.50 mole/liter · sec
   (B) 1.0 mole/liter · sec
   (C) 1.5 mole/liter · sec
   (D) 2.0 mole/liter · sec
   (E) 2.5 mole/liter · sec

*Answer: (E)*

Begin this problem by writing a balanced equation representing the reaction.

$$CH_3CHO(g) \rightarrow CH_4(g) + CO(g)$$

Next, write a rate expression.

$$\text{rate} = k(\text{conc. } CH_3CHO)^2$$

Because you know the rate and the concentration of $CH_3CHO$, solve for $k$, the rate-specific constant.

$$k = \frac{\text{rate}}{(\text{conc. } CH_3CHO)^2} \rightarrow \frac{0.10 \text{ mole/liter} \cdot \text{sec}}{(0.10 \text{ mole/liter})^2} = 10. \text{ liters/mole} \cdot \text{sec}$$

Finally, substitute the rate-specific constant and the new concentration into the rate expression.

$$\text{rate} = \frac{10. \text{ liters}}{1 \text{ mole} \cdot \text{sec}} \times \left(\frac{0.50 \text{ mole}}{1 \text{ liter}}\right)^2 = 2.5 \text{ mole/liter} \cdot \text{sec}$$

2. The rate of the chemical reaction between substances A and B is found to follow the rate law

$$\text{rate} = k[A]^2[B]$$

where $k$ is the rate constant. The concentration of A is reduced to half its original value. To make the reaction proceed at 50% of its original rate, the concentration of B should be

   (A) decreased by $1/4$
   (B) halved
   (C) kept constant
   (D) doubled
   (E) increased by a factor of 4

*Answer: (D)*

Let $X$ be what needs to be done to [B].

$$\frac{\text{rate}_{new}}{\text{rate}_{old}} = \frac{1}{2} = \frac{k([A]/2)^2 \cdot X[B]}{k[A]^2 \cdot [B]} = \frac{X}{4}$$

$$X = 2$$

3. Which of the following changes will decrease the rate of collisions between gaseous molecules of type A and B in a closed container?
   (A) Decrease the volume of the container.
   (B) Increase the temperature of the system.
   (C) Add A molecules.
   (D) Take away B molecules.
   (E) Add a catalyst.

*Answer: (D)*

With all other factors held constant, decreasing the number of molecules decreases the chance of collision. Adding a catalyst has no effect on the *rate* of collisions. It lowers the activation energy, thereby increasing the chance for *effective* molecular collisions. Furthermore, it increases the rate of production.

4. **For a certain decomposition reaction, the rate is 0.50 mole/ liter · sec when the concentration of the reactant is 0.10 M. If the reaction is second order, what will the new rate be when the concentration of the reactant is increased to 0.40 M?**
   - **(A)   0.50 mole/liter · sec**
   - **(B)   1.0 mole/liter · sec**
   - **(C)   8.0 mole/liter · sec**
   - **(D)   16 mole/liter · sec**
   - **(E)   20. mole/liter · sec**

*Answer: (C)*

The concentration of the reactant is increased by a factor of 4, from 0.10 M to 0.40 M. If the reaction is second order, the rate will then increase by a factor of $4^2 = 16$.

$$\frac{16}{1} \times \frac{0.50 \text{ mole}}{1 \text{ liter} \cdot \text{sec}} = \frac{8.0 \text{ moles}}{1 \text{ liter} \cdot \text{sec}}$$

5. **The rate-determining step of a several-step reaction mechanism has been determined to be**

$$3X(g) + 2Y(g) \rightarrow 4Z(g)$$

**When 3.0 moles of gas X and 2.0 moles of gas Y are placed in a 5.0-liter vessel, the initial rate of the reaction is found to be 0.45 mole/liter · min. What is the rate constant for the reaction?**

(A)    $$\dfrac{0.45}{\left(\dfrac{3.0}{5.0}\right)^3\left(\dfrac{2.0}{5.0}\right)^2}$$

(B)    $$\dfrac{0.45}{(3.0)(2.0)}$$

(C)    $$\dfrac{0.45}{\left(\dfrac{3.0}{5.0}\right)^2\left(\dfrac{2.0}{5.0}\right)^3}$$

(D)    $$\dfrac{0.45}{\left(\dfrac{3.0}{5.0}\right)\left(\dfrac{2.0}{5.0}\right)}$$

(E)    $$\dfrac{(3.0)^3(2.0)^3}{0.45}$$

*Answer: (A)*

*Given a reaction mechanism,* the order with respect to each reactant is its coefficient in the chemical equation for that step. The slowest step is the rate-determining step, so

$$\text{rate} = k[X]^3[Y]^2$$

$$k = \frac{\text{rate}}{[X]^3[Y]^2} = \frac{0.45 \text{ mole/liter} \cdot \text{min}}{\left(\dfrac{3.0 \text{ moles}}{5.0 \text{ liters}}\right)^3\left(\dfrac{2.0 \text{ moles}}{5.0 \text{ liters}}\right)^2}$$

6. **The reaction 2 X + Y → 3 Z was studied and the following data were obtained:**

| Experiment | X | Y | Rate (mole/liter · sec) |
|:---:|:---:|:---:|:---:|
| 1 | 3.0 | 1.5 | 1.8 |
| 2 | 1.5 | 3.0 | 0.45 |
| 3 | 1.5 | 1.5 | 0.45 |

**What is the proper rate expression?**
(A)  **rate** = $k[X][Y]$
(B)  **rate** = $k[Y]^2$
(C)  **rate** = $k[X]$
(D)  **rate** = $k[X]^2[Y]$
(E)  **rate** = $k[X]^2$

*Answer: (E)*

Examine experiments 2 and 3, wherein [X] is held constant. Note that as [Y] doubles (from 1.5 to 3.0), the rate does not change. Hence, the rate is independent of [Y] and the order is 0 for Y.

Now examine experiments 1 and 3, wherein [Y] is held constant. Note that as [X] doubles, the rate is increased by a factor of 4. In this case, the rate is proportional to the square of the concentration of the reactant. This is a second-order reactant.

Combining these reactant orders in a rate equation gives

$$\text{rate} = k[X]^2[Y]^0 = k[X]^2$$

*For Examples 7 and 8, refer to the following diagram.*

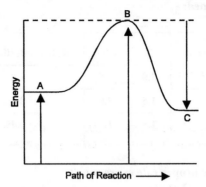

## 7. The activation energy is represented by
(A) $A$  (B) $B$   (C) $C$   (D) $B - A$   (E) $B - C$

*Answer: (D)*

The activation energy is the amount of energy that the reactants must absorb from the system in order to react. In the reaction diagram, the reactants begin at $A$. The reactants must absorb the energy from $A$ to $B$ in order to form the activated complex. The energy necessary to achieve this activated complex is the distance from $A$ to $B$ in the diagram and is mathematically the difference $(B - A)$.

8. **The enthalpy of the reaction is represented by**
    (A) $B - (C - A)$
    (B) $B$
    (C) $C - A$
    (D) $B - C$
    (E) $A - (B - C)$

*Answer: (C)*

The enthalpy of the reaction, $\Delta H$, is the difference between the enthalpies of the products and the enthalpies of the reactants.

$$\Delta H = H_{products} - H_{reactants}$$

The products are represented at point $C$ and the reactants are represented at point $A$, so the change in enthalpy is $C - A$.

9. **Given the following reaction mechanism, express the rate of the overall reaction.**

$$2\,A + 3\,C \rightarrow 4\,D + 5\,E \quad \text{slow}$$
$$A + 2\,D \rightleftharpoons 2\,A + 2\,E \quad \text{fast}$$
$$2\,E + C \rightarrow 3\,D + 2\,C \quad \text{fast}$$

    (A) $k \cdot 2[A]'''3[C]''$
    (B) $k \cdot [D]^4[E]^5 / [A]^2[C]^3$
    (C) $k \cdot [D]^4[E]^5$
    (D) $k \cdot [A]'''[C]''$
    (E) $k \cdot [A]^2[C]^3$

*Answer: (E)*

The rate is determined by the slowest step. Only when given the complete mechanisms *in steps* can you identify the slowest step and use the coefficients of the reactants as the orders in the rate equation.

**10. Referring to example 9, express the overall reaction.**
   (A) $3 C + 2 D \rightarrow 2 A + 4 E$
   (B) $3 A + 3 C \rightarrow 3 D + 4 E$
   (C) $2 A + 3 C \rightarrow A + 4 E$
   (D) $A + 2 C \rightarrow 5 D + 5 E$
   (E) $2 A + C \rightarrow D + 2 E$

*Answer: (D)*

To find the overall equation when given the reaction mechanism, simply add the reactions.

$$2 A + 3 C \rightarrow 4 D + 5 E \qquad \textbf{slow}$$
$$A + 2 D \rightleftarrows 2 A + 2 E \qquad \textbf{fast}$$
$$2 E + C \rightarrow 3 D + 2 C \qquad \textbf{fast}$$

There is a total of 3 A's on the left and 2 A's on the right: balance of 1 A on the left. There is a total of 4 C's on the left and 2 C's on the right: balance of 2 C's on the left. There is a total of 2 D's on the left and 7 D's on the right: balance of 5 D's on the right. There is a total of 2 E's on the left and 7 E's on the right: balance of 5 E's on the right.

$$A + 2 C \rightarrow 5 D + 5 E$$

## Examples: Free-Response Questions

1. The reaction

$$2 \, NO_2(g) + Cl_2(g) \rightarrow 2 \, NO_2Cl(g)$$

was studied at 20°C and the following data were obtained:

| Experiment | Initial $[NO_2]$ (mole · liter$^{-1}$) | Initial $[Cl_2]$ (mole · liter$^{-1}$) | Initial Rate of Increase of $[NO_2Cl]$ (mole · liter$^{-1}$ · sec$^{-1}$) |
|------------|------------------------------------------|------------------------------------------|------------------------------------------------------------------------------|
| 1 | 0.100 | 0.005 | $1.35 \times 10^{-7}$ |
| 2 | 0.100 | 0.010 | $2.70 \times 10^{-7}$ |
| 3 | 0.200 | 0.010 | $5.40 \times 10^{-7}$ |

(a) Write the rate law for the reaction.
(b) What is the overall order for the reaction? Explain.
(c) Calculate the rate-specific constant, including units.
(d) In Experiment 3, what is the initial rate of decrease of $[Cl_2]$?
(e) Propose a mechanism for the reaction that is consistent with the rate law expression you found in part (a).

*Answer*

1. Given: $2\ NO_2(g) + CO_2(g) \rightarrow 2\ NO_2Cl(g)$

   (a) Restatement: Rate law.

   $$\text{rate} = k[NO_2]^n[Cl_2]^m$$

   $$\begin{aligned}
   \text{Expt. 1: rate} &= 1.35 \times 10^{-7}\ \text{mole/liter} \cdot \text{sec} \\
   &= k(0.100\ \text{M})^n(0.0050\ \text{M})^m \\
   \text{Expt. 2: rate} &= 2.70 \times 10^{-7}\ \text{mole/liter} \cdot \text{sec} \\
   &= k(0.100\ \text{M})^n(0.010\ \text{M})^m \\
   \text{Expt. 3: rate} &= 5.40 \times 10^{-7}\ \text{mole/liter} \cdot \text{sec} \\
   &= k(0.200\ \text{M})^n(0.010\ \text{M})^m
   \end{aligned}$$

   $$\frac{\text{rate 2}}{\text{rate 1}} = \frac{2.70 \times 10^{-7}\ \text{mole/liter} \cdot \text{sec}}{1.35 \times 10^{-7}\ \text{mole/liter} \cdot \text{sec}}$$

   $$= \frac{\cancel{k(0.100\ \text{M})^n}(0.010\ \text{M})^m}{\cancel{k(0.100\ \text{M})^n}(0.0050\ \text{M})^m}$$

   $$= 2.00 = (2.0)^m \qquad m = 1$$

   $$\frac{\text{rate 3}}{\text{rate 2}} = \frac{5.40 \times 10^{-7}\ \text{mole/liter} \cdot \text{sec}}{2.70 \times 10^{-7}\ \text{mole/liter} \cdot \text{sec}}$$

   $$= \frac{k(0.200\ \text{M})^n\cancel{(0.010\ \text{M})^m}}{k(0.100\ \text{M})^n\cancel{(0.010\ \text{M})^m}}$$

   $$= 2.00 = (2.00)^n \qquad n = 1$$

   **rate = $k[NO_2]^1[Cl_2]^1$**

(b) Restatement: Overall order. Explain.

overall order = $m + n = 1 + 1 = 2$

The rate is proportional to the product of the concentrations of the two reactants:

$2 \, NO_2(g) + Cl_2(g) \rightarrow 2 \, NO_2Cl(g)$

$$\text{rate} = \frac{-\Delta[NO_2(g)]}{\Delta t} = k[NO_2(g)][Cl_2(g)]$$

or

$$\text{rate} = \frac{-2\Delta[Cl_2(g)]}{\Delta t} = k[NO_2(g)][Cl_2(g)]$$

(c) Restatement: Rate-specific constant $k$.

$\text{rate} = k[NO_2][Cl_2]$

$k = \text{rate}/[NO_2][Cl_2]$

$$= \frac{1.35 \times 10^{-7} \, \text{mole} \cdot \text{liter}^{-1} \cdot \text{sec}^{-1}}{(0.100 \, \text{mole} \cdot \text{liter}^{-1})(0.005 \, \text{mole} \cdot \text{liter}^{-1})}$$

$= 2.7 \times 10^{-4} \, \text{liter}/\text{mole} \cdot \text{sec}$

(d) Restatement: In experiment 3, initial rate of decrease of $[Cl_2]$.

$2 \, NO_2(g) + Cl_2(g) \rightarrow 2 \, NO_2Cl(g)$

$$\frac{-d[Cl_2]}{dt} = \frac{1}{2}\left(\frac{d[NO_2Cl]}{dt}\right)$$

$$= (5.40 \times 10^{-7})/2$$

$$= 2.7 \times 10^{-7} \, \text{mole} \cdot \text{liter}^{-1} \cdot \text{sec}^{-1}$$

(e) Restatement: Possible mechanism.

The proposed mechanism must satisfy two requirements:
(1) The sum of the steps must give a balanced equation.
(2) The mechanism must agree with the experimentally determined rate law.

$$NO_2(g) + Cl_2(g) \xrightarrow{k_1} NO_2Cl(g) + Cl(g) \qquad \text{slow}$$

$$Cl(g) + NO_2(g) \xrightarrow{k_2} NO_2Cl(g) \qquad \text{fast}$$

Requirement 1:

$$\begin{array}{r} NO_2 + Cl_2 \rightarrow NO_2Cl + \cancel{Cl} \\ \cancel{Cl} + NO_2 \rightarrow NO_2Cl \\ \hline 2NO_2 + Cl_2 \rightarrow 2\,NO_2Cl \end{array}$$

Requirement 2:

$$NO_2(g) + Cl_2(g) \rightarrow NO_2Cl + Cl$$

is the rate-determining step. This step is bimolecular.

$$\text{rate} = k_1[NO_2][Cl_2]$$

as found in part (a).

Meeting these two requirements does not prove that this <u>is</u> the mechanism for the reaction—only that it <u>could be</u>.

2. **Hydrogen peroxide, $H_2O_2$, decomposes by first-order decomposition and has a rate constant of 0.015/min at 200°C. Starting with a 0.500 M solution of $H_2O_2$, calculate:**
   (a) **The molarity of $H_2O_2$ after 10.00 min**
   (b) **The time it will take for the concentration of $H_2O_2$ to go from 0.500 M to 0.150 M**
   (c) **The half-life**

*Answer*

2. Given: $H_2O_2$, first-order decomposition

$$k = 0.015/\text{min at } 200°C$$
$$[H_2O_2]_0 = 0.500 \text{ M}$$

(a) Restatement: Calculate $[H_2O_2]$ after 10.00 min.

For first-order reactions: rate $= kX \rightarrow \dfrac{-dX}{dt} = kX$

Integrating from $X_0$ to $X$ gives

$$-\ln\left(\frac{X}{X_0}\right) = kt$$

$$= \log\left(\frac{X_0}{X}\right) = \frac{kt}{2.30}$$

$$= \log\left(\frac{0.500 \text{ M}}{X}\right) = 0.065$$

$$= \frac{0.500}{X} = 10^{0.065}$$

$$= \frac{0.500}{X} = 1.2$$

$$X = \frac{0.500}{1.2} = \mathbf{0.42 \text{ M}}$$

(b)  Restatement: Time for $H_2O_2$ to go from 0.500 M to 0.150 M.

For first-order reactions:

$$\log\left(\frac{X_0}{X}\right) = \frac{kt}{2.30}$$

$$t = \frac{2.30}{k} \log\left(\frac{X_0}{X}\right)$$

$$= \left(\frac{2.30}{0.015/\text{min}}\right) \log\left(\frac{0.500 \text{ M}}{0.150 \text{ M}}\right)$$

$$= \frac{2.30}{0.015/\text{min}} \times 0.523$$

$$= \mathbf{8.0 \times 10^1 \text{ min}}$$

(c)  Restatement: Calculate the half-life.

For first-order reactions:

$$t_{1/2} = \frac{0.693}{k} = \frac{0.693}{0.015/\text{min}} = \mathbf{46 \text{ min}}$$

# EQUILIBRIUM

## Key Terms

Words that can be used as topics in essays:

| | |
|---|---|
| 5% rule | limiting reactant |
| buffer | method of successive |
| common ion effect | approximation |
| equilibrium expression | net ionic equation |
| equivalence point | percent dissociation |
| Henderson–Hasselbalch | pH |
| equation | $pK_a$ |
| heterogeneous equilibria | $pK_b$ |
| homogeneous equilibria | pOH |
| ion product, $P$ | reaction quotient, $Q$ |
| indicator | reciprocal rule |
| $K_a$ | rule of multiple equilibria |
| $K_b$ | solubility |
| $K_c$ | spectator ions |
| $K_{eq}$ | strong acid |
| $K_p$ | strong base |
| $K_{sp}$ | van't Hoff equation |
| $K_w$ | weak acid |
| law of mass action | weak base |
| Le Chatelier's principle | |

## Key Concepts

Equations and relationships that you need to know:

- $\Delta G° = -RT \ln K = -0.0191\, T \log K_p$

  $\Delta G° \ll 0, K$ is large; $\Delta G° \gg 0, K = 0$

- $pK_a = -\log K_a$

- $HB(aq) \rightleftharpoons H^+(aq) + B^-(aq)$

  $$K_a = \frac{[H^+][B^-]}{[HB]}$$

  $$[H^+] = K_a \times \frac{[HB]}{[B^-]}$$

- $K_a \times K_b = 1.0 \times 10^{-14} = K_w = [H^+][OH^-]$

  $$K = K_1 \times K_2 \times \ldots$$

- $Q$ = ion product (or reaction quotient) = calculated as $K_{sp}$ except using initial concentrations

  $Q > K_{sp}$, supersaturated solution, precipitate forms until such point that $Q = K_{sp}$

  $Q < K_{sp}$, unsaturated solution, no precipitate

  $Q = K_{sp}$, saturated solution, no precipitate forms

- Henderson-Hasselbalch: $pH = pK_a + \log \dfrac{[A^-]}{[HA]}$

  $$= pK_a + \log \frac{[\text{base}]}{[\text{acid}]}$$

- van't Hoff equation

  $$\ln \frac{K_2}{K_1} = -\frac{\Delta H^\circ}{R}\left[\frac{1}{T_2} - \frac{1}{T_1}\right]$$

- Clausius-Clapeyron equation

  $$\ln \frac{P_2^\circ}{P_1^\circ} = -\frac{\Delta H_{\text{vap}}^\circ}{R}\left[\frac{1}{T_2} - \frac{1}{T_1}\right]$$

- $K_p = K_c(RT)^{\Delta n}$

  where $\Delta n$ = moles gaseous products − moles gaseous reactants

## Examples: Multiple-Choice Questions

1. **6.0 moles of chlorine gas are placed in a 3.0-liter flask at 1250 K. At this temperature, the chlorine molecules begin to dissociate into chlorine atoms. What is the value for $K_c$ if 50.% of the chlorine molecules dissociate when equilibrium has been achieved?**
   (A) 1.0   (B) 3.0   (C) 4.0   (D) 6.0   (E) 12.0

*Answer: (C)*

Begin by writing the balanced equation in equilibrium.

$$Cl_2(g) \rightleftarrows 2\,Cl(g)$$

Next, write an equilibrium expression.

$$K_c = \frac{[Cl]^2}{[Cl_2]}$$

Then create a chart that outlines the initial and final concentrations for the various species.

| Species | Initial Concentration | Final Concentration |
|---------|----------------------|---------------------|
| $Cl_2$ | $\dfrac{6.0 \text{ moles}}{3.0 \text{ liters}}$ $= 2.0 \text{ M}$ | $6.0 \text{ moles} - (0.5)(6.0) = 3.0 \text{ moles}$ <br><br> $\dfrac{3.0 \text{ moles}}{3.0 \text{ liters}} = 1.0 \text{ M}$ |
| $Cl$ | $\dfrac{0 \text{ moles}}{3.0 \text{ liters}} = 0 \text{ M}$ | $\dfrac{3.0 \text{ moles } Cl_2 \text{ dissociated}}{1} \times \dfrac{2 \text{ moles } Cl}{1 \text{ mole } Cl_2}$ <br><br> $= 6.0 \text{ moles } Cl \text{ at equilibrium}$ <br><br> $\dfrac{6.0 \text{ moles } Cl}{3.0 \text{ liters}} = 2.0 \text{ M}$ |

Finally, substitute the concentrations (at equilibrium) into the equilibrium expression.

$$K_c = \frac{[Cl]^2}{[Cl_2]} = \frac{(2.0)^2}{1.0} = 4.0$$

2. **6.00 moles of nitrogen gas and 6.00 moles of oxygen gas are placed in a 2.00-liter flask at 500.°C and the mixture is allowed to reach equilibrium. What is the concentration, in moles per liter, of nitrogen monoxide at equilibrium if the equilibrium constant is found to be 4.00?**
    (A) **3.00 M**   (B) **6.00 M**   (C) **8.00 M**   (D) **10.0 M**   (E) **12.0 M**

*Answer: (A)*

*Step 1:* Write the balanced equation at equilibrium.

$$N_2(g) + O_2(g) \rightleftarrows 2\,NO(g)$$

*Step 2:* Write the equilibrim expression.

$$K_{eq} = \frac{[NO]^2}{[N_2][O_2]} = 4.00$$

*Step 3:* Create a chart that shows the initial concentrations, the final concentrations, and the changes in concentration. Let $x$ represent the concentration (M) of either $N_2$ or $O_2$ (their concentrations are in a 1:1 molar ratio) that is transformed through the reaction into NO.

| Species | Initial Concentration | Change in Concentration | Final Concentration |
|---------|----------------------|-------------------------|---------------------|
| $N_2$ | 3.00 M | $-x$ | $3.00 - x$ |
| $O_2$ | 3.00 M | $-x$ | $3.00 - x$ |
| NO | 0 M | $+2x$ | $2x$ |

*Step 4:* Take the concentrations at equilibrium and substitute them into the equilibrium expression.

$$K_{eq} = \frac{[NO]^2}{[N_2][O_2]} = \frac{(2x)^2}{(3.00 - x)^2} = 4.00$$

*Step 5:* Solve for $x$ by taking the square root of both sides.

$$\frac{2x}{3.00 - x} = 2.00$$

$$2x = 6.0 - 2.00x$$

$$x = 1.50$$

*Step 6:* Plug the value for $x$ into the expression of the equilibrium concentration for NO.

$$[NO] = 2x = 2(1.50) = 3.00 \text{ M}$$

3. **Solid carbon reacts with carbon dioxide gas to produce carbon monoxide. At 1500°C, the reaction is found to be at equilibrium with a $K_p$ value of 0.50 and a total pressure of 3.5 atm. What is the proper expression for the partial pressure (in atmospheres) of the carbon dioxide?**

(A) $$\dfrac{-0.5 + \sqrt{[(0.50)^2 - 4(1)(-3.5)]}}{2(1)}$$

(B) $$\dfrac{-0.5 + \sqrt{[(0.50)^2 - 4(1)(-1.75)]}}{2(1)}$$

(C) $$\dfrac{-0.5 + \sqrt{[(0.50) - 4(1)(-1.75)]}}{2(1)}$$

(D) $$\dfrac{-0.5 + \sqrt{[(0.50)^2 - 2(1)(3.5)]}}{2(1)}$$

(E) $$\dfrac{0.5 + \sqrt{[(0.50)^2 - 4(1)(-1.75)]}}{2(1)}$$

*Answer: (B)*

*Step 1:* Write the balanced equilibrium equation.

$$C(s) + CO_2(g) \rightleftarrows 2\,CO(g)$$

*Step 2:* Write the equilibrium expression.

$$K_p = \frac{(P_{CO})^2}{P_{CO_2}} = 0.50$$

*Step 3:* Express the two unknowns, pressure of CO and pressure of $CO_2$, in terms of a single unknown, pressure of CO.

$$P_{total} = P_{CO} + P_{CO_2} = 3.5 \text{ atm}$$
$$P_{CO_2} = 3.5 \text{ atm} - P_{CO}$$

*Step 4:* Rewrite the equilibrium expression in terms of the single unknown.

$$K_p = 0.50 = \frac{(P_{CO})^2}{3.5 - P_{CO}}$$

*Step 5:* Rewrite this relationship in terms of the quadratic equation so that you can solve for the unknown $x$, the pressure of the CO.

$$x^2 = 1.75 - 0.50x$$

Putting this equation into the standard form, $ax^2 + bx + c = 0$, you get

$$x^2 + 0.50x - 1.75 = 0$$

*Step 6:* Use the quadratic equation to solve for $x$.

$$x = \frac{-0.50 \pm \sqrt{[(0.50)^2 - 4(1)(-1.75)]}}{2(1)}$$

*For Examples 4 and 5, use the following information:*

**A student prepared a 1.00 M acetic acid solution ($HC_2H_3O_2$). The student found the pH of the solution to be 2.00.**

4. **What is the $K_a$ value for the solution?**
   (A) $3.00 \times 10^{-7}$
   (B) $2.00 \times 10^{-6}$
   (C) $2.00 \times 10^{-5}$
   (D) $1.00 \times 10^{-4}$
   (E) $1.00 \times 10^{-3}$

*Answer: (D)*

*Step 1:* Write the balanced equation in a state of equilibrium.

$$HC_2H_3O_2(aq) \rightleftarrows H^+(aq) + C_2H_3O_2^-(aq)$$

*Step 2:* Write the equilibrium expression.

$$K_a = \frac{[H^+][C_2H_3O_2^-]}{[HC_2H_3O_2]}$$

*Step 3:* Use the pH of the solution to determine $[H^+]$.

$$pH = -\log[H^+] = 2.00$$
$$H^+ = 10^{-2.00} = 0.0100 \text{ M}$$

*Step 4:* Determine $[C_2H_3O_2^-]$

The molar ratio of $[H^+]$ to $[C_2H_3O_2^-]$ is 1:1, so $[C_2H_3O_2^-] = 0.0100$ M also.

*Step 5:* Substitute the concentrations into the equilibrium expression.

$$K_a = \frac{[H^+][C_2H_3O_2^-]}{[HC_2H_3O_2]} = \frac{(0.0100)^2}{0.99} \approx 1.00 \times 10^{-4}$$

**5. What is the % dissociation of the acetic acid? (Use the 5% rule.)**
   **(A) 0.05%   (B) 1.00%   (C) 1.50%   (D) 2.00%   (E) 2.50%**

*Answer: (B)*

*Step 1:* Write the generic formula for % dissociation.

$$\% \text{ dissociation} = \frac{\text{part}}{\text{whole}} \times 100\% = \frac{M_{HC_2H_3O_2 \text{ dissociated}}}{M_{HC_2H_3O_2 \text{ available}}} \times 100\%$$

*Step 2:* Substitute the known information into the generic equation and solve.

$$\% \text{ dissociation} = \frac{0.0100}{0.99} \times 100\% \approx 1.00\%$$

Note: The 5% rule is an empirical rule that states that the approximation $a - x \approx a$ is valid if $x < 0.05a$. The rule depends on the generalization that the value of the constant in the equation in which $x$ appears is seldom known to be better than 5%.

6. **Given that the first, second, and third dissociation constants for $H_3PO_4$ are $7.0 \times 10^{-3}$, $6.0 \times 10^{-8}$, and $5.0 \times 10^{-13}$, respectively, calculate $K$ for the overall reaction.**
   (A) $2.10 \times 10^{-32}$
   (B) $2.10 \times 10^{-28}$
   (C) $2.10 \times 10^{-22}$
   (D) $2.10 \times 10^{-11}$
   (E) $2.10 \times 10^{22}$

*Answer: (C)*

This problem involves the concept of multiple equilibria. The dissociation constants given in the example are related to the following reactions:

$$H_3PO_4(aq) \rightleftarrows H^+(aq) + H_2PO_4^-(aq) \qquad K_1 = 7.0 \times 10^{-3}$$

$$H_2PO_4^-(aq) \rightleftarrows H^+(aq) + HPO_4^{2-}(aq) \qquad K_2 = 6.0 \times 10^{-8}$$

$$HPO_4^{2-}(aq) \rightleftarrows H^+(aq) + PO_4^{3-}(aq) \qquad K_3 = 5.0 \times 10^{-13}$$

For multiple equilibria dissociation constants (such as polyprotic acids), $K$ for the overall reaction is the product of the equilibrium constants for the individual reactions. Therefore, $K = K_1 \times K_2 \times K_3 = 210 \times 10^{-24} = 2.10 \times 10^{-22}$, which is the equilibrium constant for the sum of three individual reactions:

$$H_3PO_4(aq) \rightleftarrows 3\,H^+(aq) + PO_4^{3-}(aq)$$

7. **A buffer is found to contain 0.35 M $NH_3$ ($K_b = 1.8 \times 10^{-5}$) and 0.20 M $NH_4Cl$. What would be the mathematical expression for $K_b$ in terms of $[NH_4^+]$, $[OH^-]$, and $[NH_3]$?**

   (A)  $1.8 \times 10^{-5} = \dfrac{(0.35 + x)(x)}{0.20}$

   (B)  $1.8 \times 10^{-5} = \dfrac{(0.35 - x)(0.20x)}{0.20}$

   (C)  $1.8 \times 10^{-5} = \dfrac{(0.20 + x)(x)}{(0.35 - x)}$

   (D)  $1.8 \times 10^{-5} = \dfrac{(0.20)(x)}{0.35}$

   (E)  $1.8 \times 10^{-5} = \dfrac{(0.20 + x)(0.35 - x)}{0.35}$

*Answer: (C)*

*Step 1:* Get a picture of the solution in equilibrium. Ammonia ($NH_3$) is a *weak* base. $NH_3$ reacts with water in accordance with the following equilibrium equation:

$$NH_3 + H_2O \rightleftarrows NH_4^+ + OH^-$$

Ammonium chloride is soluble in water (see the solubility rules on page 144). Therefore, the concentration of $NH_4^+$ and that of $Cl^-$ are both 0.20 M.

*Step 2:* Write an equilibrium expression.

$$K_b = \frac{[NH_4^+][OH^-]}{[NH_3]} = 1.8 \times 10^{-5}$$

*Step 3:* Set up a chart showing initial concentrations of the species and final concentrations at equilibrium (the $Cl^-$ does not contribute to the pH). Let $x$ represent the portion of $NH_3$ that eventually converts to $NH_4^+$. $x$ will also represent the amount by which the concentration of $NH_4^+$ increases.

| Species | Initial Concentration | Final Concentration |
|---------|----------------------|---------------------|
| $NH_3$ | 0.35 M | $0.35 - x$ |
| $NH_4^+$ | 0.20 M | $0.20 + x$ |
| $OH^-$ | ~0    M* | ~$x$ |

*Because $NH_3$ is a weak base and you are using a relatively weak solution (0.35 M), for calculating purposes you can essentially claim that $OH^-_{init}$ is 0. Further, because $[OH^-]$ and $[NH_4^+]$ at equilibrium are in a 1:1 molar ratio, the concentration of $OH^-$ will increase by the amount $x$.

*Step 4:* Substitute these chart values into the equilibrium expression.

$$K_b = \frac{[NH_4^+][OH^-]}{[NH_3]} = 1.8 \times 10^{-5} = \frac{(0.20 + x)(x)}{(0.35 - x)}$$

Note: If this question were in the free-response section (calculators allowed), and if the question asked you to solve for the pH of the buffer, you would need to solve for $x$ using the quadratic equation. $x$ would be $3.2 \times 10^{-5}$. Because $[OH^-] \approx 3.2 \times 10^{-5}$ and pOH = $-\log$ $[OH^-]$, pOH = 4.5. pH = $14.0 - $ pOH = $14.0 - 4.5 = 9.5$.

8. **Copper(II) iodate has a solubility of $3.3 \times 10^{-3}$ M at 25°C. Calculate its $K_{sp}$ value.**
   (A) $1.4 \times 10^{-7}$
   (B) $1.1 \times 10^{-5}$
   (C) $3.3 \times 10^{-3}$
   (D) $5.1 \times 10^{-1}$
   (E) $3.3 \times 10^3$

*Answer: (A)*

*Step 1:* Write the equation for the dissociation of copper(II) iodate.

$$Cu(IO_3)_2(s) \rightleftarrows Cu^{2+}(aq) + 2\,IO_3^{-}(aq)$$

*Step 2:* Write down the concentrations during the process of dissociation.

$$3.3 \times 10^{-3}\ M\ Cu(IO_3)_2 \rightarrow 3.3 \times 10^{-3}\ M\ Cu^{2+}(aq)$$

$$+ 2(3.3 \times 10^{-3}\ M)IO_3^{-}(aq)$$

$$[Cu^{2+}(aq)] = 3.3 \times 10^{-3}\ M$$

$$[IO_3^{-}(aq)] = 6.6 \times 10^{-3}\ M$$

*Step 3:* Write the equilibrium expression.

$$K_{sp} = [Cu^{2+}][IO_3^{-}]^2$$

*Step 4:* Substitute the equilibrium concentration into the $K_{sp}$ expression.

$$K_{sp} = (3.3 \times 10^{-3})(6.6 \times 10^{-3})^2 = 1.4 \times 10^{-7}$$

9. **Lead iodide has a $K_{sp}$ value of $1.08 \times 10^{-7}$ at 20°C. Calculate its solubility at 20°C.**
   (A) **$5.00 \times 10^{-8}$**
   (B) **$3.00 \times 10^{-6}$**
   (C) **$1.00 \times 10^{-4}$**
   (D) **$6.00 \times 10^{-3}$**
   (E) **$3.00 \times 10^{-3}$**

*Answer: (E)*

*Step 1:* Write the equilibrium equation for the dissociation of lead iodide.

$$PbI_2(s) \rightleftarrows Pb^{2+}(aq) + 2\,I^{-}(aq)$$

*Step 2:* Write the equilibrium expression.

$$K_{sp} = [Pb^{2+}][I^-]^2 = 1.08 \times 10^{-7}$$

*Step 3:* Set up a chart that expresses initial and final concentrations (at equilibrium) of the $Pb^{2+}(aq)$ and $I^-(aq)$.

| Species | Initial Concentration | Final Concentration at Equilibrium |
|---------|----------------------|-----------------------------------|
| $Pb^{2+}$ | 0 M | $x$ |
| $I^-$ | 0 M | $2x$ |

*Step 4:* Substitute the equilibrium concentrations of the ions into the equilibrium expression.

$$K_{sp} = [Pb^{2+}][I^-]^2 = (x)(2x)^2 = 1.08 \times 10^{-7}$$

$$4x^3 = 1.08 \times 10^{-7}$$

$$x^3 = 27 \times 10^{-9}$$

$$x = 3.0 \times 10^{-3}$$

10. **Will a precipitate form when one mixes 75.0 ml of 0.050 M PbCrO₄ solution with 75.0 ml of 0.10 M Ca(NO₃)₂? ($K_{sp}$ for CaCrO₄ = 7.1 × 10⁻⁴)**
    (A) **Yes, a precipitate will form, $Q > K_{sp}$.**
    (B) **Yes, a precipitate will form, $Q < K_{sp}$.**
    (C) **Yes, a precipitate will form, $Q = K_{sp}$.**
    (D) **No, a precipitate will not form, $Q > K_{sp}$.**
    (E) **No, a precipitate will not form, $Q < K_{sp}$.**

*Answer: (A)*

Recognize that this problem is one involving the ion product, $Q$. We calculate $Q$ in the same manner as $K_{sp}$, except that we use initial concentrations of the species instead of equilibrium concentrations. We then compare the value of $Q$ to that of $K_{sp}$.

If $Q < K_{sp}$, no precipitate forms.
If $Q = K_{sp}$, no precipitate forms.
If $Q > K_{sp}$, a precipitate forms.

*At this point you can rule out choices (B), (C), and (D) because they do not make sense. If you have forgotten how to do the problem mathematically, you should guess now; you have a 50% chance of getting the answer right.*

*Step 1:* Realize that this problem involves a possible double displacement, the possible precipitate being either $Pb(NO_3)_2$ or $CaCrO_4$. Rule out the $Pb(NO_3)_2$ because all nitrates are soluble. To answer this question, you must have the solubility table memorized.

*Step 2:* Write the net ionic equation.

$$Ca^{2+}(aq) + CrO_4^{2-}(aq) \rightarrow CaCrO_4(s)$$

*Step 3:* Write the equilibrium expression.

$$K_{sp} = [Ca^{2+}][CrO_4^{2-}]$$

*Step 4:* Determine the *initial* concentrations of the ions that *might* form the precipitate in the *mixed* solution.

$$Ca^{2+}(aq): \frac{0.075 \text{ liter}}{1} \times \frac{0.10 \text{ mole}}{1 \text{ liter}} = 7.5 \times 10^{-3} \text{ mole}$$

$$CrO_4^{2-}(aq): \frac{0.075 \text{ liter}}{1} \times \frac{0.05 \text{ mole}}{1 \text{ liter}} = 3.8 \times 10^{-3} \text{ mole}$$

The total liters of solution = 0.075 + 0.075 = 0.15 liter. Therefore,

$$[Ca^{2+}](aq): \frac{7.5 \times 10^{-3} \text{ mole}}{0.15 \text{ liter}} = 0.050 \text{ M}$$

$$[CrO_4^{2-}](aq): \frac{3.8 \times 10^{-3} \text{ mole}}{0.15 \text{ liter}} = 0.025 \text{ M}$$

*Step 5:* Determine $Q$, the ion product.

$$Q = [Ca^{2+}][CrO_4^{2-}] = [0.05][0.025] = 1.3 \times 10^{-3}$$

Because $Q > K_{sp}$, a precipitate will form.

## Examples: Free-Response Questions

*A Note to Students:* Part A of Section II of the AP chemistry exam is *always* an equilibrium problem. Part A consists of *one* equilibrium question, and you *must* do this question; there is no choice among questions. This one question is worth 25% of the grade for Section II. Needless to say, your score on this one question is very important to your success on the AP chemistry exam.

The equilibrium problem will represent one of three possible types:

Gaseous equilibrium—$K_c$ or $K_p$
Acid-base equilibrium—$K_a$ or $K_b$
Solubility—$K_{sp}$

1. **250.0 grams of solid copper(II) nitrate is placed in an empty 4.0-liter flask. Upon heating the flask to 250°C, some of the solid decomposes into solid copper(II) oxide, gaseous nitrogen(IV) oxide, and oxygen gas. At equilibrium, the pressure is measured and found to be 5.50 atmospheres.**
   (a) **Write the balanced equation for the reaction.**
   (b) **Calculate the number of moles of oxygen gas present in the flask at equilibrium.**
   (c) **Calculate the number of grams of solid copper(II) nitrate that remained in the flask at equilibrium.**
   (d) **Write the equilibrium expression for $K_p$ and calculate the value of the equilibrium constant.**
   (e) **If 420.0 grams of the copper(II) nitrate had been placed into the empty flask at 250°C, what would the total pressure have been at equilibrium?**

*Answer*

1. Given: 250.0 g $Cu(NO_3)_2$ in 4.0-liter flask
      Heated to 250°C, reaches equilibrium
      Total pressure at equilibrium = 5.50 atmospheres

   (a) Restatement: Balanced reaction.

   $$2\ Cu(NO_3)_2(s) \rightleftharpoons 2\ CuO(s) + 4\ NO_2(g) + O_2(g)$$

   (b) Restatement: Moles of $O_2(g)$ at equilibrium.

   $$PV = nRT$$

   $$n_{gas} = \frac{PV}{RT} = \frac{(5.50\ \text{atm})(4.0\ \text{liters})}{(0.0821\ \text{liter} \cdot \text{atm}/\text{mole} \cdot \text{K})(523\ \text{K})}$$

   $$= 0.51\ \text{mole gas}$$

   $$\frac{0.51\ \text{mole gas}}{1} \times \frac{1\ \text{mole oxygen gas}}{5\ \text{moles total gas}} = \textbf{0.10 mole } O_2$$

   (c) Restatement: Grams of solid $Cu(NO_3)_2$ in flask at equilibrium.

   moles of $Cu(NO_3)_2$ that decomposed:

   $$\frac{0.10\ \text{mole } O_2}{1} \times \frac{2\ \text{moles } Cu(NO_3)_2}{1\ \text{mole } O_2} = 0.20\ \text{mole } Cu(NO_3)_2$$

   mass of $Cu(NO_3)_2$ that decomposed:

   $$\frac{0.20\ \text{mole } Cu(NO_3)_2}{1} \times \frac{187.57\ \text{g } Cu(NO_3)_2}{1\ \text{mole } Cu(NO_3)_2} = 38\ \text{g } Cu(NO_3)_2$$

   mass of $Cu(NO_3)_2$ that remains in flask:

   250.0 g $Cu(NO_3)_2$ originally − 38 g $Cu(No_3)_2$ decomposed

   $$= \textbf{212 g } Cu(NO_3)_2 \textbf{ remain}$$

(d)  Restatement: Equilibrium expression for $K_p$ and value.

$$K_p = (\text{pressure } NO_2)^4 \times \text{pressure } O_2$$

Dalton's law of partial pressures:

$$\frac{4 \cancel{\text{moles}} \ NO_2(g)}{5 \text{ total } \cancel{\text{moles}} \text{ gas}} \times \frac{5.50 \text{ atm}}{1} = 4.40 \text{ atm } NO_2$$

$$5.50 \text{ atm}_{\text{tot}} - 4.40 \text{ atm}_{NO_2} = 1.10 \text{ atm } O_2$$

$$K_p = (4.40 \text{ atm})^4(1.10 \text{ atm}) = \textbf{412 atm}^5$$

(e)  Given: 420.0 grams of $Cu(NO_3)_2$ placed in flask.

Restatement: What total pressure at equilibrium?

Because the temperature was kept constant, as was the size of the flask, and because some of the original 250.0 grams of $Cu(NO_3)_2$ was left as solid in the flask at equilibrium, any extra $Cu(NO_3)_2$ introduced into the flask would remain as solid—there would be **no change in the pressure.**

2. **Magnesium hydroxide has a solubility of $9.24 \times 10^{-4}$ grams per 100 ml $H_2O$ when measured at 25°C.**
   (a) **Write a balanced equation representing magnesium hydroxide in equilibrium in a water solution.**
   (b) **Write an equilibrium expression for magnesium hydroxide in water.**
   (c) **Calculate the value of $K_{sp}$ at 25°C for magnesium hydroxide.**
   (d) **Calculate the value of pH and pOH for a saturated solution of magnesium hydroxide at 25°C.**
   (e) **Show by the use of calculations whether a precipitate would form if one were to add 75.0 ml of a $4.00 \times 10^{-4}$ M aqueous solution of magnesium chloride to 75.0 ml of a $4.00 \times 10^{-4}$ M aqueous solution of potassium hydroxide.**

*Answer*

2. Given: $Mg(OH)_2$ solubility = $9.24 \times 10^{-4}$ g/100 ml $H_2O$ at 25°C.

   (a) Restatement: Balanced equation in equilibrium.

   $$Mg(OH)_2(s) \rightleftarrows Mg^{2+}(aq) + 2OH^-(aq)$$

   (b) Restatement: Equilibrium expression.

   $$K_{sp} = [Mg^{2+}][OH^-]^2$$

   (c) Restatement: Value of $K_{sp}$.

   MW $Mg(OH)_2$ = 58.33 g/mole

   $$\frac{9.24 \times 10^{-4} \text{ g } Mg(OH)_2}{100 \text{ ml } H_2O} \times \frac{1 \text{ mole } Mg(OH)_2}{58.33 \text{ g } Mg(OH)_2} \times \frac{1000 \text{ ml } H_2O}{1 \text{ liter } H_2O}$$

   $$= 1.58 \times 10^{-4} \text{ M } Mg(OH)_2$$

   $$= 1.58 \times 10^{-4} \text{ M } Mg^{2+}$$

   $$= 2(1.58 \times 10^{-4}) = 3.16 \times 10^{-4} \text{ M } OH^-$$

   $$K_{sp} = [Mg^{2+}][OH^-]^2 = (1.58 \times 10^{-4})(3.16 \times 10^{-4})^2$$

   $$= \mathbf{1.58 \times 10^{-11}}$$

(d)  Restatement: pH and pOH.

$$pOH = -\log [OH^-]$$
$$= -\log (3.16 \times 10^{-4}) = 3.5$$
$$pH = 14.0 - pOH = 10.5$$

(e)  Given: Add 75.0 ml of $4.00 \times 10^{-4}$ M $MgCl_2$ to 75.0 ml of $4.00 \times 10^{-4}$ M KOH.

Restatement: Would a precipitate form?

$$MgCl_2 \rightarrow Mg^{2+}(aq) + 2\,Cl^-(aq)$$
$$KOH \rightarrow K^+(aq) + OH^-(aq)$$

Total volume of solution = 75.0 ml + 75.0 ml = 150.0 ml

$$M_1V_1 = M_2V_2$$

$(4.00 \times 10^{-4} \text{ mole/liter})(0.0750 \text{ liter}) = (x)(0.1500 \text{ liter})$

$$x = [Mg^{2+}] = 2.00 \times 10^{-4}$$

The same would be true for $[OH^-]$.

$Q = [Mg^{2+}][OH^-]^2 = (2.00 \times 10^{-4})^3 = 8.00 \times 10^{-12}$

$K_{sp} = 1.58 \times 10^{-11}$

**A precipitate would <u>not</u> form because $Q < K_{sp}$.**

3. **Acetic acid, $HC_2H_3O_2$, which is represented as HA, has an acid ionization constant $K_a$ of $1.74 \times 10^{-5}$.**
   (a) **Calculate the hydrogen ion concentration, $[H^+]$, in a 0.50-molar solution of acetic acid.**
   (b) **Calculate the pH and pOH of the 0.50-molar solution.**
   (c) **What percent of the acetic acid molecules do not ionize?**
   (d) **A buffer solution is designed to have a pH of 6.50. What is the $[HA]:[A^-]$ ratio in this system?**
   (e) **0.500 liter of a new buffer is made using sodium acetate. The concentration of sodium acetate in this new buffer is 0.35 M. The acetic acid concentration is 0.50 M. Finally, 1.5 grams of LiOH is added to the solution. Calculate the pH of this new buffer.**

*Answer*

3.  Given: $K_a$ for HA is $1.74 \times 10^{-5}$.

    (a) Restatement: $[H^+]$ in 0.50 M HA.

    *Step 1:* Write the balanced equation for the ionization of acetic acid, HA.

    $$HA(aq) \rightleftarrows H^+(aq) + A^-(aq)$$

    *Step 2:* Write the equilibrium expression for $K_a$.

    $$K_a = \frac{[H^+][A^-]}{[HA]}$$

    *Step 3:* Substitute into the equilibrium expression known (and unknown) information. Let $x$ equal the amount of $H^+$ that ionizes from HA. Because the molar ratio of $[H^+]:[A^-]$ is 1:1, $[A^-]$ also equals $x$, and we can approximate $0.50 - x$ as 0.50 (5% rule).

    $$1.74 \times 10^{-5} = \frac{x^2}{0.50}$$

*Step 4:* Solve for $x$.

$$x^2 = (1.74 \times 10^{-5})(0.50)$$
$$= 8.7 \times 10^{-6}$$

$$x = 3.0 \times 10^{-3} \, M = [H^+]$$

(b)  Restatement: pH and pOH in 0.50 M HA.

$$pH = -\log[H^+] = 2.5$$

$$pH + pOH = 14$$
$$pOH = 14.0 - 2.5 = 11.5$$

(c)  Restatement: % HA that does <u>not</u> ionize.

$$\% = \frac{part}{whole} \times 100 = \frac{[H^+]}{[HA]} \times 100$$

$$= \frac{3.0 \times 10^{-3}}{0.50} \times 100 = 0.60\%$$

However, 0.60% represents the percentage of the HA molecules that <u>do</u> ionize. Therefore, $100.00 - 0.60 = $ **99.40% of the HA molecules do <u>not</u> ionize.**

(d)  Given: Buffer pH = 6.50

Restatement: $[HA]/[A^-]$?

*Step 1:* Recognize the need to use the Henderson–Hasselbalch equation.

$$pH = pK_a + \log_{10} \frac{[base]}{[acid]}$$

*Step 2:* Substitute into the equation the known (and unknown) information.

$$pK_a = -\log K_a = 4.76$$

$$6.5 = 4.76 + \log \frac{[A^-]}{[HA]}$$

$$\log \frac{[A^-]}{[HA]} = 1.7 \rightarrow \frac{[A^-]}{[HA]} = 5.0 \times 10^1$$

Because the question is asking for $[HA]/[A^-]$, you need to take the reciprocal: **0.020.**

(e)  Given: 0.500 liter = volume
$$0.35 \text{ M} = [NaC_2H_3O_2] \rightarrow Na^+ + C_2H_3O_2^-$$
$$[HA] = 0.50 \text{ M}$$
1.5 g LiOH added to solution

$$\frac{1.5 \text{ g LiOH}}{1} \times \frac{1 \text{ mole LiOH}}{23.95 \text{ g LiOH}} = 0.063 \text{ mole LiOH}$$

Restatement: pH = ?

*Step 1:* Write a balanced equation expressing acetic acid at equilibrium.

$$HA(aq) \leftrightarrows H^+(aq) + A^-(aq)$$

*Step 2:* Create a chart that expresses initial and final concentrations (at equilibrium) of the species.

| Species | Initial Concentration | Final Concentration |
|---------|----------------------|---------------------|
| HA | 0.50 M | $0.50 - \dfrac{0.063}{0.500} = 0.374$ M |
| $A^-$ | 0.35 M | $0.35 + \dfrac{0.063}{0.500} = 0.48$ M |

*Step 3:* Write an equilibrium expression for the ionization of acetic acid.

$$K_a = \frac{[H^+][A^-]}{[HA]} = 1.74 \times 10^{-5} = \frac{[H^+][0.48]}{[0.374]}$$

$$[H^+] = 1.4 \times 10^{-5} \text{ M}$$

*Step 4:* Solve for the pH.

$$pH = -\log [H^+] = \textbf{4.9}$$

# ACIDS AND BASES

## Key Terms

Words that can be used as topics in essays:

| | |
|---|---|
| acid–base indicator | ion-product constant |
| acidic oxide | Lewis acid, base |
| amphoteric substance | neutralization |
| Arrhenius acid, base | organic acids |
| autoionization | oxyacids |
| base oxide | percent ionization |
| Brønsted-Lowry acid, base | pH |
| buffer | pOH |
| carboxyl group | polyprotic acid |
| common ion effect | salt |
| conjugate acid, base | salt hydrolysis |
| equivalence point | strong acid, base |
| hydronium ion | weak acid, base |

## Key Concepts

Equations and relationships that you need to know:

- $pH = -\log [H^+]$

  $pOH = -\log [OH^-]$

  $K_w = [H^+][OH^-] = 10^{-14} = K_a \cdot K_b$

  $pK_w = pH + pOH = 14$ (exact)

  $K_a = \dfrac{[H^+][A^-]}{[HA]}$ for the equation $HA(aq) \leftrightharpoons H(aq)^+ + A(aq)^-$

  $pK_a = -\log K_a$

$$pH = pK_a + \log \frac{[\text{conjugate base}]}{[\text{conjugate acid}]} = pK_a + \log \frac{[A^-]}{[HA]}$$

$$K_b = \frac{[BH^+][OH^-]}{[B]} \text{ for the equation}$$

$$B(aq) + H_2O(l) \rightleftarrows BH^+(aq) + OH^-(aq)$$

$$pK_b = -\log K_b$$

$$pOH = pK_b + \log \frac{[\text{conjugate acid}]}{[\text{conjugate base}]} = pK_b + \log \frac{[HB^+]}{[OH^-]}$$

- % ionization $= \dfrac{\text{amount ionized (M)}}{\text{initial concentration (M)}} \cdot 100\% = \dfrac{[H^+]}{[HA]_o} \cdot 100\%$

- conjugate acid $\underset{\text{gain of } H^+}{\overset{\text{loss of } H^+}{\rightleftarrows}}$ conjugate base

- **Acid-Base Theory**

|      | **Arrhenius** | **Brønsted-Lowry** | **Lewis** |
|------|---------------|---------------------|-----------|
| acid | $H^+$ supplied to water | donates $H^+$ | accepts electron pair |
| base | $OH^-$ supplied to water | accepts $H^+$ | donates electron pair |

- **Acid-Base Properties of Common Ions in Aqueous Solution**

|         | **Anions** $(-)$ | **Cations** $(+)$ |
|---------|------------------|-------------------|
| acidic  | $HSO_4^-$, $H_2PO_4^-$ | $NH_4^+$, $Mg^{2+}$, $Al^{3+}$ transition metal ions |
| basic   | $C_2H_3O_2^-$, $CN^-$, $CO_3^{2-}$ $F^-$, $HCO_3^-$, $HPO_4^{2-}$ $HS^-$, $NO_2^-$, $PO_4^{3-}$, $S^{2-}$ | none |
| neutral | $Cl^-$, $Br^-$, $I^-$, $ClO_4^-$, $NO_3^-$ $SO_4^{2-}$ | $Li^+$, $Na^+$, $K^+$, $Ca^{2+}$, $Ba^{2+}$ |

## Examples: Multiple-Choice Questions

1. **What is the OH$^-$ concentration (M) of a solution that contains 5.00 × 10$^{-3}$ mole of H$^+$ per liter?**
   (A)  $7.00 \times 10^{-14}$ M
   (B)  $1.00 \times 10^{-12}$ M
   (C)  $2.00 \times 10^{-12}$ M
   (D)  $1.00 \times 10^{-11}$ M
   (E)  $2.00 \times 10^{-11}$ M

*Answer: (C)*

$[H^+][OH^-] = 10^{-14}$. Substituting gives $(5.00 \times 10^{-3})(x) = 10^{-14}$. Solving for $x$ yields $x = 2.00 \times 10^{-12}$.

2. **Given the following equation, identify the conjugate acid.**

$$NH_3(g) + H_2O(\ell) \rightarrow NH_4^+(aq) + OH^-(aq)$$

   (A) NH$_3$   (B) H$_2$O   (C) NH$_4^+$   (D) OH$^-$   (E) H$^+$

*Answer: (C)*

The conjugate acid of a base is formed when the base acquires a proton from the acid. In this reaction, water acts as an acid because it donates a proton to the ammonia molecule. The ammonium ion (NH$_4^+$) is the conjugate acid of ammonia, a base, which receives a proton from water. The hydroxide ion is the conjugate base.

3. **Arrange the following oxyacids in order of increasing acid strength.**

$$HClO, HIO, HBrO, HClO_3, HClO_2$$

(A) $HClO > HIO > HBrO > HClO_3 > HClO_2$
(B) $HClO > HClO_2 > HClO_3 > HBrO > HIO$
(C) $HIO > HBrO > HClO > HClO_2 > HClO_3$
(D) $HBrO > HClO > HClO_3 > HClO_2 > HIO$
(E) $HClO_3 > HClO_2 > HClO > HBrO > HIO$

*Answer: (E)*

For a series of oxyacids of the same structure that differ only in the halogen, the acid strength increases with the electronegativity of the halogen. Because the electronegativity of the halogens increases as we move up the column, the order at this point would be $HClO >$ $HBrO > HIO$. For a series of oxyacids containing the same halogen, the H—O bond polarity, and hence the acid strength, increases with the oxidation state of the halogen. Therefore, in the series $HClO$, $HClO_2$, and $HClO_3$, the oxidation states of the chlorine are $+1$, $+3$, and $+5$, respectively. And thus the correct order for increasing acid strength is $HClO_3 > HClO_2 > HClO >$ $HBrO > HIO$.

4. **Given the following reversible equation, determine which species is or are Brønsted acids.**

$$CO_3^{2-}(aq) + H_2O(\ell) \rightleftarrows HCO_3^{2-}(aq) + OH^-(aq)$$

(A) $CO_3^{2-}(aq)$
(B) $H_2O(\ell)$ and $OH^-(aq)$
(C) $H_2O(\ell)$ and $HCO_3^{2-}(aq)$
(D) $CO_3^{2-}(aq)$ and $OH^-(aq)$
(E) $H_2O(\ell)$

*Answer: (C)*

Brønsted acids donate protons ($H^+$). In the equation, both $H_2O$ and $HCO_3^{2-}$ donate a $H^+$.

5. **Which of the following salts contains a basic anion?**
   (A)  NaCl
   (B)  $Ba(HSO_4)_2$
   (C)  KI
   (D)  $Li_2CO_3$
   (E)  $NH_4ClO_4$

*Answer: (D)*

See the chart on page 204. Any anion derived from a weak acid acts as a base in a water solution. The carbonate polyatomic anion, $CO_3^{2-}$, is derived from the weak acid carbonic acid, $H_2CO_3$. There are no common basic cations.

6. **Identify the net ionic product(s) produced when solutions of potassium bicarbonate ($KHCO_3$) and hydrobromic acid (HBr) are mixed.**
   (A) **KBr and $H_2CO_3$**
   (B) **$H_2CO_3$, $K^+$, and $Br^-$**
   (C) **KBr, $H_2O$, and $CO_2$**
   (D) **$K^+$, $Br^-$, $H_2O$, and $CO_2$**
   (E) **$H_2CO_3$**

*Answer: (E)*

   To write a net ionic equation for an acid–base reaction between two solutions, use the following three steps:

1. Determine the nature of the principal species in both solutions. $KHCO_3$ would ionize to produce $K^+$ and $HCO_3^-$. HBr would ionize to produce $H^+$ and $Br^-$.

2. Determine which species take part in the acid–base reaction. The bicarbonate anion ($HCO_3^-$) is basic, and the $H^+$ from the hydrobromic acid is acidic.

3. Write a balanced net ionic equation. Because $H_2CO_3$ is a weak acid, it would tend to remain as carbonic acid, especially in the presence of a strong acid like HBr. KBr is an ionic solid, soluble in water; therefore, it would exist as separate ions known as spectator ions, which are *not* written in the net ionic equation.

7. **All of the following choices are strong bases EXCEPT**
   (A) **CsOH**
   (B) **RbOH**
   (C) **Ca(OH)$_2$**
   (D) **Ba(OH)$_2$**
   (E) **Mg(OH)$_2$**

*Answer: (E)*

All hydroxides of the Group I metals are strong bases. The hydroxides of the heavier Group II metals (Ca, Sr, and Ba) are also strong bases. $Mg(OH)_2$ is not very soluble in water, yielding relatively little $OH^-(aq)$.

8. **A solution is prepared by adding 0.600 liter of $1.0 \times 10^{-3}$ M HCl to 0.400 liter of $1.0 \times 10^{-3}$ M HNO$_3$. What is the pH of the final solution?**
   (A) **1.00**   (B) **2.00**   (C) **3.00**   (D) **4.00**   (E) **5.00**

*Answer: (C)*

First, determine the volume of the mixture.

$$0.600 \text{ liter} + 0.400 \text{ liter} = 1.000 \text{ liter}$$

Next, determine the concentration of each acid.

HCl: $\dfrac{0.600 \text{ liter} \times 1.0 \times 10^{-3} \text{ M}}{1.00 \text{ liter}} = 0.000600 \text{ M}$

HNO$_3$: $\dfrac{0.400 \text{ liter} \times 1.0 \times 10^{-3} \text{ M}}{1.00 \text{ liter}} = 0.000400 \text{ M}$

Because both acids are strong (and monoprotic), the $H^+$ concentration is equal to the concentration of the acid. Therefore, $[H^+] = 6.00 \times 10^{-4}$ M $+ 4.00 \times 10^{-4}$ M $= 1.00 \times 10^{-3}$ M, and pH $= -\log [H^+] = 3.00$.

9. **Suppose that 0.500 liter of 0.0200 M HCl is mixed with 0.100 liter of 0.100 M Ba(OH)$_2$. What is the pH in the final solution after neutralization has occurred?**
   (A) 3.00    (B) 5.00    (C) 7.00    (D) 9.00    (E) 12.00

*Answer: (E)*

*Step 1:* Write a balanced reaction.

$$2 \, HCl + Ba(OH)_2 \rightarrow BaCl_2 + 2 \, H_2O$$

*Step 2:* Calculate the number of moles of H$^+$.

$$\frac{0.500 \, \text{liter}}{1} \times \frac{0.0200 \, \text{mole}}{1 \, \text{liter}} = 1.00 \times 10^{-2} \, \text{mole H}^+$$

*Step 3:* Calculate the number of moles of OH$^-$.

There should be twice as many moles of OH$^-$ as moles of Ba(OH)$_2$.

$$\frac{2 \, \text{moles OH}^-}{1 \, \text{mole Ba(OH)}_2} \times \frac{0.100 \, \text{liter}}{1} \times \frac{0.100 \, \text{mole Ba(OH)}_2}{1 \, \text{liter}}$$

$$= 0.0200 \, \text{mole OH}^-$$

*Step 4:* Write the net ionic equation.

$$H^+ + OH^- \rightarrow H_2O$$

*Step 5:* Because every mole of H$^+$ uses 1 mole of OH$^-$, calculate the number of moles of excess H$^+$ or OH$^-$.

$$2.00 \times 10^{-2} \, \text{mole OH}^- - 1.00 \times 10^{-2} \, \text{mole H}^+$$

$$= 1.00 \times 10^{-2} \, \text{mole OH}^- \text{ excess}$$

*Step 6:* Calculate the concentration of H$^+$.

$$pOH = -\log[OH^-] = -\log[1.00 \times 10^{-2}] = 2$$

$$pH = 14.00 - pOH = 14.00 - 2.00 = 12.00$$

10. **A student wants to make up 250 ml of an HNO$_3$ solution that has a pH of 2.00. How many milliliters of the 2.00 M HNO$_3$ should the student use? (The remainder of the solution is pure water.)**
    (A) **0.50 ml**
    (B) **0.75 ml**
    (C) **1.0 ml**
    (D) **1.3 ml**
    (E) **This can't be done. The 2.00 M acid is weaker than the solution required.**

*Answer: (D)*

*Step 1:* Calculate the number of moles of H$^+$ in 250 ml of a HNO$_3$ solution which has a pH of 2.00. HNO$_3$ is a monoprotic acid. pH = $-\log$ [H$^+$], so 2.00 = $-\log$ [H$^+$] and [H$^+$] = $1.00 \times 10^{-2}$ M.

$$\text{moles H}^+ = \frac{1.00 \times 10^{-2}\,\text{mole H}^+}{1\,\text{liter}} \times \frac{0.25\,\text{liter}}{1} = 2.5 \times 10^{-3}\,\text{mole H}^+$$

*Step 2:* Determine the number of milliliters of concentrated HNO$_3$ solution that is needed.

$$\frac{2.5 \times 10^{-3}\,\text{mole H}^+}{1} \times \frac{1000\,\text{ml sol'n}}{2.00\,\text{moles H}^+} = 1.3\,\text{ml sol'n}$$

**11. Calculate the mass of 1 equivalent of $Sr(OH)_2$.**

   (A)   15.21 g
   (B)   30.41 g
   (C)    60.82 g
   (D)  121.64 g
   (E)  243.28 g

*Answer: (C)*

The gram-equivalent weight (GEW) of a base is the mass of the base (in grams) that will provide 1 mole of hydroxide ions in a reaction or that will react with 1 mole of $H^+$ ions. This problem can be done by using the factor-label method.

$$\frac{121.64 \text{ g } Sr(OH)_2}{1 \text{ mole } Sr(OH)_2} \times \frac{1 \text{ mole } Sr(OH)_2}{2 \text{ equiv. } Sr(OH)_2} = \frac{60.82 \text{ g } Sr(OH)_2}{1 \text{ equiv. } Sr(OH)_2}$$

### Examples: Free-Response Questions

1. In an experiment to determine the equivalent mass of an unknown acid, a student measured out a 0.250-gram sample of an unknown solid acid and then used 45.77 ml of 0.150 M NaOH solution for neutralization to a phenolphthalein end point. Phenolphthalein is colorless in acid solutions but becomes red when the pH of the solution reaches 9 or higher. During the course of the experiment, a back-titration was further required using 1.50 ml of 0.010 M HCl.

   (a) How many moles of $OH^-$ were used in the titration?
   (b) How many moles of $H^+$ were used in the back-titration?
   (c) How many moles of $H^+$ are there in the solid acid?
   (d) What is the equivalent mass of the unknown acid?

*Answer*

1. Given: 0.250 g solid acid

   45.77 ml of 0.150 M NaOH required for phenolphthalein end point

   Back-titration: 1.50 ml of 0.010 M HCl

   (a) Restatement: Moles of $OH^-$ used in the titration.

   moles of $OH^-$ = moles of NaOH

   $$= \frac{0.04577 \text{ liter}}{1} \times \frac{0.150 \text{ mole NaOH}}{1 \text{ liter}}$$

   $$= 6.87 \times 10^{-3} \text{ mole } OH^-$$

   (b) Restatement: Moles of $H^+$ used in back-titration.

   moles of $H^+$ = moles of HCl

   $$= \frac{0.00150 \text{ liter}}{1} \times \frac{0.010 \text{ mole HCl}}{1 \text{ liter}}$$

   $$= 1.5 \times 10^{-5} \text{ mole } H^+$$

(c) Restatement: Moles of $H^+$ in solid acid.

moles $H^+$ in solid acid = moles $OH^-$ − moles $H^+$

$$= (M_{NaOH} \times V_{NaOH}) - (M_{HCl} - V_{HCl})$$

$$= 6.87 \times 10^{-3} \text{ mole } OH^- - 1.5 \times 10^{-5} \text{ mole } H^+$$

$$= \mathbf{6.86 \times 10^{-3} \text{ mole } H^+}$$

(d) Restatement: Equivalent mass of unknown acid.

$$\text{GEM} = \frac{\text{grams of acid}}{\text{moles of } H^+ \text{ furnished}}$$

$$= \frac{0.250 \text{ g acid}}{6.86 \times 10^{-3} \text{ mole } H^+}$$

$$= \mathbf{36.4 \text{ g/mole } H^+}$$

2. A student wanted to determine the molecular weight of a monoprotic, solid acid, symbolized as HA. The student carefully measured out 25.000 grams of HA and dissolved it in distilled $H_2O$ to bring the volume of the solution to exactly 500.00 ml. The student next measured out several 50.00-ml aliquots of the acid solution and then titrated it against standardized 0.100 M NaOH solution. The results of the three titrations are given in the table.

| Trial | Milliliters of HA Solution | Milliliters of NaOH Solution |
|-------|----------------------------|------------------------------|
| 1 | 49.12 | 87.45 |
| 2 | 49.00 | 84.68 |
| 3 | 48.84 | 91.23 |

(a) Calculate the number of moles of HA in the 50.00-ml aliquots.

(b) Calculate the molecular weight of the acid, HA.

(c) Calculate the pH of the 50.00-ml aliquot solution (assume complete ionization).

(d) Calculate the pOH of the 50.00-ml aliquot solution (assume complete ionization).

(e) Discuss how each of the following errors would affect the determination of the molecular weight of the acid, HA.

   (1) The balance that the student used in measuring out the 25.000 grams of HA was reading 0.010 gram too high.

   (2) There was an impurity in the acid, HA.

   (3) The NaOH solution used in titration was actually 0.150 M instead of 0.100 M.

*Answer*

2. Given: 25.000 grams of HA.
   Dissolved in $H_2O$ to make 500.00 ml of solution.
   50.00-ml aliquots (samples) of acidic solution.
   0.100 M NaOH used for titration.
   Results of titrations in given table.

(a) Restatement: Moles of HA in 50.00-ml aliquots.

   At the end of titration, moles of HA = moles of NaOH.

   $$\text{average volume of NaOH} = \frac{87.45 + 84.68 + 91.23}{3}$$

   $$= 87.79 \text{ ml}$$

   moles HA = moles NaOH = $V_{\text{NaOH}} \times M_{\text{NaOH}}$

   $$= \frac{0.08779 \text{ liter}}{1} \times \frac{0.100 \text{ mole}}{1 \text{ liter}} = \mathbf{8.78 \times 10^{-3} \text{ mole}}$$

(b) Restatement: Molecular weight of HA.

   $$MW = \frac{48.99 \text{ ml HA sol'n}^*}{8.78 \times 10^{-3} \text{ mole HA}} \times \frac{25.000 \text{ g HA}}{500.00 \text{ ml HA sol'n}}$$

   $$= \mathbf{279 \text{ g/mole}}$$

   * = average

(c) Restatement: pH of 50.00-ml aliquots (assume 100% ionization).

   Average volume of 50.00-ml aliquots = 48.99 ml

   $$[H^+] = \frac{\text{moles } H^+}{\text{liters solution}} = \frac{8.78 \times 10^{-3} \text{ mole } H^+}{0.04899 \text{ liter HA sol'n}} = 0.179 \text{ M}$$

   $$pH = -\log [H^+] = \mathbf{0.747}$$

(d) Restatement: pOH of 50.00-ml aliquot.

   $$pOH = 14.000 - pH = 14.000 - 0.747 = \mathbf{13.253}$$

(e)  Restatement: Effects of following errors.

(1)  Balance reading 0.010 gram too high.
- Student would think she or he had 25.000 grams when there were only 24.990 g.
- In the calculation of molecular weight, g/mole, grams would be too low, so the effect would be a **lower MW** than expected.

(2)  An impurity in the sample of HA.
- Student would have less HA than expected.
- In the calculation of molecular weight, g/mole, there would be less HA available than expected. Therefore, in the titration against NaOH, it would take less NaOH than expected to reach the equivalence point. This error would cause a **larger MW** than expected, because the denominator (moles) would be smaller.
- These results assume that the impurity does not have more $H^+$/mass of impurity than the HA.

(3)  NaOH was 0.150 M instead of 0.100 M.
- It would take less NaOH to reach the equivalence point because the NaOH is stronger.
- Because it would take less NaOH, the number of moles of NaOH would be less than expected, causing the denominator (moles) to be smaller than expected, making the calculated **MW larger** than expected.

# ENERGY AND SPONTANEITY

## Key Terms

Words that can be used as topics in essays:

chemical thermodynamics

endothermic

enthalpy change, $\Delta H$

entropy change, $\Delta S$

exothermic

first law of thermodynamics

free-energy change, $\Delta G$

free energy of formation, $\Delta G_f$

Gibbs–Helmholtz equation

second law of thermodynamics

surroundings

system

third law of thermodynamics

work

## Key Concepts

Equations and relationships that you need to know:

- $\Delta H° = \Sigma \Delta H_f° \text{products} - \Sigma \Delta H_f° \text{reactants}$

$\Delta S° = \Sigma \Delta S_{\text{products}}° - \Sigma \Delta S_{\text{reactants}}°$

$\Delta S_{\text{univ}} = \Delta S_{\text{sys}} + \Delta S_{\text{surr}}$
  if $> 0$, spontaneous
  if $< 0$, nonspontaneous
  if $= 0$, at equilibrium

$\Delta S_{\text{surr}} = \dfrac{-\Delta H_{\text{sys}}}{T}$ if system and surroundings are at same $T$

$\Delta G° = \Sigma \Delta G°_{\text{products}} - \Sigma \Delta G°_{\text{reactants}}$
  $\Delta G° < 0$: spontaneous in forward direction
  $\Delta G° > 0$: nonspontaneous in forward direction
  $\Delta G° = 0$: equilibrium

$\Delta G° = \Delta H° - T\Delta S°$

$\Delta E = q + w$

$\Delta G° = -RT \ln K$   where $R = 8.314 \, J/K \cdot mole$

  if $K > 1$, then $\Delta G°$ is negative; products favored at equilibrium

  if $K = 1$, then $\Delta G° = 0$; reactants and products equally favored at equilibrium

  if $K < 1$, then $\Delta G°$ is positive; reactants are favored at equilibrium

$\Delta G = \Delta G° + RT \cdot \ln Q$ where $Q$ = reaction quotient

$\Delta G° = -n \mathscr{F} E°$

  where $\mathscr{F}$ = Faradays

    $1 \mathscr{F} = 96{,}500 \, J \cdot mole^{-1} \cdot V^{-1}$

    $E°$ = standard cell potential, volts $(V)$

    $n$ = number of electrons in the half-reaction

$$\Delta S = 2.303 \, C_p \log \frac{T_2}{T_1}$$

- **Temperature's Effect on Spontaneity: $\Delta G° = \Delta H° - T\Delta S°$**

| Case | $\Delta H°$ | $\Delta S°$ | $\Delta G°$ |
|------|------|------|------|
| I | − | + | − spontaneous at all temperatures<br>ex: $2H_2O_2(\ell) \rightarrow 2H_2O(\ell) + O_2(g)$ |
| II | + | − | + nonspontaneous at all temperatures<br>ex: $3O_2(g) \rightarrow 2O_3(g)$ |
| III | + | + | + nonspontaneous at low temperatures<br>− spontaneous at high temperatures<br>ex: $H_2(g) + I_2(g) \rightarrow 2HI(g)$ |
| IV | − | − | − spontaneous at low temperatures<br>+ nonspontaneous at high temperatures<br>ex: $NH_3(g) + HCl(g) \rightarrow NH_4Cl(s)$ |

### Examples: Multiple-Choice Questions

1. **Given the following standard molar entropies measured at 25°C and 1 atm pressure, calculate $\Delta S°$ in (J/K) for the reaction**

$$2\,Al(s) + 3\,MgO(s) \rightarrow 3\,Mg(s) + Al_2O_3(s)$$

$Al(s) = 28.0\ J/K$
$MgO(s) = 27.0\ J/K$
$Mg(s) = 33.0\ J/K$
$Al_2O_3(s) = 51.0\ J/K$

(A)  $-29.0\ J/K$
(B)  $-13.0\ J/K$
(C)  $13.0\ J/K$
(D)  $69.0\ J/K$
(E)  $139\ J/K$

*Answer: (C)*

$$\Delta S° = \Sigma \Delta S°_{products} - \Sigma \Delta S°_{reactants}$$
$$\Delta S° = [3(33.0) + 51.0] - [2(28.0) + 3(27.0)] = 13.0\ J/K$$

**2. For the given reaction and the following information, calculate $\Delta G°$ at 25°C.**

$$2 \text{ PbO}(s) + 2 \text{ SO}_2(g) \rightarrow 2 \text{ PbS}(s) + 3 \text{ O}_2(g)$$

| Species | $\Delta H°$ (kJ/mole) at 25°C and 1 atm | $\Delta S°$ (J/mole · K) at 25°C and 1 atm |
|---|---|---|
| PbO(s) | −218.0 | 70.0 |
| SO$_2$(g) | −297.0 | 248.0 |
| PbS(s) | −100.0 | 91.0 |
| O$_2$(g) | — | 205.0 |

(A)  273.0 kJ
(B)  438.0 kJ
(C)  634.0 kJ
(D)  782.0 kJ
(E)  830.0 kJ

*Answer: (D)*

This problem requires us to use the Gibbs–Helmholtz equation:

$$\Delta G° = \Delta H° - T\Delta S°$$

*Step 1:* Using the given information, calculate $\Delta H°$.

$\Delta H° = \Sigma \Delta H°_{\text{products}} - \Sigma \Delta H°_{\text{reactants}}$

$\quad = [2(-100.0)] - [2(-218.0) + 2(-297.0)] = 830.0 \text{ kJ/mole}$

*Step 2:* Calculate $\Delta S°$.

$\Delta S° = \Sigma S°_{\text{products}} - \Sigma \Delta S°_{\text{reactants}}$

$\quad = [2(91.0) + 3(205.0)] - [2(70.0) + 2(248.0)]$

$\quad = 797.0 - 636.0 = 161.0 \text{ J/mole} \cdot \text{K} = 0.161 \text{ kJ/mole} \cdot \text{K}$

*Step 3:* Substitute into the Gibbs–Helmholtz equation.

$$\Delta G° = \Delta H° - T\Delta S°$$

$$= \frac{830.0 \text{ kJ}}{1 \text{ mole}} - \frac{298 \text{ K} \cdot (0.161 \text{ kJ})}{\text{mole} \cdot \text{K}} = 782.0 \text{ kJ/mole}$$

3. **Given the information that follows, calculate the standard free energy change, $\Delta G°$, for the reaction**

$$CH_4(g) + 2 O_2(g) \rightarrow 2 H_2O(\ell) + CO_2(g)$$

| Species | $\Delta H°$ (kJ/mole) at 25°C and 1 atm | $\Delta G°$ (kJ/mole) at 25°C and 1 atm |
|---|---|---|
| $CH_4(g)$ | −75.00 | −51.00 |
| $O_2(g)$ | 0 | 0 |
| $H_2O(\ell)$ | −286.00 | −237.00 |
| $CO_2(g)$ | −394.00 | −394.00 |

(A)  −919.00 kJ/mole
(B)  −817.00 kJ/mole
(C)  −408.50 kJ/mole
(D)   459.50 kJ/mole
(E)   919.00 kJ/mole

*Answer: (B)*

$$\Delta G° = \Sigma \Delta G°_{\text{products}} - \Sigma \Delta G°_{\text{reactants}}$$

$$= [2(-237.00) + (-394.00)] - (-51.00)$$

$$= -817.00 \text{ kJ/mole}$$

**4. Calculate the approximate standard free energy for the ionization of hydrofluoric acid, HF ($K_a = 1.0 \times 10^{-3}$), at 25°C.**

**(A)** $-9.0$ kJ  **(B)** $-4.0$ kJ  **(C)** $0.050$ kJ  **(D)** $4.0$ kJ  **(E)** $17$ kJ

*Answer: (E)*

At equilibrium, $\Delta G = 0 = \Delta G° + 2.303\,RT \log K$ (at equilibrium $Q = K$).

$$\Delta G° = -2.303(8.314\ \text{J} \cdot \text{K}^{-1})(298\ \text{K})(\log 1.0 \times 10^{-3})$$

Rounding,

$$\sim\ -2.3(8.3)(300)(-3.0) = 17{,}181\ \text{J} \approx 17\ \text{kJ}$$

5. **Arrange the following reactions according to increasing $\Delta S^{\circ}_{rxn}$ values.**

    1. $H_2O(g) \rightarrow H_2O(\ell)$
    2. $2\,HCl(g) \rightarrow H_2(g) + Cl_2(g)$
    3. $SiO_2(s) \rightarrow Si(s) + O_2(g)$

    **lowest————→highest**
  (A) $\Delta S^{\circ}(1) < \Delta S^{\circ}(2) < \Delta S^{\circ}(3)$
  (B) $\Delta S^{\circ}(2) < \Delta S^{\circ}(3) < \Delta S^{\circ}(1)$
  (C) $\Delta S^{\circ}(3) < \Delta S^{\circ}(1) < \Delta S^{\circ}(2)$
  (D) $\Delta S^{\circ}(1) < \Delta S^{\circ}(3) < \Delta S^{\circ}(2)$
  (E) $\Delta S^{\circ}(3) < \Delta S^{\circ}(2) < \Delta S^{\circ}(1)$

*Answer: (A)*

Entropy is a measure of the randomness or disorder of a system. The greater the disorder of a system, the greater its entropy.

In $H_2O(g) \rightarrow H_2O(\ell)$, the reaction is going from a disordered state $(g)$ to a more ordered state $(\ell)$; low entropy, $\Delta S < 0$.

In $2\,HCl(g) \rightarrow H_2(g) + Cl_2(g)$, there is no change in entropy since there are two moles of gas molecules on each side of the equation.

In $SiO_2(s) \rightarrow Si(s) + O_2(g)$, the system is becoming more disordered, apparent from the presence of gas molecules on the product side; high entropy, $\Delta S > 0$.

6. **Given for the reaction Hg($\ell$) $\rightarrow$ Hg($g$) that $\Delta H° = 61.3$ kJ · mole$^{-1}$ and $\Delta S° = 100.$ J · K$^{-1}$ · mole$^{-1}$, calculate the normal boiling point of Hg.**
   (A) 61.3 K
   (B) 163 K
   (C) 613 K
   (D) 6130 K
   (E) cannot be determined from the information provided

*Answer: (C)*

At equilibrium Hg($\ell$) $\rightleftarrows$ Hg($g$), which represents the condition of boiling, and at equilibrium $\Delta G° = 0$. The word *normal* in the question refers to conditions at 1 atm of pressure, which is reflected in the notation for standardized conditions for $\Delta S°$ and $\Delta H°$. Therefore, using the Gibbs-Helmholtz equation, $\Delta G° = \Delta H° - T\Delta S°$, we can substitute 0 for $\Delta G°$ and solve for $T$.

$$T = \frac{\Delta H°}{\Delta S°} = \frac{61{,}300 \text{ J} \cdot \text{mole}^{-1}}{100. \text{ J} \cdot \text{K}^{-1} \cdot \text{mole}^{-1}} = 613 \text{ K}$$

7. **Given the following data:**

$Fe_2O_3(s) + 3\,CO(g) \rightarrow 2\,Fe(s) + 3\,CO_2(g)$    $\Delta H^\circ = -27$ kJ/mole

$3\,Fe_2O_3(s) + CO(g) \rightarrow 2\,Fe_3O_4(s) + CO_2(g)$    $\Delta H^\circ = -61$ kJ/mole

$Fe_3O_4(s) + CO(g) \rightarrow 3\,FeO(s) + CO_2(g)$    $\Delta H^\circ = 38$ kJ/mole

| Species | $\Delta S^\circ$ $(J \cdot K^{-1} \cdot mole^{-1})$ |
|---------|------------------------------------------------------|
| $Fe_2O_3(s)$ | 87.0 |
| $CO(g)$ | 190.0 |
| $Fe(s)$ | 27.0 |
| $CO_2(g)$ | 214.0 |
| $Fe_3O_4(s)$ | 146.0 |
| $FeO(s)$ | 61.0 |

**Calculate the approximate $\Delta G^\circ$ (at 25°C) for the reaction**

$$FeO(s) + CO(g) \rightarrow Fe(s) + CO_2(g)$$

(A)  $-26$ kJ/mole

(B)  $-13$ kJ/mole

(C)   13 kJ/mole

(D)   26 kJ/mole

(E)   39 kJ/mole

*Answer: (B)*

To solve this problem, use the Gibbs–Helmholtz equation:

$$\Delta G° = \Delta H° - T\Delta S°$$

*Step 1:* Solve for $\Delta H°$. Realize that you will have to use Hess's law to determine $\Delta H°$. Be sure to multiply through the stepwise equations to achieve the lowest common denominator (6), and reverse equations where necessary.

| | | |
|---|---|---|
| $\cancel{3Fe_2O_3(s)}$ + $9\,CO(g) \rightarrow 6\,Fe(s)$ + $9\,CO_2(g)$ | −81 kJ/mole |
| $\cancel{2Fe_3O_4(s)}$ + $CO_2(g) \rightarrow \cancel{3Fe_2O_3(s)}$ + $CO(g)$ | 61 kJ/mole |
| $6\,FeO(s)$ + $2\,CO_2(g) \rightarrow \cancel{2Fe_3O_4(s)}$ + $2\,CO(g)$ | −76 kJ/mole |
| $6\,FeO(s)$ + $6\,CO(g) \rightarrow 6\,Fe(s)$ + $6\,CO_2(g)$ | −96 kJ/mole |

$$\Delta H° = \frac{-96 \text{ kJ/mole}}{6} = -16 \text{ kJ/mole}$$

*Step 2:* Solve for $\Delta S°$.

$$FeO(s) + CO(g) \rightarrow Fe(s) + CO_2(g)$$

$$\Delta S° = \Sigma \Delta S°_{products} - \Sigma \Delta S°_{reactants}$$
$$= (27.0 + 214.0) - (61.0 + 190.0) = -10.0 \text{ J} \cdot \text{K}^{-1} \cdot \text{mole}^{-1}$$

*Step 3:* Substitute $\Delta S°$ and $\Delta H°$ into the Gibbs–Helmholtz equation.

$$\Delta G° = \Delta H° - T\Delta S°$$
$$= -16 \text{ kJ/mole} - 298 \text{ K}(-0.0100 \text{ kJ} \cdot \text{K}^{-1} \cdot \text{mole}^{-1})$$
$$\approx -13 \text{ kJ/mole}$$

8. **Given the balanced equation**

$$H_2(g) + F_2(g) \rightleftarrows 2\ HF(g) \qquad \Delta G° = -546\ kJ/mole$$

**Calculate $\Delta G$ if the pressures were changed from the standard 1 atm to the following and the temperature was changed to 500°C.**

$H_2(g) = 0.50\ atm$       $F_2(g) = 2.00\ atm$       $HF(g) = 1.00\ atm$

(A) $-1090\ kJ/mole$
(B) $-546\ kJ/mole$
(C) $-273\ kJ/mole$
(D)    $546\ kJ/mole$
(E)   $1090\ kJ/mole$

*Answer: (B)*

Realize that you will need to use the equation

$$\Delta G = \Delta G° + RT \ln Q$$

*Step 1:* Solve for the reaction quotient, $Q$.

$$Q = \frac{(P_{HF(g)})^2}{(P_{H_2(g)})(P_{F_2(g)})} = \frac{(1.00)^2}{(0.50)(2.00)} = 1.00$$

$$\ln 1.00 = 0$$

*Step 2:* Substitute into the equation.

$$\Delta G = \Delta G° + RT \ln Q$$

$$= -546,000\ J + (8.3148\ J \cdot K^{-1} \cdot mole^{-1}) \cdot 773\ K(0)$$

$$= -546\ kJ/mole$$

9. If $\Delta H°$ and $\Delta S°$ are both negative, than $\Delta G°$ is
   (A) always negative
   (B) always positive
   (C) positive at low temperatures and negative at high temperatures
   (D) negative at low temperatures and positive at high temperatures
   (E) zero

*Answer: (D)*

Examine the Gibbs-Helmholtz equation $\Delta G° = \Delta H° - T\Delta S°$, to see the mathematical relationships of negative $\Delta H°$'s and $\Delta S°$'s. (Refer to page 220.)

10. Determine the entropy change that takes place when 50.0 grams of compound *x* is heated from 50.°C to 2957°C. It is found that 290.7 kilojoules of heat are absorbed.
    (A) $-461$ J/K
    (B) $0.00$ J/K
    (C) $230.$ J/K
    (D) $461$ J/K
    (E) $921$ J/K

*Answer: (C)*

Use the equation

$$\Delta S = 2.303 \, C_p \log \frac{T_2}{T_1}$$

where $C_p$ represents the heat capacity
($C_p = \Delta H / \Delta T = 290,700. \text{ J}/2907 \text{ K} = 100.0 \text{ J/K}$).

Substituting into the equation yields

$$\Delta S = 2.303 \, C_p \log \frac{T_2}{T_1}$$

$$= 2.303 \left(100.0 \, \frac{\text{J}}{\text{K}}\right) \log \frac{3230. \, \cancel{\text{K}}}{323 \, \cancel{\text{K}}} = 230. \text{ J/K}$$

## Examples: Free-Response Questions

1. Given the equation $N_2O_4(g) \rightarrow 2\,NO_2(g)$ and the following data:

| Species | $\Delta H_f^\circ (\text{kJ} \cdot \text{mole}^{-1})$ | $G_f^\circ (\text{kJ} \cdot \text{mole}^{-1})$ |
|---------|---------|---------|
| $N_2O_4(g)$ | 9.16 | 97.82 |
| $NO_2(g)$ | 33.2 | 51.30 |

(a) Calculate $\Delta G^\circ$.
(b) Calculate $\Delta H^\circ$.
(c) Calculate the equilibrium constant $K_p$ at 298 K and 1 atm.
(d) Calculate $K$ at 500°C and 1 atm.
(e) Calculate $\Delta S^\circ$ at 298 K and 1 atm.
(f) Calculate the temperature at which $\Delta G^\circ$ is equal to zero at 1 atm, assuming that $\Delta H^\circ$ and $\Delta S^\circ$ do not change significantly as the temperature increases.

*Answer*

1. Given: $\Delta H_f^\circ$ and $\Delta G_f^\circ$ information for the equation

$$N_2O_4(g) \rightarrow 2\,NO_2(g)$$

(a) Restatement: Calculate $\Delta G^\circ$.

$\Delta G^\circ = \Sigma \Delta G_f^\circ$ products $- \Sigma \Delta G_f^\circ$ reactants

$\quad = 2(51.30) - (97.82) = \textbf{4.78 kJ} \cdot \textbf{mole}^{-1}$

(b) Restatement: Calculate $\Delta H^\circ$.

$\Delta H^\circ = \Sigma \Delta H_f^\circ$ products $- \Sigma \Delta H_f^\circ$ reactants

$\quad = 2(33.2) - 9.16 = \textbf{57.2 kJ} \cdot \textbf{mole}^{-1}$

(c) Restatement: Calculate the equilibrium constant $K_p$ at 298 K and 1 atm.

$$K_p = \frac{P_{NO_2}^2}{P_{N_2O_4}} \quad \text{(where $P$ represents the partial pressure of a gas in atmospheres)}$$

$$\Delta G° = -2.303\, RT \log K \quad (R = 8.314\ \text{J} \cdot \text{K}^{-1})$$

$$\log K = \frac{\Delta G°}{-2.303\, RT} = \frac{4.78\ \cancel{\text{kJ}} \cdot \text{mole}^{-1}}{-2.303(0.008314\ \cancel{\text{kJ}} \cdot \cancel{\text{K}}^{-1})(298\ \cancel{\text{K}})}$$

$$= -0.838$$

$K_p = \mathbf{0.145}$ (at standard temperature of 298 K)

(d) Restatement: Calculate $K$ at 500°C and 1 atm.

$$\frac{\Delta H°(T_2 - T_1)}{2.303\, RT_1T_2} = \log \frac{K_{T_2}}{K_{T_1}}$$

$$\frac{57,200\ \text{J}(773\ \cancel{\text{K}} - 298\ \cancel{\text{K}})}{(2.303)(8.314\ \text{J} \cdot \cancel{\text{K}}^{-1})(773\ \cancel{\text{K}})(298\ \cancel{\text{K}})} = \log \frac{K_{773}}{K_{298}}$$

$$6.16 = \log \frac{K_{773}}{K_{298}}$$

$\log K_{773} - \log K_{298} = 6.16$
$\log K_{298} = -0.838 \quad$ from part (c)
$\log K_{773} = 6.16 + (-0.838) = 5.32$

$K = \mathbf{2.09 \times 10^5}$

(e) Restatement: Calculate $\Delta S°$ at 298 K and 1 atm.

$$\Delta G° = \Delta H° - T\Delta S°$$

$$\Delta S° = \frac{\Delta H° - \Delta G°}{T} = \frac{57,200\ \text{J} - 4,780\ \text{J}}{298\ \text{K}} = \mathbf{176\ \text{J} \cdot \text{K}^{-1}}$$

(f) Restatement: Calculate the temperature at which $\Delta G°$ is equal to zero at 1 atm, assuming that $\Delta H°$ and $\Delta S°$ do not change significantly as the temperature increases.

$$\Delta G° = H° - T\Delta S°$$

$$0 = 57{,}200\ \text{J} - T(176\ \text{J} \cdot \text{K}^{-1})$$

$$T = \frac{57{,}200\ \cancel{\text{J}}}{176\ \cancel{\text{J}} \cdot \text{K}^{-1}} = \textbf{325 K}$$

2. (a) **Define the concept of entropy.**
   (b) **From each of the pairs of substances listed, and assuming 1 mole of each substance, choose the one that would be expected to have the lower absolute entropy. Explain your choice in each case.**
   (1) **$H_2O(s)$ or $SiC(s)$ at the same temperature and pressure**
   (2) **$O_2(g)$ at 3.0 atm or $O_2(g)$ at 1.0 atm, both at the same temperature**
   (3) **$NH_3(\ell)$ or $C_6H_6(\ell)$ at the same temperature and pressure**
   (4) **$Na(s)$ or $SiO_2(s)$**

*Answer*

2. (a) Restatement: Define entropy.

Entropy, which has the symbol $\Delta S$, is a thermodynamic function that is a measure of the disorder of a system. Entropy, like enthalpy, is a state function. State functions are those quantities whose changed values are determined by their initial and final values. The quantity of entropy of a system depends on the temperature and pressure of the system. The units of entropy are commonly $J \cdot K^{-1} \cdot mole^{-1}$. If $\Delta S$ has a ° ($\Delta S°$), then it is referred to as standard molar entropy and represents the entropy at 298 K and 1 atm of pressure; for solutions, it would be at a concentration of 1 molar. The larger the value of the entropy, the greater the disorder of the system.

(b) Restatement: In each set, choose which would have the lower entropy (greatest order) and explain.

(1) **SiC(*s*)**
- $H_2O(s)$ is a polar covalent molecule. Between the individual molecules would be hydrogen bonds.
- SiC(*s*) exists as a structured and ordered covalent network.
- Melting point of SiC(*s*) is much higher than that of $H_2O$, so it would take more energy to vaporize the more ordered SiC(*s*) than to vaporize $H_2O(s)$.

(2) **$O_2(g)$ at 3.0 atm**
- At higher pressures, the oxygen molecules have less space to move within and are thus more ordered.

(3) **$NH_3(\ell)$**
- $NH_3(\ell)$ has hydrogen bonds (favors order).
- $C_6H_6(\ell)$ has more atoms and so more vibrations—thus greater disorder.

(4) **$SiO_2(s)$**
- Na(*s*) has high entropy. It exhibits metallic bonding, forming soft crystals with high amplitudes of vibration.
- $SiO_2(s)$ forms an ordered, structured covalent network.
- $SiO_2(s)$ has a very high melting point, so much more energy is necessary to break the ordered system.

# REDUCTION AND OXIDATION

## Key Terms

Words that can be used as topics in essays:

anode

cathode

disproportionation

electrolysis

electrolytic cell

electromotive force (emf)

Faraday

galvanic cell

half-equation

Nernst equation

nonspontaneous reaction

oxidation number

oxidizing agent

redox reaction

redox titration

reducing agent

spontaneous reaction

standard oxidation voltage, $E°_{ox}$

standard reduction voltage, $E°_{red}$

standard voltage, $E°$

voltage

voltaic cell

## Key Concepts

Equations and relationships that you need to know:

- $E° = E°_{ox} + E°_{red}$

- For the reaction: $aA + bB \rightarrow cC + dD$

  Nernst equation:

$$E = E° - \frac{0.0592}{n} \log \frac{(C)^c(D)^d}{(A)^a(B)^b} = E° - \frac{0.0592}{n} \log Q$$

$$= E° - \frac{RT}{n\mathscr{F}} \ln Q = E° - \frac{2.303\ RT}{n\mathscr{F}} \log Q$$

total charge $= n\mathscr{F}$

$1\mathscr{F} = 96{,}487$ coulombs/mole $= 96{,}487$ J/V $\cdot$ mole

- potential (V) = $\dfrac{\text{work (J)}}{\text{charge (C)}}$

  1 ampere = rate of flow of electrons, measured in coulombs/sec or amps

  electrical energy (work) = volts × coulombs = joules

- $E = \dfrac{-w}{q}$ where $w$ = work, $q$ = charge

- $\Delta G = w_{\max} = -n\mathscr{F}E$

- At equilibrium: $Q = K$; $E_{\text{cell}} = 0$

  $\ln K = \dfrac{n \cdot E^{\circ}_{\text{cell}}}{0.0257}$

- OIL RIG: Oxidation Is Losing; Reduction Is Gaining (electrons)

- AN OX (ANode is where OXidation occurs)
  RED CAT (REDuction occurs at the CAThode)

- Electrolytic cell—electrical energy is used to bring about a nonspontaneous electrical change. Anode is $(+)$ electrode; cathode is $(-)$ electrode.

- Voltaic (chemical) cell—electrical energy is produced by a spontaneous redox reaction. Anode is $(-)$ terminal; cathode is $(+)$ terminal.

- **Relation Between $\Delta G$, $K$, and $E^{\circ}_{\text{cell}}$**

| $\Delta G$ | $K$ | $E^{\circ}_{\text{cell}}$ | Reaction Under Standard State Conditions |
|:---:|:---:|:---:|:---:|
| $-$ | $>1$ | $+$ | Spontaneous |
| $0$ | $=1$ | $0$ | Equilibrium |
| $+$ | $<1$ | $-$ | Nonspontaneous; spontaneous in reverse direction. |

## Examples: Multiple-Choice Questions

1. **What mass of copper would be produced by the reduction of the $Cu^{2+}$ (*aq*) ion by passing 96.487 amperes of current through a solution of copper(II) chloride for 100.00 minutes? (1 Faraday = 96,487 coulombs)**
   - **(A)  95.325 g**
   - **(B)  190.65 g**
   - **(C)  285.975 g**
   - **(D)  381.30 g**
   - **(E)  cannot be determined from the information provided**

*Answer: (B)*

*Step 1:* Write the reaction that would occur at the cathode.

$$Cu^{2+}(aq) + 2e^- \rightarrow Cu(s)$$

*Step 2:* This problem can be solved by using the factor-label method: (*Note all the conversion factors that you should be comfortable with.*)

$$\frac{96.487 \text{ amperes}}{1} \times \frac{100.00 \text{ minutes}}{1} \times \frac{60 \text{ seconds}}{1 \text{ minute}}$$

$$\times \frac{1 \text{ coulomb}}{1 \text{ ampere} \cdot \text{second}} \times \frac{1 \text{ Faraday}}{96,487 \text{ coulombs}} \times \frac{1 \text{ mole e}^-}{1 \text{ Faraday}}$$

$$\times \frac{1 \text{ mole Cu}}{2 \text{ moles e}^-} \times \frac{63.55 \text{ g Cu}}{1 \text{ mole Cu}} = 190.65 \text{ g Cu}$$

2. **Find $E°$ for a cell composed of silver and gold electrodes in 1 molar solutions of their respective ions:** $E°_{red}$ **Ag** $= +0.7991$ **volts;** $E°_{red}$ **Au** $= +1.68$ **volts.**
   (A)  $-0.44$ volt
   (B)  0 volt
   (C)  0.44 volt
   (D)  0.88 volt
   (E)  2.48 volts

*Answer: (D)*

Notice that $E°_{red}$ for silver is lower than $E°_{red}$ for gold. This means that because silver is higher in the activity series, silver metal will reduce the gold ion.

*Step 1:* Write the net cell reaction.

$$Ag(s) + Au^+(aq) \rightleftarrows Ag^+(aq) + Au(s)$$

*Step 2:* Write the two half-reactions and include the $E°_{red}$ and $E°_{ox}$ values.

| | |
|---|---|
| ox: $Ag(s) \rightleftarrows Ag^+(aq) + e^-$ | $E°_{ox} = -0.7991$ volt |
| red: $Au^+(aq) + e^- \rightleftarrows Au(s)$ | $E°_{red} = \phantom{0}1.68$ volts |
| $Ag(s) + Au^+(aq) \rightleftarrows Ag^+(aq) + Au(s)$ | $E° = +0.88$ volt |

Because the sign of $E°$ is positive, the reaction will proceed spontaneously.

3. ... $FeCl_2$ + ... $KMnO_4$ + ... $HCl \rightarrow$ ... $FeCl_3$ + ... $KCl$ + ... $MnCl_2$ + ? $H_2O$

**When the equation for this reaction is balanced with the lowest whole-number coefficients, the coefficient for $H_2O$ is**
**(A) 1   (B) 2   (C) 3   (D) 4   (E) 5**

*Answer: (D)*

*Step 1:* Decide what elements are undergoing oxidation and what elements are undergoing reduction.

$$\text{ox:} \quad Fe^{2+} \rightarrow Fe^{3+}$$
$$\text{red:} \quad MnO_4^- \rightarrow Mn^{2+}$$

*Step 2:* Balance each half-reaction with respect to atoms and then charges.

$$\text{ox:} \quad Fe^{2+} \rightarrow Fe^{3+} + e^-$$

Balance the reduction half-reaction, using water to balance the O's.

$$\text{red:} \quad MnO_4^- \rightarrow Mn^{2+} + 4\,H_2O$$

Balance the H atoms with $H^+$ ions.

$$\text{red:} \quad MnO_4^- + 8\,H^+ \rightarrow Mn^{2+} + 4\,H_2O$$

Balance charges with electrons.

$$\text{red:} \quad MnO_4^- + 8\,H^+ + 5\,e^- \rightarrow Mn^{2+} + 4\,H_2O$$

*Step 3:* Equalize the number of electrons lost and gained. There were 5 $e^-$ gained in the reduction half-reaction, so there must be 5 $e^-$ lost in the oxidation half-reaction

$$\text{ox:} \quad 5\,Fe^{2+} \rightarrow 5\,Fe^{3+} + 5\,e^-$$

*Step 4:* Add the two half-reactions (cancel the electrons).

$$\text{ox:} \quad 5\,Fe^{2+} \rightarrow 5\,Fe^{3+} + \cancel{5\,e^-}$$
$$\underline{\text{red:} \quad MnO_4^- + 8H^+ + \cancel{5\,e^-} \rightarrow Mn^{2+} + 4\,H_2O}$$
$$5\,Fe^{2+} + MnO_4^- + 8\,H^+ \rightarrow 5\,Fe^{3+} + Mn^{2+} + 4\,H_2O$$

**4. Given the following notation for an electrochemical cell:**

$$Pt(s) \mid H_2(g) \mid H^+(aq) \parallel Ag^+(aq) \mid Ag(s)$$

**Which of the following represents the overall (net) cell reaction?**
**(A)** $H_2(g) + Ag^+(aq) \rightarrow 2\,H^+(aq) + Ag(s)$
**(B)** $H_2(g) + Ag(s) \rightarrow H^+(aq) + Ag^+(aq)$
**(C)** $Ag(s) + H^+(aq) \rightarrow Ag^+(aq) + H_2(g)$
**(D)** $2\,H^+(aq) + Ag(s) \rightarrow H_2(g) + Ag^+(aq)$
**(E)** **none of the above**

*Answer: (E)*

The vertical lines represent phase boundaries. By convention, the anode is written first, at the left of the double vertical lines, followed by the other components of the cell as they would appear in order from the anode to the cathode. The platinum is present to represent the presence of an inert anode. The two half-reactions that occur are

anode:  $H_2(g) \rightarrow 2\,H^+(aq) + 2\,e^-$     oxidation
            OIL (Oxidation Is Losing electrons)
            AN OX (ANode is where OXidation occurs)

cathode:  $Ag^+(aq) + e^- \rightarrow Ag(s)$     reduction
              RIG (Reduction Is Gaining electrons)
              RED CAT (REDuction occurs at the CAThode)

In adding the two half-reactions, multiply the reduction half-reaction by 2 so the electrons are in balance, giving the overall reaction

$$H_2(g) + 2\,Ag^+(aq) \rightarrow 2\,H^+(aq) + 2\,Ag(s)$$

5. **Given the following information, which of the statements is true?**

$$Cu^{2+}(aq) + e^- \rightarrow Cu^+(aq) \qquad E^\circ_{red} = 0.34 \text{ V}$$
$$2 H^+(aq) + 2 e^- \rightarrow H_2(g) \qquad E^\circ_{red} = 0.00 \text{ V}$$
$$Fe^{2+}(aq) + 2 e^- \rightarrow Fe(s) \qquad E^\circ_{red} = -0.44 \text{ V}$$
$$Ni(s) \rightarrow Ni^{2+}(aq) + 2 e^-(aq) \qquad E^\circ_{ox} = 0.25 \text{ V}$$

(A) $Cu^{2+}(aq)$ is the strongest oxidizing agent.
(B) $Cu^{2+}(aq)$ is the weakest oxidizing agent.
(C) $Ni(s)$ is the strongest oxidizing agent.
(D) $Fe(s)$ would be the weakest reducing agent.
(E) $H^+(aq)$ would be the strongest oxidizing agent.

*Answer: (A)*

The more positive the $E^\circ_{red}$ value, the greater the tendency for the substance to be reduced, and conversely, the less likely it is to be oxidized. It would help in this example to reverse the last equation so it can be easily compared to the other $E^\circ_{red}$ values. The last equation becomes $Ni^{2+}(aq) + 2e^-(aq) \rightarrow Ni(s); E^\circ_{red} = -0.25$ V.

The equation with the largest $E^\circ_{red}$ is $Cu^{2+}(aq) + e^- \rightarrow Cu^+(aq)$; $E^\circ_{red} = 0.34$ V. Thus, $Cu^{2+}(aq)$ is the strongest oxidizing agent of those listed because it has the greatest tendency to be reduced. Conversely, $Cu^+(aq)$ would be the weakest reducing agent. $Fe^{2+}(aq)$ would be the weakest oxidizing agent because it would be the most difficult species to reduce. Conversely, $Fe(s)$ would be the strongest reducing agent.

**6.** **A cell has been set up as shown in the following diagram, and $E°$ has been measured as 1.00 V at 25°C. Calculate $\Delta G°$ for the reaction.**

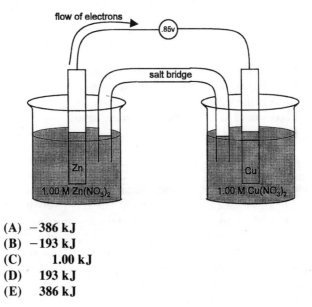

(A)　$-386$ kJ
(B)　$-193$ kJ
(C)　　$1.00$ kJ
(D)　$193$ kJ
(E)　$386$ kJ

*Answer: (B)*

The formula you need for this problem is $\Delta G° = -n\mathscr{F}E°$. The Faraday constant, $\mathscr{F}$, is equal to $9.65 \times 10^4$ joules $\cdot$ volt$^{-1}$ $\cdot$ mole$^{-1}$. $n$ is the number of electrons transferred between oxidizing and reducing agents in a balanced redox equation.

*Step 1:* Write the balanced redox equation.

$$Zn(s) + Cu^{2+}(aq) \rightarrow Zn^{2+}(aq) + Cu(s)$$

*Step 2:* Identify the variables needed for the equation.

$$\Delta G° = ? \qquad n = 2 \qquad \mathscr{F} = 9.65 \times 10^4 \text{ joules} \cdot \text{volt}^{-1} \cdot \text{mole}^{-1}$$

$$E° = 1.00 \text{ volt}$$

*Step 3:* Substitute into the equation and solve.

$$\Delta G^\circ = - \frac{(2 \text{ moles e}^-)}{1} \times \frac{9.65 \times 10^4 \text{ joules}}{\text{volt} \cdot \text{mole e}^-} \times \frac{1.00 \text{ volt}}{1}$$

$$= -1.93 \times 10^5 \text{ joules} = -193 \text{ kJ}$$

7. **Given the following diagram, determine which of the following statements is FALSE.**

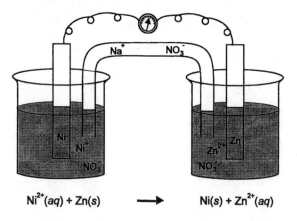

$$Ni^{2+}(aq) + Zn(s) \longrightarrow Ni(s) + Zn^{2+}(aq)$$

(A) The solid zinc electrode is being reduced to $Zn^{2+}(aq)$.

(B) The nickel electrode is the cathode.

(C) The zinc electrode is the anode.

(D) The nickel(II) ions are being reduced.

(E) The Zn electrode will be negative in charge.

*Answer: (A)*

There are two types of cells: electrolytic (which requires a battery or external power source) and voltaic (which requires no battery or external power source). The reaction in the diagram is voltaic and therefore spontaneous. In a voltaic cell, the anode is the negative terminal, and oxidation occurs at the anode. Remember the OIL portion of OIL RIG (Oxidation Is Losing electrons) and AN OX (ANode is where OXidation occurs).

$$Zn(s) \rightarrow Zn^{2+}(aq) + 2\,e^-$$

The cathode is the positive terminal in a voltaic cell, and reduction occurs at the cathode. Remember the RIG portion of OIL RIG (Reduction Is Gaining electrons) and RED CAT (REDuction occurs at the CAThode).

$$Ni^{2+}(aq) + 2\,e^- \rightarrow Ni(s)$$

**8. Given that**

$$Zn^{2+}(aq) + 2e^- \rightarrow Zn(s) \qquad E^\circ_{red} = -0.76 \text{ V}$$

$$Cr^{3+}(aq) + 3e^- \rightarrow Cr(s) \qquad E^\circ_{red} = -0.74 \text{ V}$$

**calculate the equilibrium constant $K$ for the following balanced reaction:**

$$3 \text{ Zn}(s) + 2 \text{ Cr}^{3+}(aq) \rightarrow 3 \text{ Zn}^{2+}(aq) + 2 \text{ Cr}(s)$$

(A) $K = e^{-0.02}$
(B) $K = e^{0.02}$
(C) $K = e^{4.7}$
(D) $K = e^{8.0}$
(E) **cannot be determined from the information provided**

*Answer: (C)*

*Step 1:* Determine the oxidation and reduction half-reactions and $E^\circ_{cell}$.

| | |
|---|---|
| ox: $3[\text{Zn}(s) \rightarrow \text{Zn}^{2+}(aq) + 2\,e^-]$ | $E^\circ_{ox} = +0.76 \text{ V}$ |
| red: $2[\text{Cr}^{3+}(aq) + 3\,e^- \rightarrow \text{Cr}(s)]$ | $E^\circ_{red} = -0.74 \text{ V}$ |
| $3\,\text{Zn}(s) + 2\,\text{Cr}^{3+}(aq) \rightarrow 3\,\text{Zn}^{2+}(aq) + 2\,\text{Cr}(s)$ | $E^\circ_{cell} = \quad 0.02 \text{ V}$ |

*Step 2:* Use the equation.

$$\ln K = \frac{n \cdot E^\circ_{cell}}{0.0257} = \frac{6 \cdot 0.02 \text{ V}}{0.0257} = 4.7$$

$$K = e^{4.7}$$

9. **An electric current is applied to an aqueous solution of $FeCl_2$ and $ZnCl_2$. Which of the following reactions occurs at the cathode?**

(A) $Fe^{2+}(aq) + 2 e^-(aq) \rightarrow Fe(s)$     $E°_{red} = -0.44$ V

(B) $Fe(s) \rightarrow Fe^{2+}(aq) + 2 e^-$     $E°_{ox} = 0.44$ V

(C) $Zn^{2+}(aq) + 2 e^-(aq) \rightarrow Zn(s)$     $E°_{red} = -0.76$ V

(D) $Zn(s) \rightarrow Zn^{2+}(aq) + 2 e^-$     $E°_{ox} = 0.76$ V

(E) $2 H_2O(\ell) \rightarrow O_2(g) + 4 H^+(aq) + 4 e^-$     $E°_{ox} = -1.23$ V

*Answer: (A)*

Reduction occurs at the cathode. You can eliminate choices (B), (D), and (E) because these reactions are oxidations. $E°_{red}$ for $Fe^{2+}(aq)$ is $-0.44$ V, and $E°_{red}$ for $Zn^{2+}(aq)$ is $-0.76$ V. Because $Fe^{2+}(aq)$ has the more positive $E°_{red}$ of the two choices, $Fe^{2+}(aq)$ is the more easily reduced and therefore plates out on the cathode.

**10. For the reaction**

$$Pb(s) + PbO_2(s) + 4\,H^+(aq) + 2\,SO_4{}^{2-}(aq) \rightarrow$$

$$2\,PbSO_4(s) + 2\,H_2O(\ell)$$

which is the overall reaction in a lead storage battery, $\Delta H^\circ = -315.9$ kJ/mole and $\Delta S^\circ = 263.5$ J/K $\cdot$ mole. What is the proper setup to find $E^\circ$ at 75°C?

(A) $\dfrac{-315.9 - 348(0.2635)}{-2(96.487)}$

(B) $\dfrac{-348 + 315.9(0.2635)}{2(96.487)}$

(C) $\dfrac{-348 + 315.9(0.2635)}{96.487}$

(D) $\dfrac{-2(-348) + 263.5}{96.487 + 315.9}$

(E) $\dfrac{2(315.9) - 263.5}{(96.487)(348)}$

*Answer: (A)*

Use the relationships

$$\Delta G^\circ = -n\mathscr{F}E^\circ = \Delta H^\circ - T\Delta S^\circ = -RT \ln K$$

to derive the formula

$$E^\circ = \frac{\Delta H^\circ - T\Delta S^\circ}{-n\mathscr{F}}$$

Next, take the given equation and break it down into the oxidation and reduction half-reactions so that you can discover the value for $n$, the number of moles of electrons either lost or gained.

*Anode reaction (oxidation)*

$$Pb(s) + SO_4^{2-}(aq) \rightarrow PbSO_4(s) + 2\,e^-$$

*Cathode reaction (reduction)*

$$PbO_2(s) + SO_4^{2-}(aq) + 4\,H^+(aq) + 2\,e^- \rightarrow PbSO_4(s) + 2\,H_2O(\ell)$$

$$\overline{Pb(s) + PbO_2(s) + 4\,H^+(aq) + 2\,SO_4^{2-}(aq) \rightarrow 2\,PbSO_4(s) + 2\,H_2O(\ell)}$$

Now substitute all the known information into the derived equation.

$$E° = \frac{H° - T\Delta S°}{-n\mathscr{F}} = \frac{-315.9 \text{ kJ/mole} - 348 \text{ K } (0.2635 \text{ kJ/K} \cdot \text{mole})}{-2(96.487 \text{ kJ/V} \cdot \text{mole})}$$

### Examples: Free-Response Questions

1. A student places a copper electrode in a 1 M solution of $CuSO_4$ and in another beaker places a silver electrode in a 1 M solution of $AgNO_3$. A salt bridge composed of $Na_2SO_4$ connects the two beakers. The voltage measured across the electrodes is found to be $+0.42$ volt.
   (a) Draw a diagram of this cell.
   (b) Describe what is happening at the cathode. (Include any equations that may be useful.)
   (c) Describe what is happening at the anode. (Include any equations that may be useful.)
   (d) Write the balanced overall cell equation.
   (e) Write the standard cell notation.
   (f) The student adds 4 M ammonia to the copper sulfate solution, producing the complex ion $Cu(NH_3)_4^{2+}(aq)$. The student remeasures the cell potential and discovers the voltage to be 0.88 volt. What is the $Cu^{2+}(aq)$ concentration in the cell after the ammonia has been added?

*Answer*

1. Given: Cu electrode in 1 M $CuSO_4$.
            Ag electrode in 1 M $AgNO_3$.
            Voltage = 0.42 volt.

   (a) Restatement: Diagram the cell.

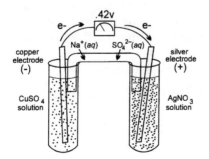

(b) Restatement: What happens at the cathode?

Reduction always occurs at the cathode. Note that $E°_{red}$ for silver is +0.7991 volt, according to the Table of Standard Reduction Potentials. $E°_{red}$ for copper is +0.337. This means that the copper metal is higher in the activity series than the silver metal, so copper metal will reduce the silver ion. The equation that describes reduction (or the cathode reaction) is therefore

$$\text{red:} \quad Ag^+(aq) + e^- \rightarrow Ag(s)$$

(c) Restatement: What happens at the anode?

Oxidation occurs at the anode. Silver is lower in the activity series than copper. Therefore, the oxidation half-reaction is

$$\text{ox:} \quad Cu(s) \rightarrow Cu^{2+}(aq) + 2\,e^-$$

(d) Restatement: Overall cell equation.

Combining these two half-equations into one cell equation produces

ox: $Cu(s) \rightarrow Cu^{2+}(aq) + 2e^-$        $E°_{ox} = -0.337$
red: $2Ag^+(aq) + 2e^- \rightarrow 2Ag(s)$       $E°_{red} = +0.7991$

$$\overline{Cu(s) + 2\,Ag^+(aq) \rightarrow Cu^{2+}(aq) + 2\,Ag(s)} \quad E°_{cell} = +0.462$$

The overall theoretical $E°_{cell}$ is $0.7991 - 0.337 = +0.462$ volt. Because this reaction is spontaneous, as was discovered when the cell was measured, producing the experimentally determined 0.42 volt, this is in agreement with our cell designations.

(e) Restatement: Cell notation.

$$Cu(s) \,|\, Cu^{2+}(aq) \,\|\, Ag^+(aq) \,|\, Ag(s)$$

(f) Given:

4 M $NH_3(aq)$ added to $CuSO_4$ solution $\rightarrow Cu(NH_3)_4^{2+}(aq)$

Voltage = 0.88 volt

Restatement: Calculate $[Cu^{2+}(aq)]$.

Because this cell is not operating under standard conditions, you will need to use the Nernst equation:

$$E_{cell} = E_{cell}^\circ - \frac{0.0592}{n} \log Q$$

The variables take on the following values:

$$E_{cell} = 0.88 \text{ volt}$$

$$E_{cell}^\circ = 0.46 \text{ volt}$$

$$Q = \frac{[Cu^{2+}(aq)]}{[Ag^+(aq)]^2} = \frac{x}{1^2} = x$$

Substituting into the Nernst equation yields

$$0.88 = 0.46 - \frac{0.0592}{2} \log x$$

$$0.0296 \log x = -0.42$$

$$\log x = -\frac{0.42}{0.0296} = -14$$

So            $[Cu^{2+}(aq)] = \mathbf{1.0 \times 10^{-14} \, M}$

2. **The ferrous ion, $Fe^{2+}(aq)$, reacts with the permanganate ion, $MnO_4^-(aq)$, in an acidic solution to produce the ferric ion, $Fe^{3+}(aq)$. A 6.893-gram sample of ore was mechanically crushed and then treated with concentrated hydrochloric acid, which oxidized all of the iron in the ore to the ferrous ion, $Fe^{2+}(aq)$. Next, the acid solution containing all of the ferrous ions was titrated with 0.100 M $KMnO_4$ solution. The end point was reached when 13.889 ml of the potassium permanganate solution was used.**
   (a) **Write the oxidation half-reaction.**
   (b) **Write the reduction half-reaction.**
   (c) **Write the balanced final redox reaction.**
   (d) **Identify the oxidizing agent, the reducing agent, the species oxidized, and the species reduced.**
   (e) **Calculate the number of moles of iron in the sample of ore.**
   (f) **Calculate the mass percent of iron in the ore.**

*Answer*

2. Given: $Fe^{2+}(aq) + MnO_4^-(aq) \rightarrow Fe^{3+}(aq)$
   6.893 grams of ore.
   All of the iron in the ore was converted to $Fe^{2+}(aq)$.
   $Fe^{2+}(aq)$ treated with 0.001 M $KMnO_4$ solution $\rightarrow$ $Fe^{3+}(aq)$.
   13.889 ml of $KMnO_4$ required to reach end point.

   (a) Restatement: Oxidation half-reaction.

   $$Fe^{2+}(aq) \rightarrow Fe^{3+}(aq) \qquad \text{OIL (Oxidation Is Losing)}$$

   (b) Restatement: Reduction half-reaction.

   $$MnO_4^-(aq) \rightarrow Mn^{2+}(aq) \qquad \text{RIG (Reduction Is Gaining)}$$

(c) Restatement: Balanced redox reaction.

ox:   $Fe^{2+} \rightarrow Fe^{3+} + e^-$

red:   $MnO_4^- \rightarrow Mn^{2+} + 4\,H_2O$    (balance O's)

$MnO_4^- + 8\,H^+ \rightarrow Mn^{2+} + 4\,H_2O$    (balance H's)

$MnO_4^- + 8\,H^+ + 5\,e^- \rightarrow Mn^{2+} + 4\,H_2O$

(balance charge)

ox:   $5\,Fe^{2+}(aq) \rightarrow 5\,Fe^{3+}(aq) + \cancel{5\,e^-}$

red:   $MnO_4^- + 8\,H^+ + \cancel{5\,e^-} \rightarrow Mn^{2+} + 4\,H_2O$

$\overline{MnO_4^- + 8H^+ + 5\,Fe^{2+} \rightarrow Mn^{2+} + 4\,H_2O + 5\,Fe^{3+}}$

(d) Restatement: Identify:

| | |
|---|---|
| oxidizing agent: $MnO_4^-(aq)$ | a species that accepts electrons from another |
| reducing agent: $Fe^{2+}(aq)$ | a species that furnishes electrons to another |
| species oxidized: $Fe^{2+}(aq)$ | Oxidation Is Losing (electrons) |
| species reduced: $MnO_4^-(aq)$ | Reduction Is Gaining (electrons). |

(e) Restatement: Moles of iron in the sample of ore.

This problem can be done by using the factor-label method.

$$\frac{13.889 \ \cancel{\text{ml KMnO}_4 \text{ sol'n}}}{1} \times \frac{1 \ \cancel{\text{liter KMnO}_4 \text{ sol'n}}}{1000 \ \cancel{\text{ml KMnO}_4 \text{ sol'n}}}$$

$$\times \frac{0.100 \ \cancel{\text{mole KMnO}_4}}{1 \ \cancel{\text{liter KMnO}_4 \text{ sol'n}}} \times \frac{5 \ \text{moles Fe}^{2+}}{1 \ \cancel{\text{mole KMnO}_4}}$$

$$= 6.94 \times 10^{-3} \ \text{mole Fe}^{2+} = \mathbf{6.94 \times 10^{-3} \ mole \ Fe}$$

(because *all* of the Fe was converted to $Fe^{2+}$)

(f) Restatement: Mass percent of iron in the ore.

$$\% = \frac{\text{part}}{\text{whole}} \times 100\% = \frac{0.00694 \ \cancel{\text{mole Fe}}}{6.893 \ \text{g ore}} \times \frac{55.85 \ \text{g Fe}}{1 \ \cancel{\text{mole Fe}}}$$

$$\times 100\% = \mathbf{5.62\%}$$

# ORGANIC CHEMISTRY

*Note to the student:* You will find *very little* organic chemistry in either Section I or Section II of the AP chemistry exam. According to the Educational Testing Service, "Physical and chemical properties of simple organic compounds should be included as exemplary material for the study of other areas such as bonding, equilibria involving weak acids, kinetics, colligative properties, and stoichiometric determinations of empirical and molecular formulas. (*Reactions specific to organic chemistry are NOT tested.*)"

What this means is that you will *not* be tested on advanced organic chemistry concepts such as organic synthesis, nucleophilic substitutions, electrophilic additions, or molecular rearrangements. Rather, if you were given an acid-dissociation constant ($K_a$) problem, the AP chemistry exam might include an organic acid such as acetic acid ($HC_2H_3O_2$) instead of an inorganic acid such as boric acid ($H_3BO_3$). However, *the mechanisms of the problem would remain unchanged.*

In a thermochemistry problem, you might be given the equation

$$C_2H_4(g) + H_2(g) \rightarrow C_2H_6(g) \qquad \Delta H^\circ = -137\,\text{kJ}$$

to work with, but the mechanics of the operations are the same regardless of whether you work with inorganic or organic species.

Every once in a while you may run into an organic chemistry problem in question 4 of Section II, on writing equations. An example is "Write an equation that describes burning methanol in air." You would need to know the chemical formula and structural formula of methanol in order to do this problem. Writing organic reactions is covered in more detail in the chapter entitled "Writing and Predicting Chemical Reactions."

In short, then, in the area of organic chemistry you should know

- simple nomenclature
- functional groups
- various types of reactions (addition, substitution, elimination, condensation, and polymerization)
- how to draw various types of isomers: geometric, positional, functional, structural, stereo, and optical.

## Key Terms

Words that can be used as topics in essays:

| | |
|---|---|
| addition reaction | elimination reaction |
| alcohol | enantiomer |
| aldehyde | ester |
| aliphatic hydrocarbon | ether |
| alkane | free radical |
| alkene | functional group |
| alkyne | hydrocarbon |
| amine | isomerization |
| aromatic hydrocarbon | isomers (functional, geometric, |
| aryl group | positional, structural, |
| branched-chain hydrocarbon | optical) |
| carboxylic acid | ketone |
| chiral center | saturated hydrocarbon |
| condensation reaction | substitution reaction |
| cycloalkane | thiols |
| dimer | unsaturated hydrocarbon |

## Key Concepts

Equations and relationships that you need to know:

- **Functional Groups**

| | Functional Group | General Formula | Example |
|---|---|---|---|
| Acids | $\overset{O}{\underset{\|}{-C}}-O-H$ | $R-\overset{O}{\underset{\|}{C}}-O-H$ | acetic acid $H-\overset{H}{\underset{H}{\overset{\|}{C}}}-\overset{O}{\overset{\|}{C}}-OH$ |
| Alcohol | $-O-H$ | $R-O-H$ | methanol $H-\overset{H}{\underset{H}{\overset{\|}{C}}}-OH$ |
| Aldehyde | $-\overset{O}{\overset{\|}{C}}-H$ | $R-\overset{O}{\overset{\|}{C}}-H$ | formaldehyde $H-\overset{O}{\overset{\|}{C}}-H$ |
| Amide | $-\overset{O}{\overset{\|}{C}}-N\overset{H}{\underset{H}{}}$ | $R-\overset{O}{\overset{\|}{C}}-N\overset{H}{\underset{H}{}}$ | acetamide $H-\overset{H}{\underset{H}{\overset{\|}{C}}}-\overset{O}{\overset{\|}{C}}-N\overset{H}{\underset{H}{}}$ |
| Amine | $-\overset{\|}{N}-$ | $R-N\overset{R'}{\underset{R''}{}}$ | methylamine $H-\overset{H}{\underset{H}{\overset{\|}{C}}}-N\overset{H}{\underset{H}{}}$ |
| Disulfide | $-S-S-$ | $R-S-S-R'$ | dimethyl disulfide $H-\overset{H}{\underset{H}{\overset{\|}{C}}}-S-S-\overset{H}{\underset{H}{\overset{\|}{C}}}-H$ |
| Ester | $-\overset{O}{\overset{\|}{C}}-O-$ | $R-\overset{O}{\overset{\|}{C}}-O-R'$ | ethyl acetate $H-\overset{H}{\underset{H}{\overset{\|}{C}}}-\overset{O}{\overset{\|}{C}}-O-\overset{H}{\underset{H}{\overset{\|}{C}}}-\overset{H}{\underset{H}{\overset{\|}{C}}}-H$ |
| Ether | $-O-$ | $R-O-R'$ | methyl ethyl ether $H-\overset{H}{\underset{H}{\overset{\|}{C}}}-O-\overset{H}{\underset{H}{\overset{\|}{C}}}-\overset{H}{\underset{H}{\overset{\|}{C}}}-H$ |
| Ketone | $-\overset{O}{\overset{\|}{C}}-$ | $R-\overset{O}{\overset{\|}{C}}-R'$ | methyl ethyl ketone $H-\overset{H}{\underset{H}{\overset{\|}{C}}}-\overset{O}{\overset{\|}{C}}-\overset{H}{\underset{H}{\overset{\|}{C}}}-\overset{H}{\underset{H}{\overset{\|}{C}}}-H$ |
| Salt (Carbox-ylate) | $-\overset{O}{\overset{\|}{C}}-O^-\cdots M^+$ | $R-\overset{O}{\overset{\|}{C}}-O^-\cdots M^+$ | sodium acetate $H-\overset{H}{\underset{H}{\overset{\|}{C}}}-\overset{O}{\overset{\|}{C}}-O^-\cdots Na^+$ |
| Thiol | $-S-H$ | $R-S-H$ | ethanethiol $H-\overset{H}{\underset{H}{\overset{\|}{C}}}-\overset{H}{\underset{H}{\overset{\|}{C}}}-S-H$ |

- **Types of Isomers**

Structural

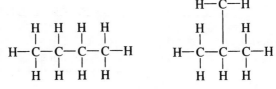

Geometric

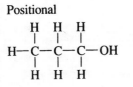
*cis*

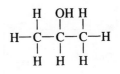
*trans*

Positional

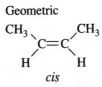

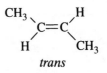

Functional

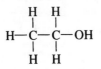

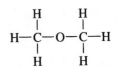

## Examples: Multiple-Choice Questions

*Directions:* The first lettered list consists of the answer choices for questions 1–5, the second list gives the answer choices for questions 6–10, and the third list gives the answer choices for questions 11–14. Select the letter of the one choice that properly identifies the given compound (questions 1–5), describes the given reaction (questions 6–10), or identifies the product of the reaction (questions 11–14). A choice may be used once, more than once, or not at all in each set.

### Questions 1–5

 (A) **Alcohol**
 (B) **Aldehyde**
 (C) **Carboxylic acid**
 (D) **Ester**
 (E) **Ether**

$$\begin{array}{c}\quad\;\; H \\ \quad\;\; | \\ 1.\; H-C-C-O-H \\ \quad\;\; | \;\;\; \| \\ \quad\;\; H \;\; O \end{array}$$

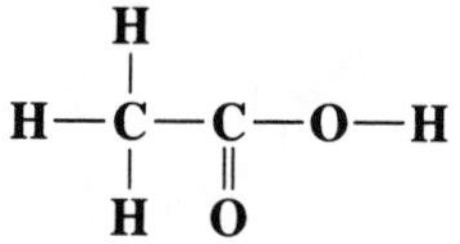

*Answer: (C)*

The functional group of a carboxylic acid is

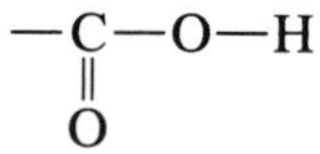

$$\begin{array}{c} -C-O-H \\ \| \\ O \end{array}$$

The name of this compound is acetic acid.

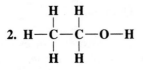

*Answer: (A)*

The functional group of an alcohol is

$$-O-H$$

The name of this alcohol is ethyl alcohol.

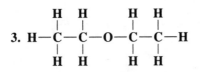

*Answer: (E)*

The functional group of an ether is

$$-O-$$

The name of this ether is diethyl ether.

$$\begin{array}{c} H \\ | \\ H-C-C-H \\ | \quad \| \\ H \quad O \end{array}$$

4.

*Answer: (B)*

The functional group of an aldehyde is

$$\begin{array}{c} -C-H \\ \| \\ O \end{array}$$

The name of this aldehyde is acetaldehyde.

5.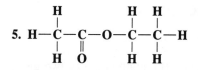

*Answer: (D)*

The functional group of an ester is

The name of this ester is ethyl acetate.

*Questions 6–10*

    (A) **Addition reaction**
    (B) **Elimination reaction**
    (C) **Condensation reaction**
    (D) **Substitution reaction**
    (E) **Polymerization reaction**

**6.** $C_2H_5OH(aq) + HCl(aq) \rightarrow C_2H_5Cl(\ell) + H_2O(\ell)$

*Answer: (D)*

A substitution reaction occurs when an atom or group of atoms in a molecule is replaced by a different atom or group.

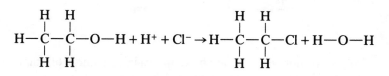

**7.** $CH_2{=}CH_2 + Br_2 \rightarrow \overset{\displaystyle Br}{\underset{|}{C}}H_2{-}\overset{\displaystyle Br}{\underset{|}{C}}H_2$

*Answer: (A)*

In addition reactions, a small molecule adds across a double or triple bond.

**8. $C_2H_5Cl(g) \rightarrow C_2H_4(g) + HCl(g)$**

*Answer: (B)*

An elimination reaction involves the elimination of two groups from adjacent carbon atoms, converting a saturated molecule into an unsaturated molecule. It is essentially the reverse of an addition reaction.

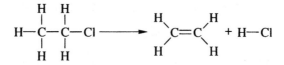

**9. $CH_3OH(\ell) + CH_3OH(\ell) \rightarrow CH_3OCH_3(\ell) + H_2O(\ell)$**

*Answer: (C)*

Condensation reactions occur when two molecules combine by splitting out a small molecule such as water.

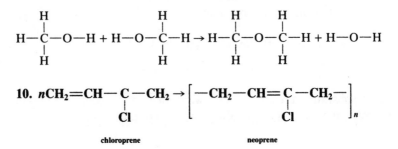

**10.** $n CH_2{=}CH{-}\underset{\underset{Cl}{|}}{C}{-}CH_2 \rightarrow \left[ {-}CH_2{-}CH{=}\underset{\underset{Cl}{|}}{C}{-}CH_2{-} \right]_n$

chloroprene                    neoprene

*Answer: (E)*

Polymerization reactions are built up of a large number of simple molecules known as monomers, which have reacted with one another.

*Questions 11–14*

    (A) **alcohol**
    (B) **carboxylic acid**
    (C) **ester**
    (D) **ether**
    (E) **ketone**

**11. The product of the reaction of an alcohol and a carboxylic acid.**

*Answer: (C)*

An example of esterification is the production of ethyl acetate by the reaction of ethanol with acetic acid.

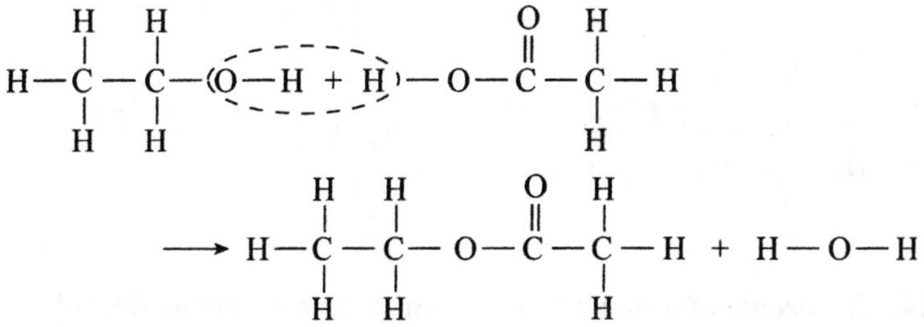

**12. The product of the reaction of an alkene and water.**

*Answer: (A)*

An example is the production of ethanol by the addition of water to ethylene.

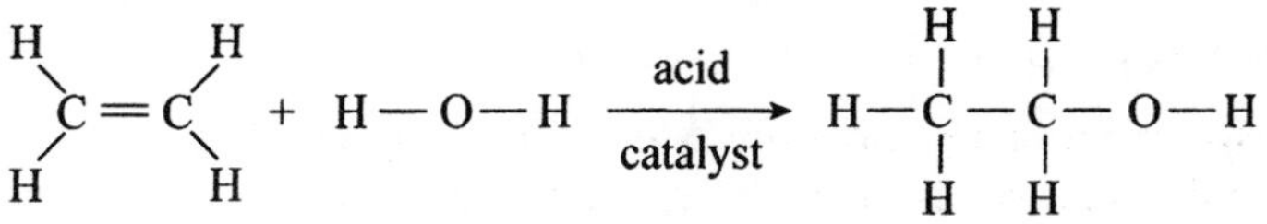

**13. The product formed by the oxidation of a secondary alcohol.**

*Answer: (E)*

A secondary alcohol has the general structure

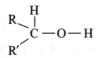

where the R and R' (which may be the same or different) represent hydrocarbon fragments. An example is the oxidation of isopropyl alcohol to acetone.

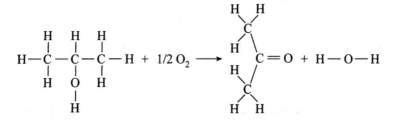

**14. The product formed by the condensation reaction of alcohols.**

*Answer: (D)*

A condensation reaction is characterized by the joining of two molecules and the elimination of a water molecule. In the example below, two methyl alcohol molecules react to form dimethyl ether.

# NUCLEAR CHEMISTRY

## Key Terms

Words that can be used as topics in essays:

| | |
|---|---|
| alpha particle, $\alpha$ | isotopes |
| beta particle, $\beta$ | mass defect |
| binding energy | nuclear transformation |
| chain reaction | nucleon |
| decay series | nuclide |
| Einstein equation | positron |
| electron capture | rate of decay |
| fission | transmutation |
| fusion | transuranium elements |
| gamma radiation, $\gamma$ | zone of stability |
| half-life | |

## Key Concepts

- $t_{1/2} = \dfrac{0.693}{k}$

- $\ln\left(\dfrac{x}{x_0}\right) = kt$

    where

    $x_0$ = original number of nuclides at time 0
    $x$ = number of nuclides at time $t$

- $\log\dfrac{x_0}{x} = \dfrac{kt}{2.30}$

- $E = mc^2$

- $c = 3.00 \times 10^8\,\text{m} \cdot \text{sec}^{-1}$

    $c^2 = 9.00 \times 10^{10}\,\text{kJ} \cdot \text{g}^{-1}$

## • Symbols

| | |
|---|---|
| proton | $_1^1\text{p}$ or $_1^1\text{H}$ |
| neutron | $_0^1\text{n}$ |
| electron ($\beta$ particle) | $_{-1}^0\text{e}$ or $_{-1}^0\beta$ or $\text{e}^-$ |
| positron | $_1^0\text{e}$ or $_1^0\beta$ |
| $\alpha$ particle | $_2^4\text{He}$ or $_2^4\alpha$ |
| gamma rays | $\gamma$ |
| deuteron | $_1^2\text{H}$ |
| triton | $_1^3\text{H}$ |

## Examples: Multiple-Choice Questions

*Questions 1–3*

   (A) $\gamma$   (B) $^1_1\text{H}$   (C) $^1_0\text{n}$   (D) $^4_2\text{He}$   (E) $2\,^1_0\text{n}$

1. $^{54}_{26}\text{Fe} + ? \rightarrow\ ^{56}_{26}\text{Fe} + 2\,^1_1\text{H}$

*Answer: (D)*

Think of the yield sign (arrow) as an equal sign. The superscript represents the mass number. The sum of the mass numbers on both sides of the arrow must be equal. The subscript represents the atomic number, and as with mass numbers, the sum of the numbers on both sides of the arrow must be equal.

mass: $54 + \underline{4} = 56 + 2(1)$
atomic number: $26 + \underline{2} = 26 + 2(1)$

2. $^{65}_{29}\text{Cu} + ^{1}_{0}\text{n} \rightarrow ^{64}_{29}\text{Cu} + ?$

*Answer: (E)*

   mass: $65 + 1 = 64 + \underline{2(1)}$
   atomic number: $29 + \underline{0} = 29 + \underline{2(0)}$

3. $^{14}_{7}\text{N} + ^{1}_{1}\text{H} \rightarrow ^{15}_{8}\text{O} + ?$

*Answer: (A)*

   mass: $14 + 1 = 15 + \underline{0}$
   atomic number: $7 + \underline{1} = 8 + \underline{0}$

4. Choose the one FALSE statement.

   (A) Nuclei with an even number of protons and an even number of neutrons tend to be stable.
   (B) "γ" rays are high-energy photons.
   (C) Nuclei with too few neutrons per proton tend to undergo positron ($^{0}_{1}\beta$) emission.
   (D) Light nuclides are stable when the atomic number (Z) equals the mass number minus the atomic number (A − Z).
   (E) Nuclei with too many neutrons per proton tend to undergo positron ($^{0}_{1}\beta$) emission.

*Answer: (E)*

Positron production occurs for nuclides that are below the zone of stability (those nuclides whose neutron/proton ratios are too small). The net effect of positron emission is to change a proton to a neutron. An example of positron emission would be

$$^{22}_{11}\text{Na} \rightarrow {^0_1}\text{e} + {^{22}_{10}}\text{Ne}$$

Nuclides with too many neutrons per proton tend to undergo $\beta$ particle production. The net effect of $\beta$ particle production is to change a neutron to a proton. Examples of $\beta$ particle production are

$$^{234}_{90}\text{Th} \rightarrow {^{234}_{91}}\text{Pa} + {^{\ 0}_{-1}}\text{e}$$

$$^{131}_{53}\text{I} \rightarrow {^{131}_{54}}\text{Xe} + {^{\ 0}_{-1}}\text{e}$$

*Questions 5–9*

(A) $^{201}_{80}Hg + ^{0}_{-1}e \rightarrow ^{201}_{79}Au + ^{0}_{0}\gamma$

(B) $^{11}_{6}C \rightarrow ^{0}_{1}e + ^{11}_{5}B$

(C) $^{237}_{93}Np \rightarrow ^{4}_{2}He + ^{233}_{91}Pa$

(D) $^{235}_{92}U + ^{1}_{0}n \rightarrow ^{142}_{56}Ba + ^{91}_{36}Kr + 3\,^{1}_{0}n$

(E) $^{214}_{83}Bi \rightarrow ^{214}_{84}Po + ^{0}_{-1}e$

**5. Alpha ($\alpha$) particle production.**

*Answer: (C)*

An alpha particle is a helium nucleus.

### 6.  Beta (β) particle production.

*Answer: (E)*

A β particle is an electron. An unstable nuclide in β particle production creates an electron as it releases energy in the decay process. This electron is created from the decay process, rather than being present before the decay occurs.

## 7. Electron capture.

*Answer: (A)*

Electron capture is a process by which one of the inner-orbital electrons is captured by the nucleus.

## 8. Fission.

*Answer: (D)*

Fission is the process whereby a heavy nucleus splits into two nuclei with smaller mass numbers.

## 9. Positron production.

*Answer: (B)*

A positron is a particle with the same mass as an electron but with the opposite charge. The net effect of positron production is to change a proton to a neutron.

10. **The half-life of C is 5770 years. What percent of the original radioactivity would be present after 28,850 years?**

   (A) **1.56%**   (B) **3.12%**   (C) **6.26%**   (D) **12.5%**   (E) **25.0%**

*Answer: (B)*

This problem can be solved using the factor-label method.

$$\frac{28{,}850 \text{ years}}{1} \times \frac{1 \text{ half-life}}{5770 \text{ years}} = 5.00 \text{ half-lives}$$

In 5.00 half-lives, the radioactivity is reduced by

$$\left(\frac{1}{2}\right)^{5.00} = 0.0312 \times 100 = 3.12\%$$

11. **Which of the following choices correctly describes the *decreasing* ability of the radiation to penetrate a sheet of lead that is 3 inches thick?**
    (A) **alpha particles > beta particles > gamma rays**
    (B) **gamma rays > alpha particles > beta particles**
    (C) **alpha particles > gamma rays > beta particles**
    (D) **beta particles > alpha particles > gamma rays**
    (E) **gamma rays > beta particles > alpha particles**

*Answer: (E)*

Gamma rays ($\gamma$) have high penetrating power and are not deflected by electric or magnetic fields. Beta particles ($\beta$) have a lower ionizing power and greater penetrating power than alpha particles ($\alpha$).

## Examples: Free-Response Questions

1. $^{208}_{81}Tl$ undergoes β decay. The half-life is 3.1 min.
   (a) Write the nuclear equation.
   (b) How long will it take for 1.00 gram of $^{208}_{81}Tl$ to be reduced to 0.20 gram by decay?
   (c) Given 11.00 grams of pure $^{208}_{81}Tl$ initially, how many grams of pure $^{208}_{81}Tl$ will remain after 23.0 min?

*Answer*

1. Given: $^{208}_{81}Tl$ (β decay)        $t_{1/2} = 3.1$ min

   (a) Restatement: Nuclear equation.

$$^{208}_{81}Tl \rightarrow \, ^{208}_{82}Pb + \, ^{0}_{-1}e$$

   (b) Restatement: Time for 1.00 g to reduce to 0.20 g.

$$\ln \frac{[A]_0}{[A]} = \ln \frac{1.00}{0.20} = kt \qquad 0.693 = kt_{1/2}$$

$$k = \frac{0.693}{3.1 \text{ min}} = 0.22 \text{ min}^{-1}$$

$$t = \ln \frac{1.00}{0.20} \times \frac{1}{0.22 \text{ min}^{-1}} = \textbf{7.3 min}$$

   (c) Given: 11.00 g of $^{208}_{81}Tl$ initially.

   Restatement: How many grams remain after 23 min?

$$k = \frac{0.693}{3.1 \text{ min}} = 0.22 \text{ min}^{-1} \qquad \log \frac{x_0}{x} = \frac{kt}{2.303}$$

$$\log \frac{11.00}{x} = \frac{0.22 \text{ min}^{-1} \times 23 \text{ min}}{2.303} = 2.2$$

$$\log \frac{11}{x_0} = 2.2 \rightarrow \frac{11}{x_0} = 10^{2.2}$$

$$x_0 = \textbf{0.069 g}$$

**2. Radon-222 can be produced from the α decay of radium-226.**

    **(a) Write the nuclear reaction.**

    **(b) Calculate $\Delta E$ (in kJ) when 7.00 g of $^{226}_{88}$Ra decays.**

$$^4_2\text{He} = 4.0015 \text{ g/mole}$$

$$^{222}_{86}\text{Rn} = 221.9703 \text{ g/mole}$$

$$^{226}_{88}\text{Ra} = 225.9771 \text{ g/mole}$$

    **(c) Calculate the mass defect of $^{226}_{88}$Ra.**

$$1 \text{ mole protons} = 1.00728 \text{ g}$$

$$1 \text{ mole neutrons} = 1.00867 \text{ g}$$

$$\text{atomic mass } ^{226}_{88}\text{Ra} = 225.9771 \text{ g/mole}$$

    **(d) Calculate the binding energy (in kJ/mole) of $^{226}_{88}$Ra.**

    **(e) $^{226}_{88}$Ra has a half-life of $1.62 \times 10^3$ yr. Calculate the first-order rate constant.**

    **(f) Calculate the fraction of $^{226}_{88}$Ra that will remain after 100.0 yr.**

*Answer*

2. Given: $^{222}_{86}$Rn produced by alpha decay of $^{226}_{88}$Ra.

    (a) Restatement: Nuclear reaction.

$$^{226}_{88}\text{Ra} \rightarrow ^{222}_{86}\text{Rn} + ^4_2\text{He}$$

(b) Given: 7.00 g of $^{226}_{88}$Ra decays.

Restatement: Calculate $\Delta E$ (in kJ).

$$\Delta E = \Delta mc^2$$

$$= 9.00 \times 10^{10} \frac{kJ}{g} \times \Delta m$$

$\Delta m =$      mass products     $-$ mass reactants

$= 4.0015$ g $+ 221.9703$ g $-$    $225.9771$ g

$= -0.0053$ g

$$\Delta E = \frac{7.00 \text{ g } ^{226}_{88}\text{Ra}}{1} \times \frac{1 \text{ mole } ^{226}_{88}\text{Ra}}{225.9771 \text{ g } ^{226}_{88}\text{Ra}} \times \frac{-0.0053 \text{ g}}{1 \text{ mole } ^{226}_{88}\text{Ra}}$$

$$\times \frac{9.00 \times 10^{10} \text{ kJ}}{g} = -1.5 \times 10^7 \text{ kJ}$$

(c) Restatement: Mass defect of $^{226}_{88}$Ra.

88 moles protons $= 88 \times 1.00728$ g $=$     88.6406 g

138 moles neutrons $= 138 \times 1.00867$ g $= +139.196$ g

                                              227.837 g

mass defect $= 227.837$ g $- 225.9771$ g $= \mathbf{1.860}$ **g**

(d) Restatement: Calculate binding energy (kJ/mole) of $^{226}_{88}$Ra.

$$\Delta E = \frac{9.00 \times 10^{10} \text{ kJ}}{g} \times \frac{1.860 \text{ g}}{1 \text{ mole}} = \mathbf{1.67 \times 10^{11} \text{ kJ/mole}}$$

(e) Given $^{226}_{88}$Ra has $t_{1/2} = 1.62 \times 10^3$ yr.

Restatement: Rate constant for $^{226}_{88}$Ra.

$$k = \frac{0.693}{1.62 \times 10^3 \text{ yr}} = \mathbf{4.28 \times 10^{-4} \text{ yr}}$$

(f) Restatement: Fraction of $^{226}_{88}$Ra that remains after 100.0 yr.

$$\ln = \frac{x_0}{x} = kt = 4.28 \times 10^{-4}\,\text{yr}^{-1} \times 100.0\,\text{yr} = 4.28 \times 10^{-2}$$

$$e^{0.0428} = 1.04$$

fraction remaining: $\dfrac{x_0}{x} = \dfrac{1.000}{1.04} = 0.962 = \textbf{96.2\%}$

# WRITING AND PREDICTING CHEMICAL REACTIONS

Question 1 of Section II (also known as Part A) of the AP chemistry exam is *always* a question on writing reactions. The directions for this question follow.

1. You may NOT use a calculator for this section of the exam. You will be given 10 minutes to answer FIVE of the eight options in this part. (Answers to more than five options will not be scored.)

   Give the formulas to show the reactants and the products for FIVE of the following chemical reactions. Each of the reactions occurs in aqueous solution unless otherwise indicated. Represent substances in solution as ions if the substance is extensively ionized. Omit formulas for any ions or molecules that are unchanged by the reaction. In all cases a reaction occurs. You need not balance.

   Example: A strip of magnesium is added to a solution of silver nitrate.

   $$Mg + Ag^+ \rightarrow Mg^{2+} + Ag$$

The question is scored according to the following guide:

- Each of the five reactions you choose is worth a maximum of 3 points—15 points in all.
- One point is given if the reactants are correct.
- Two points are given if the products are correct.
- If the equation is correct but the charge on the ions is incorrect, 1 point is deducted.
- Part A represents 15% of your score for Section II.

In order to do well on this question, *you must know the solubility rules!* See page 144 of this book. Also, in the sections that follow, I have tried to give you *general* rules for predicting the products when the reactants are given. These guidelines will not work for 100% of the questions on the AP exam, but they should get you through at least four or five of the eight you are presented with—and that's all you need.

## I. Metals Combining with Nonmetals

### Metal + Nonmetal → Salt* (Metal Ion$^+$ + Nonmetal Ion$^-$)

### Reactions of Alkali Metals and Alkaline Earth Metals

| Group IA Metal (M)  + | Combining Substance | → | Reaction |
|---|---|---|---|
| All | Hydrogen | | $2\,M(s) + H_2(g) \rightarrow 2\,MH(s)$ |
| All | Halogen | | $2\,M(s) + X_2 \rightarrow 2\,MX(s)$ |
| Li | Nitrogen | | $6\,Li(s) + N_2(g) \rightarrow 2Li_3N(s)$ |
| All | Sulfur | | $2\,M(s) + S(s) \rightarrow M_2S(s)$ |
| Li | Oxygen | | $4\,Li(s) + O_2(g) \rightarrow 2\,Li_2O(s)$ |
| Na | Oxygen | | $2\,Na(s) + O_2(g) \rightarrow Na_2O_2(s)$ |
| K, Rb, Cs | Oxygen | | $M(s) + O_2(g) \rightarrow MO_2(s)$ |
| All | Water | | $2\,M(s) + 2\,H_2O \rightarrow 2\,M^+(aq)$ $+2\,OH^-(aq) + H_2(g)$ |

| Group IIA Metal (M)  + | Combining Substance | → | Reaction |
|---|---|---|---|
| Ca, Sr, Ba | Hydrogen | | $M(s) + H_2(g) \rightarrow MH_2(s)$ |
| All | Halogens | | $M(s) + X_2 \rightarrow MX_2(s)$ |
| Mg, Ca, Sr, Ba | Nitrogen | | $3\,M(s) + N_2(g) \rightarrow M_3N_2(s)$ |
| Mg, Ca, Sr, Ba | Sulfur | | $M(s) + S(s) \rightarrow MS(s)$ |
| Be, Mg, Ca, Sr, Ba | Oxygen | | $2\,M(s) + O_2(g) \rightarrow 2\,MO(s)$ |
| Ba | Oxygen | | $Ba(s) + O_2(g) \rightarrow BaO_2(s)$ |
| Ca, Sr, Ba | Water | | $M(s) + 2H_2O \rightarrow M^{2+}(aq) +$ $2\,OH^-(aq) + H_2(g)$ |
| Mg | Water | | $Mg(s) + H_2O(g) \rightarrow MgO(s)$ $+ H_2(g)$ |

$M$ = symbol for the metal, $X$ = any halogen

---

*By definition, a salt is an ionic compound made up of a cation other than $H^+$ and an anion other than $OH^-$ or $O^{2-}$. However, in these examples a "salt" represents *any* ionic (metal–nonmetal) compound.

1. Calcium metal is heated in the presence of nitrogen gas:

$Ca + N_2 \rightarrow Ca_3N_2$

2. Solid potassium is added to a flask of oxygen gas:

$K + O_2 \rightarrow KO_2$

This reaction is also true for rubidium and cesium. (Note: These are superoxides.)

3. A piece of solid magnesium is added to water:

$Mg + H_2O \rightarrow MgO + H_2$

## II. Combustion

### Substance + Oxygen Gas → Oxide of Element

The usual products are the oxides of the elements present in the original substance in their *higher* valence states. When N, Cl, Br, and I are present in the original compound, they are usually released as free elements, *not* as the oxides.

1. Solid copper(II) sulfide is heated strongly in oxygen gas:

$CuS + O_2 \rightarrow CuO + SO_2$

or

$\rightarrow Cu_2O + SO_2$

2. Carbon disulfide gas is burned in excess oxygen gas:

$CS_2 + O_2 \rightarrow CO_2 + SO_2$

3. Methanol is burned completely in air:

$CH_3OH + O_2 \rightarrow CO_2 + H_2O$

All alcohols (as well as hydrocarbons and carbohydrates) burn in oxygen gas to produce $CO_2$ and $H_2O$.

4. Silane is combusted in a stream of oxygen gas:

$SiH_4 + O_2 \rightarrow SiO_2 + H_2O$

### III. Metallic Oxide + $H_2O$ → Base (Metallic Hydroxide)

1. Lithium oxide is added to water:

$Li_2O + H_2O \rightarrow Li^+ + OH^-$

2. A solid piece of potassium oxide is dropped into cold water:

$K_2O + H_2O \rightarrow K^+ + OH^-$

### IV. Nonmetallic Oxide + $H_2O$ → Acid

1. Dinitrogen pentoxide is added to water:

$N_2O_5 + H_2O \rightarrow H^+ + NO_3^-$

2. Carbon dioxide gas is bubbled through water:

$CO_2 + H_2O \rightarrow H_2CO_3$    (carbonic acid)

or

$\rightarrow H^+ + HCO_3^-$    (weak acid)

3. Sulfur trioxide gas is bubbled through water:

$SO_3 + H_2O \rightarrow H^+ + SO_4^{2-}$

4. Phosphorus(V) oxytrichloride is added to water:

$POCl_3 + H_2O \rightarrow H_3PO_4 + H^+ + Cl^-$

or

$\rightarrow H^+ + H_2PO_4^- + Cl^-$

or

$\rightarrow H^+ + HPO_4^{2-} + Cl^-$

### V. Metallic Oxide + Acid → Salt + H$_2$O

1. Ferric oxide is added to hydrochloric acid:

   $Fe_2O_3 + HCl \rightarrow Fe^{3+} + Cl^- + H_2O$

2. Copper(II) oxide is added to nitric acid:

   $CuO + HNO_3 \rightarrow Cu^{2+} + NO_3^- + H_2O$

### VI. Nonmetallic Oxide + Base → Salt + H$_2$O

1. Carbon dioxide gas is bubbled through a solution of sodium hydroxide:

   $CO_2 + OH^- \rightarrow CO_3^{2-} + H_2O$

2. Sulfur dioxide gas is bubbled through a solution of lithium hydroxide:

   $SO_2 + OH^- \rightarrow SO_3^{2-} + H_2O$

### VII. Metallic Oxide + Nonmetallic Oxide → Salt

1. Magnesium oxide is heated strongly in carbon dioxide gas:

   $MgO + CO_2 \rightarrow MgCO_3$

2. Calcium oxide is heated in an environment of sulfur trioxide gas:

   $CaO + SO_3 \rightarrow CaSO_4$

### VIII. Acid + Base → Salt + Water (Neutralization)

1. Hydrochloric acid is added to potassium hydroxide:

   $H^+ + OH^- \rightarrow H_2O$

2. Equal volumes of 0.5 M sulfuric acid and 0.5 M sodium hydroxide are mixed:

$$HSO_4^- + OH^- \rightarrow SO_4^{2-} + H_2O$$

or

$$H^+ + OH^- \rightarrow H_2O$$

3. Hot nitric acid is added to solid sodium hydroxide:

$$H^+ + OH^- \rightarrow H_2O$$

### IX. Acid + Metal → Salt + Hydrogen

1. Sulfuric acid is added to a solid strip of zinc:

$$H^+ + Zn \rightarrow H_2 + Zn^{2+}$$

2. A piece of magnesium is dropped into a beaker of 6 M hydrochloric acid:

$$Mg + H^+ \rightarrow Mg^{2+} + H_2$$

3. Calcium metal is added to a solution of 4 M HCl:

$$Ca + H^+ \rightarrow Ca^{2+} + H_2$$

*Some Common Departures*

4. Lead shot is dropped into hot, concentrated sulfuric acid:

$$Pb + H^+ + SO_4^{2-} \rightarrow PbSO_4 + SO_2 + H_2O$$

Note the departure from the general guideline.

5. Solid copper shavings are added to a concentrated nitric acid solution. (This reaction is well known and is covered quite extensively in textbooks. Note how it departs from the guideline.)

$$Cu + H^+ + NO_3^- \rightarrow Cu^{2+} + H_2O + NO$$

## X. Base + Amphoteric Metal → Salt + Hydrogen Gas

Amphoteric metals (such as Al, Zn, Pb, and Hg) have properties that may be intermediate between those of metals and those of nonmetals. They will react with a base to form a complex ion with oxygen. *This is a rare problem.*

1. A piece of solid aluminum is added to a 6 M solution of sodium hydroxide:

   $Al + OH^- → AlO_3^{3-} + H_2$

2. A solid piece of zinc is added to a 6 M solution of potassium hydroxide:

   $Zn + OH^- → ZnO_2^{2-} + H_2$

$$\text{XI.} \quad \frac{\text{Strong}}{\text{Acid}} + \frac{\text{Salt of}}{\text{Weak Acid}} → \frac{\text{Salt of}}{\text{Strong Acid}} + \frac{\text{Weak}}{\text{Acid}}$$

1. Hydrochloric acid is added to potassium acetate:

   $H^+ + Ac^- → HAc$     (Do not dissociate a weak acid.)

2. A 9 M nitric acid solution is added to a solution of potassium carbonate:

   $H^+ + CO_3^{2-} → H_2CO_3$

$$\text{XII.} \quad \frac{\text{Weak}}{\text{Acid}} + \frac{\text{Weak}}{\text{Base}} → \frac{\text{Conjugate}}{\text{Base}} + \frac{\text{Conjugate}}{\text{Acid}}$$

1. A solution of ammonia is mixed with an equimolar solution of hydrofluoric acid:

   $NH_3 + HF → NH_4^+ + F^-$

2. Acetic acid is added to a solution of ammonia:

   $HC_2H_3O_2 + NH_3 → C_2H_3O_2^- + NH_4^+$

### XIII. Weak Acid + Strong Base → Water + Conjugate Base

1. Hydrofluoric acid is added to a solution of sodium hydroxide:

   $HF + OH^- \rightarrow H_2O + F^-$

2. A solution of vinegar (acetic acid) is titrated with lye (sodium hydroxide):

   $HC_2H_3O_2 + OH^- \rightarrow H_2O + C_2H_3O_2^-$

3. Nitrous acid is added to sodium hydroxide:

   $HNO_2 + OH^- \rightarrow H_2O + NO_2^-$

### XIV. Strong Acid + Weak Base → Conjugate Acid (Weak Acid)

1. Hydrochloric acid is added to a solution of ammonia:

   $H^+ + NH_3 \rightarrow NH_4^+$

2. Sulfuric acid is added to a solution of sodium fluoride:

   $H^+ + F^- \rightarrow HF$

3. Hydrochloric acid is added to sodium carbonate:

   $H^+ + CO_3^{2-} \rightarrow HCO_3^-$

   or

   $\rightarrow H_2CO_3$

   or

   $\rightarrow CO_2 + H_2O$

4. Sodium acetate is added to a weak solution of nitric acid:

   $C_2H_3O_2^- + H^+ \rightarrow HC_2H_3O_2$

## XV. Precipitation Reactions

These problems involve mixing two solutions. Each solution is a water solution of an ionic compound. From the mixture of the two solutions, at least one insoluble precipitate will form. The other ions present are probably soluble and are called spectator ions; they are not included in the net ionic equation. *You must know your solubility rules to do these problems.* (Refer to page 144.)

1. A solution of silver nitrate is added to a solution of hydrochloric acid:

   $Ag^+ + Cl^- \rightarrow AgCl$    (All nitrates are soluble.)

2. Silver nitrate is added to a solution of potassium chromate:

   $Ag^+ + CrO_4^{2-} \rightarrow Ag_2CrO_4$

3. Lead nitrate is added to a solution of sodium chloride:

   $Pb^{2+} + Cl^- \rightarrow PbCl_2$

4. Iron(III) nitrate is added to a strong sodium hydroxide solution:

   $Fe^{3+} + OH^- \rightarrow Fe(OH)_3$

5. Strontium chloride is added to a solution of sodium sulfate:

   $Sr^{2+} + SO_4^{2-} \rightarrow SrSO_4$

## XVI. Redox Reactions
### (4–20: Common Oxidation State Changes)

1. A strip of zinc metal is added to a solution of copper(II) nitrate:

   $Zn + Cu^{2+} \rightarrow Zn^{2+} + Cu$

2. A piece of aluminum is dropped into a solution of lead chloride:

   $Al + Pb^{2+} \rightarrow Pb + Al^{3+}$

3. Chlorine gas is bubbled through a solution of sodium iodide:

$$Cl_2 + I^- \rightarrow I_2 + Cl^-$$

4. $Cl_2 \xrightarrow{\text{dilute basic sol'n}} ClO^-$

5. $Cl_2 \xrightarrow{\text{conc. basic sol'n}} ClO_2^-$

6. $Cl^- \rightarrow Cl_2$
   (or other
   hallide)

7. $Na \rightarrow Na^+$
   (free
   metal)

8. $NO_2^- \rightarrow NO_3^-$

9. $HNO_3 \rightarrow NO_2$
   (conc.)

10. $HNO_3 \rightarrow NO$
    (dilute)

11. $Sn^{2+} \rightarrow Sn^{4+}$

12. $MnO_4^- \rightarrow Mn^{2+}$
    (in acid sol'n)

13. $MnO_2 \rightarrow Mn^{2+}$
    (in acid sol'n)

14. $MnO_4^- \rightarrow MnO_2$
    (in neutral or
    basic sol'n)

15. $H_2SO_4 \rightarrow SO_2$
    (hot, conc.)

16. $SO_3^{2-}$ or $SO_2(aq) \rightarrow SO_4^{2-}$

17. $Na_2O_2 \rightarrow NaOH$

18. $H_2O_2 \rightarrow H_2O + O_2$

19. $HClO_4 \rightarrow Cl^-$

20. $Cr_2O_7^{2-} \rightarrow Cr^{3+}$
    (in acid)

## XVII. Synthesis Reactions (A + B → AB)

1. Solid calcium oxide is added to silicon dioxide and the mixture is heated strongly:

   $CaO + SiO_2 \rightarrow CaSiO_3$

2. Hydrogen gas is mixed with oxygen gas and the mixture is sparked:

   $H_2 + O_2 \rightarrow H_2O$

3. Boron trichloride gas and ammonia gas are mixed:

   $BCl_3 + NH_3 \rightarrow BCl_3NH_3$

   If this compound is not familiar, try drawing a Lewis diagram to see how it is put together.

## XVIII. Decomposition (AB → A + B)

1. A sample of calcium carbonate is heated:

   $CaCO_3 \rightarrow CaO + CO_2$

2. Hydrogen peroxide is gently warmed:

$$H_2O_2 \rightarrow H_2O + O_2$$

3. Manganese dioxide (acting as a catalyst) is added to a solid sample of potassium chlorate and the mixture is then heated:

$$KClO_3 \xrightarrow{MnO_2} KCl + O_2$$

4. Solid aluminum hydroxide is heated:

$$Al(OH)_3 \rightarrow Al_2O_3 + H_2O$$

### XIX. Single Displacement (A + BC → AC + B)

1. Chlorine gas is bubbled through a strong solution of potassium bromide:

$$Cl_2 + Br^- \rightarrow Cl^- + Br_2$$

Note: This is also a redox reaction.

2. Powdered lead is added to a warm solution of copper(II) sulfate:

$$Pb + Cu^{2+} + SO_4^{2-} \rightarrow PbSO_4 + Cu$$

3. Strontium turnings are added to a 4 M sulfuric acid solution:

$$Sr + H^+ + SO_4^{2-} \rightarrow SrSO_4 + H_2$$

4. Silver is added to a solution of hydrochloric acid:

$$Ag + H^+ + Cl^- \rightarrow AgCl + H_2$$

## XX. Complex Ions*

1. A concentrated solution of ammonia is added to a solution of zinc nitrate:

$$Zn^{2+} + NH_3 \rightarrow Zn(NH_3)_4{}^{2+}$$

$$or$$

$$Zn^{2+} + NH_3 + H_2O \rightarrow Zn(OH)_2 + NH_4{}^+$$

2. A solution of iron(III) iodide is added to a solution of ammonium thiocyanate:

$$Fe^{3+} + SCN^- \rightarrow Fe(SCN)_6{}^{3-}$$

3. A solution of copper(II) nitrate is added to a strong solution of ammonia:

$$Cu^{2+} + NH_3 \rightarrow Cu(NH_3)_4{}^{2+}$$

4. A concentrated potassium hydroxide solution is added to solid aluminum hydroxide:

$$OH^- + Al(OH)_3 \rightarrow Al(OH)_4{}^-$$

---

*Ligands are generally electron pair donors (Lewis bases). Important ligands are $NH_3$, $CN^-$, and $OH^-$. Ligands bond to a central atom that is usually the positive ion of a transition metal, forming complex ions and coordination compounds. On the AP exam, the number of ligands attached to a central metal ion is often twice the oxidation number of the central metal ion.

## XXI. Organic Substitution

1.  Chlorine gas is added to a flask of methane gas and heated:

    $CH_4 + Cl_2 \rightarrow CH_3Cl + HCl$

    or

    $\rightarrow CH_2Cl_2$

    or

    $\rightarrow CHCl_3$

    or

    $\rightarrow CCl_4$

2.  Chloromethane is bubbled through a solution of warm ammonia:

    $CH_3Cl + NH_3 \rightarrow CH_3NH_2 + HCl$

    or

    $[CH_3NH_3]^+Cl^-$

    or

    $\rightarrow [CH_3NH_3]^+ + Cl^-$

## XXII. Organic Addition

1.  Hot steam is mixed with propene gas:

    $C_3H_6 + H_2O \rightarrow C_3H_7OH$

2.  Ethene gas is heated in the presence of chlorine gas:

    $C_2H_4 + Cl_2 \rightarrow C_2H_4Cl_2$

## XXIII. Organic Elimination

1. Ethanol is heated in the presence of sulfuric acid:

$$C_2H_5OH \xrightarrow{H_2SO_4} C_2H_4 + H_2O$$

2. Chloroethane is heated:

$$C_2H_5Cl \rightarrow C_2H_4 + HCl$$

## XXIV. Organic Condensation

1. Methanol is mixed with acetic acid and then gently warmed:

$$CH_3OH + CH_3COOH \xrightarrow{\text{esterification}} CH_3COOCH_3 + H_2O$$

2. Methyl alcohol is mixed with a small amount of sulfuric acid and then warmed gently:

$$CH_3OH + HOCH_3 \rightarrow CH_3OCH_3 + H_2O$$

## XXIII. Organic Elimination

...

$$HOOC \cdots H_2O \cdots$$

...

## ... dehydration

...

$$ \cdots H_2O + \cdots CH_2=CH_2 \cdots $$

...

# Part III:
# AP Chemistry Practice Test

ANSWER SHEET FOR THE PRACTICE TEST
(Remove This Sheet and Use It to Mark Your Answers)

# SECTION I
## MULTIPLE-CHOICE QUESTIONS

**Part A**             **Part B**

| Part A |
| --- |
| 1 Ⓐ Ⓑ Ⓒ Ⓓ Ⓔ |
| 2 Ⓐ Ⓑ Ⓒ Ⓓ Ⓔ |
| 3 Ⓐ Ⓑ Ⓒ Ⓓ Ⓔ |
| 4 Ⓐ Ⓑ Ⓒ Ⓓ Ⓔ |
| 5 Ⓐ Ⓑ Ⓒ Ⓓ Ⓔ |
| 6 Ⓐ Ⓑ Ⓒ Ⓓ Ⓔ |
| 7 Ⓐ Ⓑ Ⓒ Ⓓ Ⓔ |
| 8 Ⓐ Ⓑ Ⓒ Ⓓ Ⓔ |
| 9 Ⓐ Ⓑ Ⓒ Ⓓ Ⓔ |
| 10 Ⓐ Ⓑ Ⓒ Ⓓ Ⓔ |
| 11 Ⓐ Ⓑ Ⓒ Ⓓ Ⓔ |
| 12 Ⓐ Ⓑ Ⓒ Ⓓ Ⓔ |
| 13 Ⓐ Ⓑ Ⓒ Ⓓ Ⓔ |
| 14 Ⓐ Ⓑ Ⓒ Ⓓ Ⓔ |
| 15 Ⓐ Ⓑ Ⓒ Ⓓ Ⓔ |
| 16 Ⓐ Ⓑ Ⓒ Ⓓ Ⓔ |

| Part B | |
| --- | --- |
| 17 Ⓐ Ⓑ Ⓒ Ⓓ Ⓔ | 47 Ⓐ Ⓑ Ⓒ Ⓓ Ⓔ |
| 18 Ⓐ Ⓑ Ⓒ Ⓓ Ⓔ | 48 Ⓐ Ⓑ Ⓒ Ⓓ Ⓔ |
| 19 Ⓐ Ⓑ Ⓒ Ⓓ Ⓔ | 49 Ⓐ Ⓑ Ⓒ Ⓓ Ⓔ |
| 20 Ⓐ Ⓑ Ⓒ Ⓓ Ⓔ | 50 Ⓐ Ⓑ Ⓒ Ⓓ Ⓔ |
| 21 Ⓐ Ⓑ Ⓒ Ⓓ Ⓔ | 51 Ⓐ Ⓑ Ⓒ Ⓓ Ⓔ |
| 22 Ⓐ Ⓑ Ⓒ Ⓓ Ⓔ | 52 Ⓐ Ⓑ Ⓒ Ⓓ Ⓔ |
| 23 Ⓐ Ⓑ Ⓒ Ⓓ Ⓔ | 53 Ⓐ Ⓑ Ⓒ Ⓓ Ⓔ |
| 24 Ⓐ Ⓑ Ⓒ Ⓓ Ⓔ | 54 Ⓐ Ⓑ Ⓒ Ⓓ Ⓔ |
| 25 Ⓐ Ⓑ Ⓒ Ⓓ Ⓔ | 55 Ⓐ Ⓑ Ⓒ Ⓓ Ⓔ |
| 26 Ⓐ Ⓑ Ⓒ Ⓓ Ⓔ | 56 Ⓐ Ⓑ Ⓒ Ⓓ Ⓔ |
| 27 Ⓐ Ⓑ Ⓒ Ⓓ Ⓔ | 57 Ⓐ Ⓑ Ⓒ Ⓓ Ⓔ |
| 28 Ⓐ Ⓑ Ⓒ Ⓓ Ⓔ | 58 Ⓐ Ⓑ Ⓒ Ⓓ Ⓔ |
| 29 Ⓐ Ⓑ Ⓒ Ⓓ Ⓔ | 59 Ⓐ Ⓑ Ⓒ Ⓓ Ⓔ |
| 30 Ⓐ Ⓑ Ⓒ Ⓓ Ⓔ | 60 Ⓐ Ⓑ Ⓒ Ⓓ Ⓔ |
| 31 Ⓐ Ⓑ Ⓒ Ⓓ Ⓔ | 61 Ⓐ Ⓑ Ⓒ Ⓓ Ⓔ |
| 32 Ⓐ Ⓑ Ⓒ Ⓓ Ⓔ | 62 Ⓐ Ⓑ Ⓒ Ⓓ Ⓔ |
| 33 Ⓐ Ⓑ Ⓒ Ⓓ Ⓔ | 63 Ⓐ Ⓑ Ⓒ Ⓓ Ⓔ |
| 34 Ⓐ Ⓑ Ⓒ Ⓓ Ⓔ | 64 Ⓐ Ⓑ Ⓒ Ⓓ Ⓔ |
| 35 Ⓐ Ⓑ Ⓒ Ⓓ Ⓔ | 65 Ⓐ Ⓑ Ⓒ Ⓓ Ⓔ |
| 36 Ⓐ Ⓑ Ⓒ Ⓓ Ⓔ | 66 Ⓐ Ⓑ Ⓒ Ⓓ Ⓔ |
| 37 Ⓐ Ⓑ Ⓒ Ⓓ Ⓔ | 67 Ⓐ Ⓑ Ⓒ Ⓓ Ⓔ |
| 38 Ⓐ Ⓑ Ⓒ Ⓓ Ⓔ | 68 Ⓐ Ⓑ Ⓒ Ⓓ Ⓔ |
| 39 Ⓐ Ⓑ Ⓒ Ⓓ Ⓔ | 69 Ⓐ Ⓑ Ⓒ Ⓓ Ⓔ |
| 40 Ⓐ Ⓑ Ⓒ Ⓓ Ⓔ | 70 Ⓐ Ⓑ Ⓒ Ⓓ Ⓔ |
| 41 Ⓐ Ⓑ Ⓒ Ⓓ Ⓔ | 71 Ⓐ Ⓑ Ⓒ Ⓓ Ⓔ |
| 42 Ⓐ Ⓑ Ⓒ Ⓓ Ⓔ | 72 Ⓐ Ⓑ Ⓒ Ⓓ Ⓔ |
| 43 Ⓐ Ⓑ Ⓒ Ⓓ Ⓔ | 73 Ⓐ Ⓑ Ⓒ Ⓓ Ⓔ |
| 44 Ⓐ Ⓑ Ⓒ Ⓓ Ⓔ | 74 Ⓐ Ⓑ Ⓒ Ⓓ Ⓔ |
| 45 Ⓐ Ⓑ Ⓒ Ⓓ Ⓔ | 75 Ⓐ Ⓑ Ⓒ Ⓓ Ⓔ |
| 46 Ⓐ Ⓑ Ⓒ Ⓓ Ⓔ | |

301

# SECTION I (MULTIPLE-CHOICE QUESTIONS)

**Time: 1 hour and 30 minutes**
**75 questions**
**45% of total grade**
**No calculators allowed**

This section consists of 75 multiple-choice questions. Mark your answers carefully on the answer sheet.

<u>General Instructions</u>

Do not open this booklet until you are told to do so by the proctor.

Be sure to write your answers for Section I on the separate answer sheet. Use the test booklet for your scratchwork or notes, but remember that no credit will be given for work, notes, or answers written only in the test booklet. Once you have selected an answer, blacken thoroughly the corresponding circle on the answer sheet. To change an answer, erase your previous mark completely, and then record your new answer. Mark only one answer for each question.

| <u>Example</u> | <u>Sample Answer</u> |
|---|---|
| The Pacific is | Ⓐ Ⓑ ● Ⓓ Ⓔ |
| (A) a river | |
| (B) a lake | |
| (C) an ocean | |
| (D) a sea | |
| (E) a gulf | |

To discourage haphazard guessing on this section of the exam, a quarter of a point is subtracted for every wrong answer, but no points are subtracted if you leave the answer blank. Even so, if you can eliminate one or more of the choices for a question, it may be to your advantage to guess.

Because it is not expected that all test takers will complete this section, do not spend too much time on difficult questions. Answer first the questions you can answer readily, and then, if you have time, return to the difficult questions later. Don't get stuck on one question. Work quickly but accurately. Use your time effectively. The following table is provided for your use in answering questions in Section I.

## PERIODIC TABLE OF THE CHEMICAL ELEMENTS

| 1 H Hydrogen 1.01 | | | | | | | | |
|---|---|---|---|---|---|---|---|---|
| 3 Li Lithium 6.94 | 4 Be Beryllium 9.01 | | | | | | | |
| 11 Na Sodium 22.99 | 12 Mg Magnesium 24.31 | | | | | | | |
| 19 K Potassium 39.10 | 20 Ca Calcium 40.08 | 21 Sc Scandium 44.96 | 22 Ti Titanium 47.90 | 23 V Vanadium 50.94 | 24 Cr Chromium 52.00 | 25 Mn Manganese 54.94 | 26 Fe Iron 55.85 | 27 Co Cobalt 58.93 |
| 37 Rb Rubidium 85.47 | 38 Sr Strontium 87.62 | 39 Y Yttrium 88.91 | 40 Zr Zirconium 91.22 | 41 Nb Niobium 92.91 | 42 Mo Molybdenum 95.94 | 43 Tc Technetium (99) | 44 Ru Ruthenium 101.07 | 45 Rh Rhodium 102.91 |
| 55 Cs Cesium 132.91 | 56 Ba Barium 137.34 | 57 La Lanthanum 138.91 | 72 Hf Hafnium 178.49 | 73 Ta Tantalum 180.95 | 74 W Tungsten 183.85 | 75 Re Rhenium 186.21 | 76 Os Osmium 190.2 | 77 Ir Iridium 192.22 |
| 87 Fr Francium (223) | 88 Ra Radium (226) | 89 Ac Actinium (227) | 104 (261) | 105 (262) | 106 (263) Names not yet established for these elements | 107 (262) | 108 (265) | 109 (266) |

| | 58 Ce Cerium 140.12 | 59 Pr Praseodymium 140.91 | 60 Nd Neodymium 144.24 | 61 Pm Promethium (147) | 62 Sm Samarium 150.35 | 63 Eu Europium 151.96 |
|---|---|---|---|---|---|---|
| Lanthanides | | | | | | |
| Actinides | 90 Th Thorium (232) | 91 Pa Protactinium (231) | 92 U Uranium (238) | 93 Np Neptunium (237) | 94 Pu Plutonium (242) | 95 Am Americium (243) |

| | | | | | | | 2<br>**He**<br>Helium<br>4.00 |
|---|---|---|---|---|---|---|---|
| | | 5<br>**B**<br>Boron<br>10.81 | 6<br>**C**<br>Carbon<br>12.01 | 7<br>**N**<br>Nitrogen<br>14.01 | 8<br>**O**<br>Oxygen<br>16.00 | 9<br>**F**<br>Fluorine<br>19.00 | 10<br>**Ne**<br>Neon<br>20.18 |
| | | 13<br>**Al**<br>Aluminum<br>26.98 | 14<br>**Si**<br>Silicon<br>28.09 | 15<br>**P**<br>Phosphorus<br>30.97 | 16<br>**S**<br>Sulfur<br>32.06 | 17<br>**Cl**<br>Chlorine<br>35.45 | 18<br>**Ar**<br>Argon<br>39.95 |

| 28<br>**Ni**<br>Nickel<br>58.71 | 29<br>**Cu**<br>Copper<br>63.55 | 30<br>**Zn**<br>Zinc<br>65.38 | 31<br>**Ga**<br>Gallium<br>69.72 | 32<br>**Ge**<br>Germanium<br>72.59 | 33<br>**As**<br>Arsenic<br>74.92 | 34<br>**Se**<br>Selenium<br>78.96 | 35<br>**Br**<br>Bromine<br>79.90 | 36<br>**Kr**<br>Krypton<br>83.80 |
|---|---|---|---|---|---|---|---|---|
| 46<br>**Pd**<br>Palladium<br>106.42 | 47<br>**Ag**<br>Silver<br>107.87 | 48<br>**Cd**<br>Cadmium<br>112.41 | 49<br>**In**<br>Indium<br>114.82 | 50<br>**Sn**<br>Tin<br>118.69 | 51<br>**Sb**<br>Antimony<br>121.75 | 52<br>**Te**<br>Tellurium<br>127.60 | 53<br>**I**<br>Iodine<br>126.90 | 54<br>**Xe**<br>Xenon<br>131.30 |
| 78<br>**Pt**<br>Platinum<br>195.09 | 79<br>**Au**<br>Gold<br>196.97 | 80<br>**Hg**<br>Mercury<br>200.59 | 81<br>**Tl**<br>Thallium<br>204.37 | 82<br>**Pb**<br>Lead<br>207.19 | 83<br>**Bi**<br>Bismuth<br>208.98 | 84<br>**Po**<br>Polonium<br>(210) | 85<br>**At**<br>Astatine<br>(210) | 86<br>**Rn**<br>Radon<br>(222) |

| 64<br>**Gd**<br>Gadolinium<br>157.25 | 65<br>**Tb**<br>Terbium<br>158.93 | 66<br>**Dy**<br>Dysprosium<br>162.50 | 67<br>**Ho**<br>Holmium<br>164.93 | 68<br>**Er**<br>Erbium<br>167.26 | 69<br>**Tm**<br>Thulium<br>168.93 | 70<br>**Yb**<br>Ytterbium<br>173.04 | 71<br>**Lu**<br>Lutetium<br>174.97 |
|---|---|---|---|---|---|---|---|
| 96<br>**Cm**<br>Curium<br>(247) | 97<br>**Bk**<br>Berkelium<br>(247) | 98<br>**Cf**<br>Californium<br>(251) | 99<br>**Es**<br>Einsteinium<br>(254) | 100<br>**Fm**<br>Fermium<br>(257) | 101<br>**Md**<br>Mendelevium<br>(258) | 102<br>**No**<br>Nobelium<br>(259) | 103<br>**Lr**<br>Lawrencium<br>(260) |

<u>Note</u>: Unless otherwise stated, assume that for all questions involving solutions and/or chemical equations, the system is in water and at room temperature.

## Part A

<u>Directions</u>: Each group of lettered answer choices below refers to the numbered statements or questions that immediately follow. For each question or statement, select the one lettered choice that is the best answer and fill in the corresponding circle on the answer sheet. An answer choice may be used once, more than once, or not at all in each set of questions.

<u>Questions 1–3</u>

     (A)  F
     (B)  Co
     (C)  Sr
     (D)  Be
     (E)  O

1. Which has the lowest ionization energy?

2. Which has the fewest negative oxidation states?

3. Which has the smallest ionic radius?

Questions 4–8

    (A) $SO_2$
    (B) $SiH_4$
    (C) $CO_2$
    (D) $Be_2$
    (E) NO

4. In which of the choices is there polar double bonding in a nonpolar molecule?

5. In which molecule does resonance occur?

6. In which molecule is the bond order 2½?

7. Which of the molecules has four $sp^3$ hybrid bonds?

8. Which molecule would you expect to be unstable on the basis of molecular orbital theory?

Questions 9–11

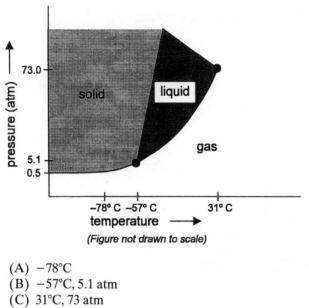

*(Figure not drawn to scale)*

(A)  −78°C
(B)  −57°C, 5.1 atm
(C)  31°C, 73 atm
(D)  31°C
(E)  None of the above.

9. What does the phase diagram above show to be the normal boiling point of carbon dioxide?

10. Which point represents the critical point?

11. Which point represents the triple point?

Questions 12–16

Directions: Predict the change in entropy.

     (A) The change in entropy will be positive.
     (B) The change in entropy will be zero.
     (C) The change in entropy will be negative.
     (D) The change in entropy cannot be determined from the information given.

12. $Cl_2 \rightarrow 2\, Cl(g)$

13. $H_2(g)$ at 5.0 atm $\rightarrow H_2(g)$ at 1.0 atm

14. Sublimation of solid $CO_2$

15. $2\, H_2(g) + O_2(g) \rightarrow 2\, H_2O(g)$

16. $PCl_5(g) \rightleftharpoons PCl_3(g) + Cl_2(g)$

## Part B

Directions: Each of the following questions or incomplete statements has five possible answer choices or completions. In each case, select the one choice that is best and fill in the corresponding circle on the answer sheet.

17. Unknown element X combines with oxygen to form the compound $XO_2$. If 44.0 grams of element X combine with 8.00 grams of oxygen, what is the atomic mass of element X?
    (A) 16 amu
    (B) 44 amu
    (C) 88 amu
    (D) 176 amu
    (E) 352 amu

18. When water evaporates at constant pressure, the sign of the change in enthalpy
    (A) is negative
    (B) is positive
    (C) depends on the temperature
    (D) depends on the volume of the container
    (E) does not exist; that is, the enthalpy change is zero

19. Which of the following statements is NOT correct?
    (A) At constant temperature, the pressure of a certain amount of gas increases with increasing volume.
    (B) At constant volume, the pressure of a certain amount of gas increases with increasing temperature.
    (C) At constant pressure, the volume of a certain amount of gas increases with increasing temperature.
    (D) In dealing with gas laws, the most convenient scale of temperature to use is the Kelvin temperature scale.
    (E) Equal numbers of molecules of all gases exert about the same pressure at a certain temperature and volume.

20. Within a period, an increase in atomic number is usually accompanied by
    (A) a decrease in atomic radius and an increase in electronegativity
    (B) an increase in atomic radius and an increase in electronegativity
    (C) a decrease in atomic radius and a decrease in electronegativity
    (D) an increase in atomic radius and a decrease in electronegativity
    (E) None of these answer choices is correct.

21. A molecule exhibits $sp^3d^2$ hybridization in its bonding structure. The most probable geometric shape of this molecule is
    (A) triangular bipyramidal
    (B) T-shaped
    (C) octahedral
    (D) linear
    (E) hexagonal

22. What is the proper name of $[Co(NH_3)_5Br]Cl_2$?
    (A) Cobaltpentaamine bromo-dichloride
    (B) Pentaamminecobalt(III) bromo-dichloride
    (C) Dichlorocobalt(V) bromodichloride
    (D) Dichloropentaaminecobalt(III) bromide
    (E) Pentaaminebromocobalt(III) chloride

23. Which one of the following does NOT show hydrogen bonding?
    (A) Ammonia, $NH_3$
    (B) Hydrazine, $N_2H_4$
    (C) Hydrogen peroxide, $H_2O_2$
    (D) Dimethyl ether, $CH_3OCH_3$
    (E) Methyl alcohol, $CH_3OH$

24. How many moles of solid $Ca(NO_3)_2$ should be added to 450 milliliters of 0.35 M $Al(NO_3)_3$ to increase the concentration of the $NO_3^-$ ion to 1.7 M? (Assume that the volume of the solution remains constant).
    (A) 0.07 mole
    (B) 0.14 mole
    (C) 0.29 mole
    (D) 0.45 mole
    (E) 0.77 mole

Questions 25–29

$$A(g) + 2 B(g) + 3 C(g) \rightarrow 4 D(g) + 5 E(g)$$

$$\text{rate of formation of } E = \frac{d[E]}{dt} = k[A]^2[B]$$

25. If one were to double the concentration of B, the rate of the reaction shown above would increase by a factor of
   (A) ½   (B) 1   (C) 2   (D) 4   (E) 8

26. $\dfrac{-d[B]}{dt}$ is equal to

   (A) $\dfrac{-d[A]}{dt}$

   (B) $\dfrac{-d[C]}{dt}$

   (C) $\dfrac{d^{1/2}[D]}{dt}$

   (D) $\dfrac{d^{1/5}[E]}{dt}$

   (E) none of these

27. To decrease the rate constant $k$, one could
   (A) increase [E]
   (B) decrease [B]
   (C) decrease the temperature
   (D) increase the volume
   (E) increase the pressure

28. If one were to reduce the volume of a container by $\frac{1}{3}$, the rate of the reaction would increase by a factor of
    (A)  3
    (B)  9
    (C) 16
    (D) 27
    (E) Reducing the volume of the container has no effect on the rate.

29. Sulfur trioxide gas dissociates into sulfur dioxide gas and oxygen gas at 1250°C. In an experiment, 3.60 moles of sulfur trioxide were placed into an evacuated 3.0-liter flask. The concentration of sulfur dioxide gas measured at equilibrium was found to be 0.20 M. What is the equilibrium constant, $K_c$, for the reaction?
    (A)  $1.6 \times 10^{-4}$
    (B)  $1.0 \times 10^{-3}$
    (C)  $2.0 \times 10^{-3}$
    (D)  $4.0 \times 10^{-3}$
    (E)  $8.0 \times 10^{-3}$

30. A solution has a pH of 11.0. What is the hydrogen ion concentration?
    (A) $1.0 \times 10^{-11}$ M
    (B) $1.0 \times 10^{-3}$ M
    (C) 0.0 M
    (D) $1.0 \times 10^{3}$ M
    (E) $1.0 \times 10^{11}$ M

31.

| Species | $\Delta H°$ (kJ/mole) at 25°C and 1 atm | $\Delta S°$ (J/K) at 25°C and 1 atm |
|---------|------------------|------------------|
| $BaCO_3(s)$ | −1170. | 100.00 |
| $BaO(s)$ | −600. | 70.00 |
| $CO_2(g)$ | −400. | 200. |

At what temperature does $\Delta G°$ become zero for the following reaction:

$$BaCO_3(s) \rightarrow BaO(s) + CO_2(g)$$

    (A) 0 K
    (B) $1.0 \times 10^{1}$ K
    (C) $1.0 \times 10^{2}$ K
    (D) $1.0 \times 10^{3}$ K
    (E) $1.0 \times 10^{4}$ K

32. Calculate the rate constant for the radioactive disintegration of an isotope that has a half-life of 6930 years.
    (A) $1.00 \times 10^{-5}$ yr$^{-1}$
    (B) $1.00 \times 10^{-4}$ yr$^{-1}$
    (C) $1.00 \times 10^{-3}$ yr$^{-1}$
    (D) $1.00 \times 10^{3}$ yr$^{-1}$
    (E) $1.00 \times 10^{4}$ yr$^{-1}$

Questions 33–37

    (A) Amide
    (B) Amine
    (C) Ketone
    (D) Thiol
    (E) Salt

33.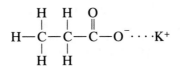

34.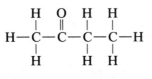

35.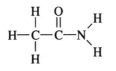

36.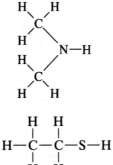

37.

38. A mining company supplies an ore that is 15.915% chalcocite, $Cu_2S$, by weight. How many metric tons of ore should be purchased in order to produce $6.0 \times 10^2$ metric tons of an alloy containing 12.709% Cu?
   (A)  $5.0 \times 10^{-1}$ metric tons
   (B)  $1.0 \times 10^1$ metric tons
   (C)  $2.0 \times 10^2$ metric tons
   (D)  $3.0 \times 10^2$ metric tons
   (E)  $6.0 \times 10^2$ metric tons

39. At constant temperature and pressure, the heats of formation of $H_2O(g)$, $CO_2(g)$, and $C_2H_6(g)$ (in kilocalories per mole) are as follows:

| Species | $\Delta H_f (kcal/mole)$ |
|---------|--------------------------|
| $H_2O(g)$ | $-60.0$ |
| $CO_2(g)$ | $-94.0$ |
| $C_2H_6(g)$ | $-20.0$ |

If $\Delta H$ values are negative for exothermic reactions, what is $\Delta H$ (in kcal/mole) for 1 mole of $C_2H_6$ gas to oxidize to carbon dioxide gas and water vapor (same temperature and pressure)?
   (A)  $-1340.0$ kcal/mole
   (B)   $-696.0$ kcal/mole
   (C)   $-348.0$ kcal/mole
   (D)   $-134.0$ kcal/mole
   (E)    $348.0$ kcal/mole

40. Which one of the following is NOT an assumption of the kinetic theory of gases?
    (A) Gas particles are negligibly small.
    (B) Gas particles undergo a decrease in kinetic energy when passed from a region of high pressure to a region of low pressure.
    (C) Gas particles are in constant motion.
    (D) Gas particles don't attract each other.
    (E) Gas particles undergo elastic collisions.

41. How many electrons can be accommodated in all the atomic orbitals that correspond to the principal quantum number 4?
    (A) 2   (B) 8   (C) 18   (D) 32   (E) 40

42. A linear molecule can have the general formulas AA, AB, or $AB_2$. Given a molecule with the general formula $AB_2$, which one of the following would be the most useful in determining whether the molecule was bent or linear?
    (A) Ionization energies
    (B) Electron affinities
    (C) Dipole moments
    (D) Electronegativities
    (E) Bond energies

43. What is the charge of Zn in $Zn(H_2O)_3(OH)^+$?
    (A) 0   (B) +1   (C) +2   (D) +3   (E) +5

44. A certain organic compound has a vapor pressure of 132 mm Hg at 54°C. To determine the vapor pressure of 2.00 moles of the compound at 37°C, taking the heat of vaporization for the compound to be $4.33 \times 10^4$ J/mole, you would use
    (A) the Arrhenius equation
    (B) the Clausius-Clapeyron equation
    (C) the combined gas laws
    (D) the ideal gas law
    (E) Raoult's law

45. What is the molality of a 10.% $C_6H_2O$ (MW = 90.) solution?
    (A)    0.012 m
    (B)    0.12 m
    (C)    1.2 m
    (D)   12 m
    (E)   Not enough information is provided.

46. If a 10. cm$^3$ sample of unknown contains 1 cm$^3$ of 0.1 M AlCl$_3$, then the concentration of Al$^{3+}$ in the unknown is about
    (A)  0.001 M
    (B)  0.01 M
    (C)  0.1 M
    (D)  1 M
    (E)  10. M

47. If a reactant concentration is doubled, and the reaction rate increases by a factor of 8, the exponent for that reactant in the rate law should be
    (A)  ¼
    (B)  ½
    (C)  2
    (D)  3
    (E)  4

48. For the reaction

$$2 NO(g) + O_2(g) \rightarrow 2 NO_2(g)$$

which two of the following possible intermediate mechanisms would support this reaction?

1.  $2 NO(g) \rightarrow N_2O_2(g)$

2.  $NO(g) + O_2(g) \rightarrow NO_3(g)$

3.  $2 NO_2(g) \rightarrow N_2O_2(g) + O_2(g)$

4.  $NO_3(g) + NO(g) \rightarrow 2 NO_2(g)$

5.  $NO(g) \rightarrow NO(g) + O_2(g)$

    (A)  1 and 2
    (B)  2 and 3
    (C)  3 and 4
    (D)  2 and 4
    (E)  1 and 4

49. The value of $K_a$ for lactic acid, HLac, is $1.5 \times 10^{-5}$. What is the value of $K_b$ for the lactate anion, $Lac^-$?
    (A) $1.0 \times 10^{-14}$
    (B) $8.5 \times 10^{-10}$
    (C) $6.7 \times 10^{-10}$
    (D) $8.5 \times 10^{10}$
    (E) It cannot be determined from the information provided.

50. How many grams of NaOH are required to neutralize 700 ml of 3.0 N HCl?
    (A)   2.1 grams
    (B)  21 grams
    (C)  42 grams
    (D)  84 grams
    (E) 102 grams

51. Solid calcium carbonate decomposes to produce solid calcium oxide and carbon dioxide gas. The value of $\Delta G°$ for this reaction is 130.24 kJ/mole. Calculate $\Delta G$ at 100°C for this reaction if the pressure of the carbon dioxide gas is 1.00 atm.
    (A) $-998.56$ kJ/mole
    (B) $-604.2$ kJ/mole
    (C)    56.31 kJ/mole
    (D)   130.24 kJ/mole
    (E)   256.24 kJ/mole

52. Which of the following choices represents $^{239}_{94}Pu$ producing a positron?
    (A) $^{239}_{94}Pu \rightarrow {}^{235}_{94}Pu + {}^{4}_{2}He$
    (B) $^{239}_{94}Pu \rightarrow {}^{0}_{-1}e + {}^{239}_{93}Np$
    (C) $^{239}_{94}Pu + {}^{0}_{-1}e \rightarrow {}^{239}_{93}Np$
    (D) $^{239}_{94}Pu \rightarrow {}^{0}_{1}e + {}^{239}_{93}Np$
    (E) $^{239}_{94}Pu + {}^{4}_{2}He \rightarrow {}^{235}_{92}U$

53. $Ni(s)|Ni^{2+}(aq)||Ag^+(aq)|Ag(s)$

$Ni^{2+} + 2e^- \rightarrow Ni(s) \qquad E^\circ_{red} = -0.25$ volt

$Ag^+ + e^- \rightarrow Ag(s) \qquad E^\circ_{red} = 0.80$ volt

Which of the following statements is true of the above reaction?
(A) The reaction is spontaneous, $E^\circ = 1.05$ volts.
(B) The reaction is nonspontaneous, $E^\circ = -1.05$ volts.
(C) The reaction is spontaneous, $E^\circ = -1.05$ volts.
(D) The reaction is spontaneous, $E^\circ = 0.55$ volt.
(E) The reaction is nonspontaneous, $E^\circ = -0.55$ volt.

54. An excess of $S_8(s)$ is heated with a metallic element until the metal reacts completely. All excess sulfur is combusted to a gaseous compound and escapes from the crucible. Given the information that follows, determine the most probable formula for the residue.

> mass of crucible, lid, and metal = 55.00 grams
> mass of crucible and lid = 41.00 grams
> mass of crucible, lid, and residue = 62.00 grams

(A) CuS
(B) $Cu_2S$
(C) FeS
(D) $Fe_2S_3$
(E) Not enough information is given to solve the problem.

55. When 3.00 grams of a certain metal are completely oxidized, 3.80 grams of its oxide are produced. The specific heat of the metal is $0.052$ cal/g · °C. What is the approximate atomic weight of this metal?
(A)   35 g/mole
(B)   65 g/mole
(C) 115 g/mole
(D) 150 g/mole
(E) 180 g/mole

56. The density of a gas is directly proportional to its
    (A) pressure
    (B) volume
    (C) kinetic energy
    (D) temperature
    (E) molecular mass

57. The valence electron configuration of element A is $3s^2\,3p^1$ and that of B is $3s^2\,3p^4$. What is the probable empirical formula for a compound of the two elements?
    (A) $A_2B$  (B) $AB_2$  (C) $A_3B_2$  (D) $A_2B_3$  (E) $AB$

58. Which formula correctly represents the diamminediaquadibromochromium(III) ion?
    (A) $[Cr(H_2O)_2(NH_3)_2Br_2]^+$
    (B) $[(NH_3)_2(H_2O)_2Br_2Cr]^{3+}$
    (C) $[Cr(H_2O)_2(NH_3)_2Br_2]^{3+}$
    (D) $[(NH_3)_2(H_2O)_2Br_2Cr]^+$
    (E) $[Cr(H_2O)_2(NH_3)_2Br_2]^{2+}$

59. According to Raoult's law, which statement is false?
    (A) The vapor pressure of a solvent over a solution is less than that of the pure solvent.
    (B) Ionic solids ionize in water, increasing the effect of all colligative properties.
    (C) The vapor pressure of a pure solvent when measured over a solution decreases as the mole fraction increases.
    (D) The solubility of a gas increases as the temperature decreases.
    (E) The solubility of a gas in solution increases as the pressure of the gas increases.

60. Calculate the volume of a 36.45% solution of hydrochloric acid (density = 1.50 g/ml) required to prepare 9.0 liters of a 5.0-molar solution.
    (A) 0.5 liter
    (B) 1.0 liter
    (C) 2.0 liters
    (D) 2.5 liters
    (E) 3.0 liters

61. Dinitrogen pentoxide decomposes according to the following balanced equation:

$$N_2O_5(g) \rightarrow 2\,NO_2(g) + \tfrac{1}{2}\,O_2(g)$$

The rate of decomposition was found to be 0.80 mole · liter$^{-1}$ · sec$^{-1}$ at a given concentration and temperature. What would the rate be for the formation of oxygen gas under the same conditions?
    (A) 0.20 mole · liter$^{-1}$ · sec$^{-1}$
    (B) 0.40 mole · liter$^{-1}$ · sec$^{-1}$
    (C) 0.80 mole · liter$^{-1}$ · sec$^{-1}$
    (D) 1.60 mole · liter$^{-1}$ · sec$^{-1}$
    (E) 3.20 mole · liter$^{-1}$ · sec$^{-1}$

62. The $K_{sp}$ of lead (II) chloride is $2.4 \times 10^{-4}$. What conclusion can be made about the concentration of [Cl$^-$] in a solution of lead chloride if [Pb$^{2+}$] = 1.0 M?
    (A) [Cl$^-$] can have any value.
    (B) [Cl$^-$] cannot be greater than $(K_{sp})^{1/2}$.
    (C) [Cl$^-$] cannot be less than $(K_{sp})^{1/2}$.
    (D) [Cl$^-$] cannot be equal to $(K_{sp})^{1/2}$.
    (E) [Cl$^-$] must also be equal to 1.0 M.

Directions: For Questions 63–65, use the following information:

25.0 ml of a sample of vinegar (a solution of $HC_2H_3O_2$, MW = 60.00 g · mole$^{-1}$) is neutralized by 50.0 ml of a 0.50 N NaOH solution.

63. What is the normality of the acid?
    (A) 0.25 N
    (B) 0.50 N
    (C) 0.75 N
    (D) 1.0 N
    (E) 2.0 N

64. Calculate the number of grams of acetic acid per liter of the vinegar.
    (A)  5.0 grams
    (B) 25. grams
    (C) 30. grams
    (D) 50. grams
    (E) 60. grams

65. Calculate the weight percentage of acetic acid in the vinegar. The vinegar has a density of 1.0 g/ml.
    (A) 1.0%  (B) 1.5%  (C) 2.5%  (D) 6.0%  (E) 6.5%

66. When a solid melts, which of the following is true?
    (A) $\Delta H > 0, \Delta S > 0$
    (B) $\Delta H < 0, \Delta S < 0$
    (C) $\Delta H > 0, \Delta S < 0$
    (D) $\Delta H < 0, \Delta S > 0$
    (E) More information is required before we can specify the signs of $\Delta H$ and $\Delta S$.

67. For the following reaction

$$Zn(s) + 2\,Ag^+(aq) \rightarrow Zn^{2+}(aq) + 2\,Ag(s)$$

the standard voltage ($E^\circ_{cell}$) has been calculated to be 1.56 volts. To decrease the voltage from the cell to 1.00 volt, one could

    (A) increase the size of the zinc electrode
    (B) reduce the coefficients of the reactions so that it reads

$$1/2\,Zn(s) + Ag^+(aq) \rightarrow 1/2\,Zn^{2+}(aq) + Ag(s)$$

    (C) decrease the concentration of the silver ion in solution
    (D) increase the concentration of the silver ion in solution
    (E) decrease the concentration of the zinc ion in solution

68. A radioactive isotope has a half-life of 6.93 years and decays by beta emission. Determine the approximate fraction of the sample that is left undecayed at the end of 11.5 years.
    (A)  1%
    (B)  5%
    (C) 30%
    (D) 75%
    (E) 99%

69. The solubility product constant at 25°C for AgCl is $1.6 \times 10^{-10}$ $mol^2 \cdot L^{-2}$ and that for AgI is $8.0 \times 10^{-17}$ $mol^2 \cdot L^{-2}$. Determine the equilibrium constant for the reaction of silver chloride with silver iodide.
    (A)  $1.3 \times 10^{-26}$ $mol^2 \cdot L^{-2}$
    (B)  $5.0 \times 10^{-7}$ $mol^2 \cdot L^{-2}$
    (C)  $1.0 \times 10^3$ $mol^2 \cdot L^{-2}$
    (D)  $2.0 \times 10^6$ $mol^2 \cdot L^{-2}$
    (E)  $1.3 \times 10^{16}$ $mol^2 \cdot L^{-2}$

70.

| Species | Bond Energy (kcal/mole) |
|---------|-------------------------|
| F—F | 33 |
| H—H | 103 |
| H—F | 135 |

Calculate the value of $\Delta H$ for the following reaction:

$$H_2(g) + F_2(g) \rightarrow 2\,HF(g)$$

(A) $-406$ kcal/mole
(B) $-320$ kcal/mole
(C) $-271$ kcal/mole
(D) $-134$ kcal/mole
(E)    $-1.00$ kcal/mole

71. What happens to the velocities of different molecules as the temperature of a gas increases?
   (A) The velocities of all component molecules increase equally.
   (B) The velocity range among different molecules at higher temperatures is smaller than that at lower temperatures.
   (C) The effect on the velocities of the molecules depends on whether the pressure remains constant.
   (D) The velocity range among different molecules at higher temperatures is wider than the range at lower temperatures.
   (E) None of these answer choices is correct.

72. For the isoelectronic series $S^{2-}$, $Cl^-$, Ar, $K^+$, and $Sc^{3+}$, which species requires the least energy to remove an outer electron?
   (A) $S^{2-}$   (B) $Cl^-$   (C) Ar   (D) $K^+$   (E) $Sc^{3+}$

73. The silver ion in the complex $[Ag(CN)_2]^-$ has a coordination number of
   (A) 2   (B) 3   (C) 4   (D) 5   (E) 6

74. Cesium (atomic radius = 0.255 nm) crystallizes with a body-centered cubic unit cell. What is the length of a side of the cell? ($\sqrt{3} = 1.73$)
   (A) 0.450 nm
   (B) 0.500 nm
   (C) 0.600 nm
   (D) 0.800 nm
   (E) 0.900 nm

75. How many grams of $H_3PO_4$ are required to make 100.0 ml of a 0.100 N $H_3PO_4$ solution?
   (A) 0.0164 g
   (B) 0.164 g
   (C) 0.327 g
   (D) 0.654 g
   (E) 1.31 g

**STOP.** IF YOU FINISH BEFORE TIME IS CALLED, CHECK YOUR WORK ON THIS SECTION ONLY. DO NOT WORK ON ANY OTHER SECTION IN THE TEST.

# SECTION II (FREE-RESPONSE QUESTIONS)

## Part A
## Writing and Predicting Chemical Reactions

**Time: 10 minutes**
**8% of total grade**

1.  You will be given exactly 10 minutes to complete this part of the exam. After 10 minutes, your paper will be collected.

You are given eight options in this part. Select and answer only FIVE of these options. (No more than five options will be scored.)

Give the formulas to show the reactants and the products for FIVE of the following chemical reactions. Each of the reactions occurs in aqueous solution unless otherwise indicated. Represent substances in solution as ions if the substance is extensively ionized. Omit formulas for any ions or molecules that are unchanged by the reaction. In all cases, a reaction occurs. You need not balance.

Example: A strip of magnesium is added to a solution of silver nitrate.

$$Mg + Ag^+ \rightarrow Mg^{2+} + Ag$$

(a)  A piece of solid tin is heated in the presence of chlorine gas.
(b)  Ethane is burned in the presence of air.
(c)  Solid copper shavings are added to a concentrated nitric acid solution.
(d)  Dilute sulfuric acid is added to a solution of mercuric nitrate.
(e)  Sulfur trioxide gas is heated in the presence of solid calcium oxide.
(f)  Copper sulfate pentahydrate is strongly heated.
(g)  A strong ammonia solution is added to a suspension of zinc hydroxide.
(h)  Ethane gas is heated in the presence of bromine gas.

# SECTION II (FREE-RESPONSE QUESTIONS)

**Parts B, C, and D**
**Time: 85 minutes**
**A programmable calculator is allowed**
**Calculators will not be cleared**
**47% of the total grade**

## General Instructions

You will be given 85 minutes to complete Parts B, C, and D. You may move freely from one question to another during the allotted 85 minutes.

A periodic table, an electrochemical series, a water vapor pressure table, and a table of chemistry equations and constants are included as reference materials.

Write CLEARLY and LEGIBLY as you answer each question. You may use a pencil or pen to write your answers. In correcting your writing, you may simply cross out the incorrect word or words to save time.

Material in the following tables is provided for your use in answering Parts B, C, and D in Section II.

# PERIODIC TABLE OF THE CHEMICAL ELEMENTS

| 1 | | | | | | | | |
|---|---|---|---|---|---|---|---|---|
| **H** | | | | | | | | |
| Hydrogen | | | | | | | | |
| 1.01 | | | | | | | | |
| 3 | 4 | | | | | | | |
| **Li** | **Be** | | | | | | | |
| Lithium | Beryllium | | | | | | | |
| 6.94 | 9.01 | | | | | | | |
| 11 | 12 | | | | | | | |
| **Na** | **Mg** | | | | | | | |
| Sodium | Magnesium | | | | | | | |
| 22.99 | 24.31 | | | | | | | |
| 19 | 20 | 21 | 22 | 23 | 24 | 25 | 26 | 27 |
| **K** | **Ca** | **Sc** | **Ti** | **V** | **Cr** | **Mn** | **Fe** | **Co** |
| Potassium | Calcium | Scandium | Titanium | Vanadium | Chromium | Manganese | Iron | Cobalt |
| 39.10 | 40.08 | 44.96 | 47.90 | 50.94 | 52.00 | 54.94 | 55.85 | 58.93 |
| 37 | 38 | 39 | 40 | 41 | 42 | 43 | 44 | 45 |
| **Rb** | **Sr** | **Y** | **Zr** | **Nb** | **Mo** | **Tc** | **Ru** | **Rh** |
| Rubidium | Strontium | Yttrium | Zirconium | Niobium | Molybdenum | Technetium | Ruthenium | Rhodium |
| 85.47 | 87.62 | 88.91 | 91.22 | 92.91 | 95.94 | (99) | 101.07 | 102.91 |
| 55 | 56 | 57 | 72 | 73 | 74 | 75 | 76 | 77 |
| **Cs** | **Ba** | **La** | **Hf** | **Ta** | **W** | **Re** | **Os** | **Ir** |
| Cesium | Barium | Lanthanum | Hafnium | Tantalum | Tungsten | Rhenium | Osmium | Iridium |
| 132.91 | 137.34 | 138.91 | 178.49 | 180.95 | 183.85 | 186.21 | 190.2 | 192.22 |
| 87 | 88 | 89 | 104 | 105 | 106 | 107 | 108 | 109 |
| **Fr** | **Ra** | **Ac** | | | Names not yet established for these elements | | | |
| Francium | Radium | Actinium | | | | | | |
| (223) | (226) | (227) | (261) | (262) | (263) | (262) | (265) | (266) |

| | 58 | 59 | 60 | 61 | 62 | 63 |
|---|---|---|---|---|---|---|
| Lanthanides | **Ce** | **Pr** | **Nd** | **Pm** | **Sm** | **Eu** |
| | Cerium | Praseodymium | Neodymium | Promethium | Samarium | Europium |
| | 140.12 | 140.91 | 144.24 | (147) | 150.35 | 151.96 |
| | 90 | 91 | 92 | 93 | 94 | 95 |
| Actinides | **Th** | **Pa** | **U** | **Np** | **Pu** | **Am** |
| | Thorium | Protactinium | Uranium | Neptunium | Plutonium | Americium |
| | (232) | (231) | (238) | (237) | (242) | (243) |

| | | | | | | | | 2<br>**He**<br>Helium<br>4.00 |
|---|---|---|---|---|---|---|---|---|
| | | | 5<br>**B**<br>Boron<br>10.81 | 6<br>**C**<br>Carbon<br>12.01 | 7<br>**N**<br>Nitrogen<br>14.01 | 8<br>**O**<br>Oxygen<br>16.00 | 9<br>**F**<br>Fluorine<br>19.00 | 10<br>**Ne**<br>Neon<br>20.18 |
| | | | 13<br>**Al**<br>Aluminum<br>26.98 | 14<br>**Si**<br>Silicon<br>28.09 | 15<br>**P**<br>Phosphorus<br>30.97 | 16<br>**S**<br>Sulfur<br>32.06 | 17<br>**Cl**<br>Chlorine<br>35.45 | 18<br>**Ar**<br>Argon<br>39.95 |
| 28<br>**Ni**<br>Nickel<br>58.71 | 29<br>**Cu**<br>Copper<br>63.55 | 30<br>**Zn**<br>Zinc<br>65.38 | 31<br>**Ga**<br>Gallium<br>69.72 | 32<br>**Ge**<br>Germanium<br>72.59 | 33<br>**As**<br>Arsenic<br>74.92 | 34<br>**Se**<br>Selenium<br>78.96 | 35<br>**Br**<br>Bromine<br>79.90 | 36<br>**Kr**<br>Krypton<br>83.80 |
| 46<br>**Pd**<br>Palladium<br>106.42 | 47<br>**Ag**<br>Silver<br>107.87 | 48<br>**Cd**<br>Cadmium<br>112.41 | 49<br>**In**<br>Indium<br>114.82 | 50<br>**Sn**<br>Tin<br>118.69 | 51<br>**Sb**<br>Antimony<br>121.75 | 52<br>**Te**<br>Tellurium<br>127.60 | 53<br>**I**<br>Iodine<br>126.90 | 54<br>**Xe**<br>Xenon<br>131.30 |
| 78<br>**Pt**<br>Platinum<br>195.09 | 79<br>**Au**<br>Gold<br>196.97 | 80<br>**Hg**<br>Mercury<br>200.59 | 81<br>**Tl**<br>Thallium<br>204.37 | 82<br>**Pb**<br>Lead<br>207.19 | 83<br>**Bi**<br>Bismuth<br>208.98 | 84<br>**Po**<br>Polonium<br>(210) | 85<br>**At**<br>Astatine<br>(210) | 86<br>**Rn**<br>Radon<br>(222) |

| 64<br>**Gd**<br>Gadolinium<br>157.25 | 65<br>**Tb**<br>Terbium<br>158.93 | 66<br>**Dy**<br>Dysprosium<br>162.50 | 67<br>**Ho**<br>Holmium<br>164.93 | 68<br>**Er**<br>Erbium<br>167.26 | 69<br>**Tm**<br>Thulium<br>168.93 | 70<br>**Yb**<br>Ytterbium<br>173.04 | 71<br>**Lu**<br>Lutetium<br>174.97 |
|---|---|---|---|---|---|---|---|
| 96<br>**Cm**<br>Curium<br>(247) | 97<br>**Bk**<br>Berkelium<br>(247) | 98<br>**Cf**<br>Californium<br>(251) | 99<br>**Es**<br>Einsteinium<br>(254) | 100<br>**Fm**<br>Fermium<br>(257) | 101<br>**Md**<br>Mendelevium<br>(258) | 102<br>**No**<br>Nobelium<br>(259) | 103<br>**Lr**<br>Lawrencium<br>(260) |

$E°_{red}$ POTENTIALS IN WATER SOLUTION AT 25°C

| | | | |
|---|---|---|---|
| $Li^+ + e^-$ | → | $Li(s)$ | −3.05 |
| $Cs^+ + e^-$ | → | $Cs(s)$ | −2.92 |
| $K^+ + e^-$ | → | $K(s)$ | −2.92 |
| $Sr^{2+} + 2e^-$ | → | $Sr(s)$ | −2.89 |
| $Ca^{2+} + 2e^-$ | → | $Ca(s)$ | −2.87 |
| $Na^+ + e^-$ | → | $Na(s)$ | −2.71 |
| $Mg^{2+} + 2e^-$ | → | $Mg(s)$ | −2.37 |
| $Al^{3+} + 3e^-$ | → | $Al(s)$ | −1.66 |
| $Mn^{2+} + 2e^-$ | → | $Mn(s)$ | −1.18 |
| $Zn^{2+} + 2e^-$ | → | $Zn(s)$ | −0.76 |
| $Fe^{2+} + 2e^-$ | → | $Fe(s)$ | −0.44 |
| $Cr^{3+} + e^-$ | → | $Cr^{2+}$ | −0.41 |
| $Ni^{2+} + 2e^-$ | → | $Ni(s)$ | −0.25 |
| $Sn^{2+} + 2e^-$ | → | $Sn(s)$ | −0.14 |
| $Pb^{2+} + 2e^-$ | → | $Pb(s)$ | −0.13 |
| $2\,H^+ + 2e^-$ | → | $H_2(g)$ | 0.00 |
| $S(s) + 2\,H^+ + 2e^-$ | → | $H_2S$ | 0.14 |
| $Sn^{4+} + 2e^-$ | → | $Sn^{2+}$ | 0.15 |
| $Cu^{2+} + e^-$ | → | $Cu^+$ | 0.16 |
| $Cu^{2+} + 2e^-$ | → | $Cu(s)$ | 0.34 |
| $Cu^+ + e^-$ | → | $Cu(s)$ | 0.52 |
| $Fe^{3+} + e^-$ | → | $Fe^{2+}$ | 0.77 |
| $Ag^+ + e^-$ | → | $Ag(s)$ | 0.80 |
| $Hg^{2+} + 2e^-$ | → | $Hg(\ell)$ | 0.85 |
| $Br_2(\ell) + 2e^-$ | → | $2\,Br^-$ | 1.07 |
| $O_2(g) + 4\,H^+ + 4e^-$ | → | $2\,H_2O$ | 1.23 |
| $Cl_2(g) + 2e^-$ | → | $2\,Cl^-$ | 1.36 |
| $F_2(g) + 2e^-$ | → | $2\,F^-$ | 2.87 |

## WATER VAPOR PRESSURE

| Temperature (°C) | Water Vapor Pressure (mm Hg) |
|---|---|
| 0 | 4.6 |
| 10 | 9.2 |
| 15 | 12.7 |
| 20 | 17.4 |
| 30 | 31.5 |
| 35 | 41.8 |
| 40 | 55.0 |
| 50 | 92.2 |
| 60 | 149.2 |

## EQUATIONS AND CONSTANTS

### ATOMIC STRUCTURE

$$\Delta E = h\nu \qquad c = \lambda\nu \qquad \lambda = \frac{h}{mv} \qquad p = mv$$

$$E_n = \frac{-2.178 \times 10^{-18}}{n^2} \text{ joule}$$

$E$ = energy $\qquad\qquad$ $p$ = momentum
$\nu$ = frequency (Greek nu) $\qquad$ $v$ = velocity (Italic v)
$\lambda$ = wavelength $\qquad\qquad$ $m$ = mass
$n$ = principal quantum number

speed of light: $c = 3.00 \times 10^8$ m/s
Planck's constant: $h = 6.63 \times 10^{-34}$ joule $\cdot$ s
Boltzmann's constant: $k = 1.38 \times 10^{-23}$ joule/K
Avogadro's number = $6.022 \times 10^{23}$/mole
electron charge: $e = -1.602 \times 10^{-19}$ coulomb
1 electron volt/atom = 96.5 kilojoules/mole

## EQUILIBRIUM

$$K_a = \frac{[H^+][A^-]}{[HA]} \qquad K_b = \frac{[OH^-][HB^+]}{[B]}$$

$$K_w = [OH^-][H^+] = 10^{-14} \text{ at } 25°C = K_a \cdot K_b$$

$$pH = -\log[H^+] \qquad pOH = -\log[OH^-] \qquad 14 = pH + pOH$$

$$pH = pK_a + \log\frac{[A^-]}{[HA]} \qquad pOH = pK_b + \log\frac{[HB^+]}{[B]}$$

$$pK_a = -\log K_a \qquad pK_b = -\log K_b$$

$$K_p = K_c(RT)^{\Delta n}, \text{ where } \Delta n = \text{moles product gas} - \text{moles reactant gas}$$

$K_a$ (weak acid) $\qquad K_p$ (gas pressure)

$K_b$ (weak base) $\qquad K_c$ (molar concentration)

$K_w$ (water)

## THERMOCHEMISTRY

$$\Delta S° = \Sigma S°_{products} - \Sigma S°_{reactants}$$

$$\Delta H° = \Sigma \Delta H°_{f\,products} - \Sigma \Delta H°_{f\,reactants}$$

$$\Delta G° = \Sigma \Delta G°_{f\,products} - \Sigma \Delta G°_{f\,reactants}$$

$$\Delta G° = \Delta H° - T\Delta S° = -RT \ln K = -2.303\,RT \log K = -n\mathscr{F}E°$$

$$\Delta G = \Delta G° + RT \ln Q = \Delta G° + 2.303\,RT \log Q$$

$$q = m \cdot c \cdot \Delta T \qquad C_p = \frac{\Delta H}{\Delta T}$$

$S°$ = standard entropy $\qquad n$ = moles

$H°$ = standard enthalpy $\qquad m$ = mass

$G°$ = standard free energy $\quad q$ = heat

$E°$ = standard voltage $\qquad c$ = specific heat capacity

$T$ = absolute temperature $\quad C_p$ = molar heat capacity at constant pressure

## GASES, LIQUIDS, AND SOLUTIONS

$$PV = nRT \qquad \left(P + \frac{n^2a}{V^2}\right)(V - nb) = nRT$$

$P_A = P_{\text{total}} \cdot X_A$, where $X_A = \dfrac{\text{moles A}}{\text{total moles}}$

$P_{\text{total}} = P_A + P_B + P_C + \cdots$

$n = \dfrac{m}{M}$

$K = {}^{\circ}C + 273$

$\dfrac{P_1V_1}{T_1} = \dfrac{P_2V_2}{T_2}$

$D = \dfrac{m}{V}$

$u_{rms} = \sqrt{\dfrac{3kT}{m}} = \sqrt{\dfrac{3RT}{M}}$

$$KE \text{ per molecule} = \tfrac{1}{2}mv^2 \qquad KE \text{ per mole} = \tfrac{3}{2}RTn$$

$\dfrac{r_1}{r_2} = \sqrt{\dfrac{M_2}{M_1}}$

molarity: $M$ = moles solute/liter solution

molality = moles solute/kilogram solvent

$$\Delta T_f = i \cdot K_f \cdot \text{molality} \qquad \Delta T_b = i \cdot K_b \cdot \text{molality}$$

$\pi = \dfrac{nRT}{V} i$

$P$ = pressure
$V$ = volume
$T$ = absolute temperature
$n$ = number of moles
$D$ = density
$m$ = mass

$v$ = velocity
$u_{rms}$ = root mean square velocity
$KE$ = kinetic energy
$r$ = rate of effusion
M = molar mass
$\pi$ = osmotic pressure
$i$ = van't Hoff factor
$K_f$ = molal freezing-point depression constant
$K_b$ = molal boiling-point elevation constant
$Q$ = reaction quotient
Gas constant: $R$ = 8.31 joules/(mole · K)
$\qquad\qquad\quad$ = 0.0821 (liter · atm)/(mole · K)
$\qquad\qquad\quad$ = 8.31 (volt · coulomb)/(mole · K)
Boltzmann's constant: $k = 1.38 \times 10^{-23}$ joule/K
$K_f$ for $H_2O$ = 1.86 (K · kg)/mole
$K_b$ for $H_2O$ = 0.512 (K · kg)/mole
STP = 273 K and 1.000 atmospheres

## OXIDATION-REDUCTION AND ELECTROCHEMISTRY

$$Q = \frac{[C]^c[D]^d}{[A]^a[B]^b}, \text{ where } a\text{A} + b\text{B} \rightarrow c\text{C} + d\text{D}$$

$$I = \frac{q}{t}$$

$$E_{\text{cell}} = E^\circ_{\text{cell}} - \frac{RT}{n\mathscr{F}} \ln Q = E^\circ_{\text{cell}} - \frac{0.0592}{n} \log Q \text{ at } 25^\circ\text{C}$$

$$\log K = \frac{nE^\circ}{0.0592}$$

$I$ = current (amperes)
$Q$ = charge (coulombs)
$t$ = time (seconds)
$E^\circ$ = standard potential
$K$ = equilibrium constant
1 Faraday ($\mathscr{F}$) = 96,500 coulombs/mole

## Part B

(11 percent of total grade)

Solve the following problem.

2. Ethylamine reacts with water as follows:

$$C_2H_5NH_2(\ell) + H_2O(\ell) \rightleftarrows C_2H_5NH_3^+(aq) + OH^-(aq)$$

The base-dissociation constant, $K_b$, for the ethylamine ion is $5.6 \times 10^{-4}$.

(a) A student carefully measures out 65.987 ml of a 0.250 M solution of ethylamine. Calculate the $OH^-$ ion concentration.

(b) Calculate the pOH of the solution.

(c) Calculate the % ionization of the ethylamine in the solution in part (a).

(d) What would be the pH of a solution made by adding 15.000 grams of ethylammonium bromide ($C_2H_5NH_3Br$) to 250.00 ml of a 0.100-molar solution of ethylamine?

(e) If a student adds 0.125 grams of solid silver bromide to the solution in part (a), will silver hydroxide form as a precipitate? The value of $K_{sp}$ for silver hydroxide is $1.52 \times 10^{-8}$.

**Part C**

(11 percent of total grade)

Solve ONE of the two problems in this part. (A second problem will not be scored.)

3. Water is introduced into a test tube that contains 2.51 grams of $SbCl_3$. The products of the reaction are collected, analyzed, and found to be

   - 1.906 grams of a solid containing only antimony, oxygen, and chlorine.
   - 0.802 grams of a single gas that is found to be 97.20% by weight chlorine and 2.75% by weight hydrogen.

     (a) Determine the simplest formula for the gas.
     (b) What fraction of the chlorine atoms are found in the solid compound, and what fraction are found in the gas phase, after the reaction?
     (c) What is the formula of the solid product?
     (d) Write a balanced equation for the reaction. Assume that the empirical formula of the gas is the true formula.

4. Methyl alcohol oxidizes to produce methanoic (formic) acid and water according to the following reaction and structural diagram:

$$CH_3OH(aq) + O_2(g) \rightarrow HCOOH(aq) + H_2O(\ell)$$

Given the following data:

| Substance | $\Delta H_f^\circ$ (kJ/mole) | $\Delta S^\circ$ (J/K · mole) |
|---|---|---|
| $CH_3OH(aq)$ | −238.6 | 127 |
| $O_2(g)$ | 0 | 205.0 |
| $HCOOH(aq)$ | −409 | 129.0 |
| $H_2O(\ell)$ | −285.84 | 69.94 |

(a) Calculate $\Delta H^\circ$ for the oxidation of methyl alcohol.
(b) Calculate $\Delta S^\circ$ for the oxidation of methyl alcohol.
(c) (1) Is the reaction spontaneous at 25°C? Explain.
    (2) If the temperature were increased to 100°C, would the reaction be spontaneous? Explain.
(d) The heat of fusion of methanoic acid is 12.7 kJ/mole, and its freezing point is 8.3°C. Calculate $\Delta S^\circ$ for the reaction

$$HCOOH(\ell) \rightarrow HCOOH(s)$$

(e) (1) What is the standard molar entropy of $HCOOH(s)$?
    $\Delta S^\circ$ $HCOOH(\ell) = 109.1$ J/mole · K.
    (2) Is the magnitude of $S^\circ$ for $HCOOH(s)$ in agreement with the magnitude of $S^\circ$ for $HCOOH(\ell)$? Explain.
(f) Calculate $\Delta G^\circ$ for the ionization of methanoic acid at 25°C. $K_a = 1.9 \times 10^{-4}$.

## Part D

(25 percent of total grade)

You are given five topics. One topic is required. Then you are to select and answer only TWO of the remaining four topics. (Answers to additional topics will not be scored.)

The recommended time for this part of the test is about 40 minutes. Use convincing English to present your answers logically and coherently. The accuracy and importance of the detail given will be the basis for judging your response. The appropriateness of the descriptive material used will also be an important factor. Responses that are specific, using illustrative examples and equations, are preferred to responses that are general, broad, or vague.

**Answer the following essay question.**

5. When 1.00 mole of hydrochloric acid is mixed with 1.00 mole of sodium hydroxide, 13.4 kilocalories of heat is released. Describe a laboratory experiment that could measure this value accurately.

**Select two of the following four essay questions.** (Additional essays will not be scored.)

6. Give a brief explanation for each of the following:
   (a) Water can act either as an acid or as a base.
   (b) HF is a weaker acid than HCl.
   (c) For the triprotic acid $H_3PO_4$, $K_{a1}$ is $7.5 \times 10^{-3}$ whereas $K_{a2}$ is $6.2 \times 10^{-8}$.
   (d) Pure HCl is not an acid.
   (e) $HClO_4$ is a stronger acid than $HClO_3$, $HSO_3^-$, or $H_2SO_3$.

7. If one completely vaporizes a measured amount of a volatile liquid, the molecular weight of the liquid can be determined by measuring the volume, temperature, and pressure of the resulting gas. When using this procedure, one must use the ideal gas equation and assume that the gas behaves ideally. However, if the temperature of the gas is only slightly above the boiling point of the liquid, the gas deviates from ideal behavior. Explain the postulates of the ideal gas equation and explain why, if measured just above the boiling point, the molecular weight deviates from the true value.

8. Interpret each of the following four examples using modern bonding principles.
   (a) $C_2H_2$ and $C_2H_6$ both contain two carbon atoms. However, the bond between the two carbons in $C_2H_2$ is significantly shorter than that between the two carbons in $C_2H_6$.
   (b) The bond angle in the hydronium ion, $H_3O^+$, is less than 109.5°, the angle of a tetrahedron.
   (c) The lengths of the bonds between the carbon and the oxygens in the carbonate ion, $CO_3^{2-}$, are all equal and are longer than one might expect to find in the carbon monoxide molecule, CO.
   (d) The $CNO^-$ ion is linear.

9. The boiling points of the following compounds increase in the order in which they are listed below:

$$F_2 < PH_3 < H_2O$$

Discuss the theoretical considerations involved, and use them to account for this order.

## END OF EXAMINATION

## ANSWER KEY FOR THE PRACTICE TEST

## SECTION I (MULTIPLE-CHOICE QUESTIONS)

### Part A

| | | |
|---|---|---|
| 1. C | 7. B | 13. A |
| 2. A | 8. D | 14. A |
| 3. D | 9. E | 15. C |
| 4. C | 10. C | 16. B |
| 5. A | 11. B | |
| 6. E | 12. A | |

### Part B

| | | |
|---|---|---|
| 17. D | 37. D | 57. D |
| 18. B | 38. E | 58. A |
| 19. A | 39. C | 59. C |
| 20. A | 40. B | 60. E |
| 21. C | 41. D | 61. B |
| 22. E | 42. C | 62. B |
| 23. D | 43. C | 63. D |
| 24. B | 44. B | 64. E |
| 25. C | 45. C | 65. D |
| 26. C | 46. B | 66. A |
| 27. C | 47. D | 67. C |
| 28. D | 48. D | 68. C |
| 29. D | 49. C | 69. D |
| 30. A | 50. D | 70. D |
| 31. D | 51. D | 71. D |
| 32. B | 52. D | 72. A |
| 33. E | 53. A | 73. A |
| 34. C | 54. A | 74. C |
| 35. A | 55. C | 75. C |
| 36. B | 56. A | |

## PREDICTING YOUR AP SCORE

The table below shows historical statistical relationships between students' results on the multiple-choice portion (Section I) of the AP chemistry exam and their overall AP score. The AP grade ranges from 1 to 5, with 3, 4, or 5 generally considered to be passing. Over the years, around 60% of the students who take the AP chemistry exam receive a 3, 4, or 5.

After you've taken the multiple-choice practice exam under timed conditions, count the number of questions you got correct. From this number, subtract the number of wrong answers × 1/4. Do *not* count items left blank as wrong. Then refer to this table to find your "probable" overall AP grade. For example, if you get 39 questions correct, based on historical statistics you have a 25% chance of receiving an overall score of 3, a 63% chance of receiving an overall score of 4, and a 12% chance of receiving an overall score of 5. Note that your actual results may be different from the grade this table predicts. Also, remember that the free-response section represents 55% of your AP grade.

No attempt is made here to combine your specific results on the practice AP chemistry free-response questions (Section II) with your multiple-choice results (which is beyond the scope of this book). However, you should have your AP chemistry instructor review your essays before you take the AP exam so that he or she can give you additional pointers.

| Number of Multiple-Choice Questions Correct* | Overall AP Grade | | | | |
|---|---|---|---|---|---|
| | 1 | 2 | 3 | 4 | 5 |
| 47 to 75 | 0% | 0% | 1% | 21% | 78% |
| 37 to 46 | 0% | 0% | 25% | 63% | 12% |
| 24 to 36 | 0% | 19% | 69% | 12% | 0% |
| 13 to 23 | 15% | 70% | 15% | 0% | 0% |
| 0 to 12 | 86% | 14% | 0% | 0% | 0% |
| Percent of Test Takers Receiving Grade | 13% | 19% | 36% | 19% | 13% |

*Corrected for wrong answers

# ANSWERS AND EXPLANATIONS FOR THE PRACTICE TEST

## SECTION I (MULTIPLE-CHOICE QUESTIONS)

### Part A

1. (C) Shielding and large ionic radius minimize electrostatic attraction.

2. (A) F has only one negative oxidation state ($-1$).

3. (D) $Be^{2+}$ now has electrons in the first energy level only.

4. (C)

$$\ddot{O}{=}C{=}\ddot{O}$$

Oxygen is more electronegative than carbon, resulting in polar bonding. Because there are no unshared pairs of electrons for carbon, a linear molecule results.

5. (A)

$$:\!\ddot{O}\!\diagup^{\,\ddot{S}}\!\diagdown_{\ddot{O}}\!: \longrightarrow \cdot\ddot{O}\!\diagup^{\,\ddot{S}}\!\diagdown_{\ddot{O}}\!:$$

If you missed this question, review the topic of resonance in your textbook.

6. (E)

$$\text{bond order} = \frac{\begin{array}{c}\text{number of} \\ \text{bonding electrons}\end{array} - \begin{array}{c}\text{number of} \\ \text{antibonding electrons}\end{array}}{2}$$

$$= \frac{8 - 3}{2} = 2\frac{1}{2}$$

7. (B)

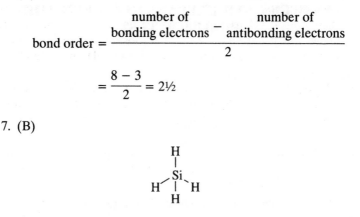

Silicon, in order to bond four hydrogen atoms to itself, must exhibit $sp^3$ hybridization.

8. (D) Two of the four valence electrons would go to the $\sigma_{2s}$ bonding orbital, and the other two would go to the $\sigma_{2s}^*$ antibonding orbital. The electron configuration would be $(\sigma_{2s})^2(\sigma_{2s}^*)^2$.

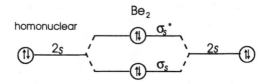

9. (E) "Normal" means 1 atm (760 mm Hg) pressure. Boiling occurs at a temperature at which the substance's vapor pressure becomes equal to the pressure above its surface. On this phase diagram, at 1 atm pressure, there is no intercept on a line separating the liquid phase from the gas phase. In other words, carbon dioxide cannot be liquefied at 1 atm pressure. It is in the liquid form only under very high pressures. At 1.0 atm pressure, solid $CO_2$ will sublime—that is, go directly to the gas phase.

10. (C) The critical point is the point at which the liquid–gas curve ends at a point at which the temperature and pressure have their critical values. Critical temperature is the temperature above which the liquid state of a substance no longer exists. Critical pressure is the pressure at the critical temperature.

11. (B) All three phases are in equilibrium at the triple point. The solid $CO_2$ sublimes if warmed at any pressure below 5.1 atm. Above 5.1 atm, the solid melts if warmed.

12. (A) The greater the disorder of the system, the larger the entropy. There is an increase in the number of molecules and thus greater disorder.

13. (A) Entropy increases upon expansion. The molecules under 1.0 atm of pressure are more free to move around—less constricted.

14. (A) Sublimation means the change from the ordered solid phase to the random gas phase.

15. (C) There are three molecules on the left for every two on the right. Things are becoming more ordered on the right.

16. (B) The system is in equilibrium. The rate of the forward reaction equals the rate of the reverse reaction. No one particular side is becoming more (or less) ordered than the other. No additional stress is being placed on the system.

**Part B**

17. (D) 8.00 g of oxygen *atoms* represent 0.500 moles.

$$\frac{8.00 \text{ g O}}{0.500 \text{ mole O}} \times \frac{2 \text{ moles O}}{1 \text{ mole X}} \times \frac{44.0 \text{ g X}}{8.00 \text{ g O}} = 176 \text{ gX/mole X}$$

18. (B) Remember that in an endothermic process, energy is being absorbed. All endothermic changes are defined with a + sign. Going from the liquid to the gaseous phase requires energy and thus is endothermic.

19. (A) Remember Boyle's law: As the volume decreases (at constant temperature), the pressure increases.

20. (A) The atomic radius decreases because of increasing effective nuclear charge and electrostatic attraction. There are more protons and electrons, so electrons are needed to create a complete shell; thus, there is an increase in electronegativity.

21. (C) Refer to the table entitled "Geometry and Hybridization Patterns," page 102.

22. **(E)** $NH_3$ is a neutral ligand; the bromide and the chloride ion both have a $-1$ charge. Cobalt would have to have a $+3$ charge in this compound for the complex compound to be electrically neutral.

### Naming Complex Compounds

1. Name the cation before the anion.

2. Name the ligands before the metal ion.

3. For the ligands:
    a. Add -o to the root name of the anion—in this case, bromo.
    b. Use aquo for $H_2O$, amine for $NH_3$, carbonyl for CO, nitrosyl for NO.
    c. Use the name of the ligand for other neutral ligands.
    d. Name the ligands alphabetically.

4. Use prefixes to denote the number of ligands of the same kind present.
    a. mono-, di-, tri-, tetra-, penta-, hexa- (here, pentaamine).
    b. bis-, tris-, tetrakis for complex ligands.

5. Use Roman numerals to designate the oxidation state of the metal ion [cobalt(III)].

6. Add -ate as a suffix to the metal if the complex ion is an anion.

23. **(D)** Hydrogen bonding is a very strong *inter*molecular force that occurs between an H atom of one molecule that is bonded to either a fluorine, an oxygen, or a nitrogen atom. In choice (D), the hydrogens are bonded to carbon, not to F, O, or N.

24. (B) The molarity of a solution multiplied by its volume equals the number of moles of solute. In this case, 450 ml of 0.35 M $Al(NO_3)_3$ can be shown as

$$\frac{0.35 \text{ mole } Al(NO_3)_3}{1 \text{ liter solution}} \times \frac{0.45 \text{ liter solution}}{1} = 0.16 \text{ mole } Al(NO_3)_3$$

$Al(NO_3)_3$ is completely soluble, so there would be three times the number of moles of nitrate ions present in the solution because

$$Al(NO_3)_3 \rightarrow Al^{3+}(aq) + 3 NO_3^-(aq)$$

Therefore, the number of moles of nitrate ions in the original solution would be $0.16 \times 3 = 0.48$.

The number of moles of nitrate ions needs to be brought up to 0.77 because the volume did not change (it remained at 0.45 liter).

$$\frac{1.7 \text{ moles } NO_3^-}{1 \text{ liter solution}} \times \frac{0.45 \text{ liter solution}}{1}$$

$$= 0.77 \text{ mole of } NO_3^- \text{ in final solution}$$

The solution begins with 0.48 mole of nitrate ions and must end up with 0.77 moles of nitrate ions; therefore, the solution needs an additional 0.29 mole of nitrate ions:

$$(0.77 - 0.48) = 0.29 \text{ mole } NO_3^- \text{ needed}$$

Calcium nitrate, $Ca(NO_3)_2$, produces 2 moles of nitrate ions in solution for each mole of solid calcium nitrate added to the solution. Therefore, because 0.29 mole of $NO_3^-$ is needed, you will need $0.29/2 = 0.14$ mole of solid $Ca(NO_3)_2$.

25. (C) In examining the rate expression, note that B is first-order, so the rate is directly proportional to the concentration of the reactant. Holding [A] constant, doubling [B] would double the rate.

26. (C) The term $-d[B]/dt$ represents the rate of decrease in the concentration of B as time elapses. For every mole of B that is lost on the reactant side, $\frac{1}{2} \times 4$, or 2, moles of D are gained on the product side over the same amount of time ($dt$).

27. (C) The rate constant is independent of the concentration of the reactants. However, $k$ depends on two factors:

   • The nature of the reaction. "Fast" reactions typically have large rate constants.
   • The temperature. Usually $k$ increases with an increase in temperature.

   With all other variables held constant, choice (D) would reduce the rate of molecular collisions, but increasing the volume is analogous to decreasing the concentration.

28. (D) The overall order of the reaction is the sum of the orders of the individual reactants. Here, $[A]^2[B]^1 = 2 + 1 = 3$. For reactions with an overall order of 3, the rate is proportional to the cube of the concentration of the reactants. Reducing the volume by $1/3$ effectively triples their concentration: $3(\text{conc})^{3(\text{order})} = 27$.

29. (D)

*Step 1:* Write the balanced equation in equilibrium:

$$2 SO_3(g) \rightleftarrows 2 SO_2(g) + O_2(g)$$

*Step 2:* Write the equilibrium expression:

$$K_c = \frac{[SO_2]^2[O_2]}{[SO_3]^2}$$

*Step 3:* Create a chart showing initial and final concentrations.

| Species | Initial Concentration | Final Concentration |
|---------|----------------------|---------------------|
| $SO_3$ | 1.20 M | 1.20 M − 0.20 M = 1.00 M |
| $SO_2$ | 0 M | 0.20 M |
| $O_2$ | 0 M | 0.10 M |

*Step 4:* Substitute the final equilibrium concentrations into the equilibrium expression.

$$K_c = \frac{[SO_2]^2[O_2]}{[SO_3]^2} = \frac{(0.20)^2(0.10)}{(1.00)^2} = 4.0 \times 10^{-3}$$

30. (A) Remember, $\log [H^+] = -pH$, so $[H^+] = 10^{-pH}$.

31. (D) When $\Delta G° = 0$,

$$T = \frac{\Delta H°}{\Delta S°} = \frac{[(-600.) + (-400.)] - [-1170.]}{[(0.0700) + (0.2000)] - [0.10000]}$$
$$= 1.00 \times 10^3 \text{ K}$$

32. (B)

$$k = \frac{0.693}{t_{1/2}} = \frac{0.693}{6930 \text{ yr}} = 1.00 \times 10^{-4} \text{ yr}^{-1}$$

33. (E) The functional group of a salt is

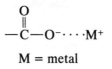

M = metal

The name of this compound is potassium propionate.

34. (C) The functional group of a ketone is

$$\overset{\overset{\displaystyle O}{\|}}{-\text{C}-}$$

The name of this ketone is methyl ethyl ketone.

35. (A) The functional group of an amide is

The name of this amide is acetamide.

36. (B) The functional group of an amine is

$$-\overset{|}{\text{N}}-$$

The name of this amine is dimethylamine.

37. (D) The functional group of a thiol is

$$-S-H$$

The name of this thiol is ethanethiol.

38. (E) Do this problem by using the factor-label method (m.t. stands for metric tons, 1 m.t. = $10^3$ kg).

$$\frac{6.0 \times 10^2 \text{ m.t. alloy}}{1} \times \frac{12.709 \text{ m.t. Cu}}{100. \text{ m.t. alloy}} \times \frac{159.15 \text{ m.t. Cu}_2\text{S}}{127.09 \text{ m.t. Cu}}$$

$$\times \frac{100. \text{ m.t. ore}}{15.915 \text{ m.t. Cu}_2\text{S}} = 6.0 \times 10^2 \text{ m.t. ore}$$

39. (C) Begin this problem by balancing the reaction.

$$2 \text{ C}_2\text{H}_6(g) + 7 \text{ O}_2(g) \rightarrow 4 \text{ CO}_2(g) + 6 \text{ H}_2\text{O}(g)$$

Because $\Delta H° = \Sigma \Delta H_f°$ products $- \Sigma \Delta H_f°$ reactants, you can substitute at this point.

$$\Delta H° = [4(-94.0) + 6(-60.0)] - 2(20.0) = -696.0$$

However, remember that the question calls for the answer per mole of $\text{C}_2\text{H}_6$. Thus, because the balanced equation is written for 2 moles of $\text{C}_2\text{H}_6$, simply divide $-696.0$ by 2 and you get the answer $-348.0$.

40. (B) Review the postulates of the kinetic molecular theory of gases, which are listed on page 71.

41. (D) A principal quantum number of 4 tells you that you are in the fourth energy level. The fourth energy level contains electrons in the $s$, $p$, $d$, and $f$ orbitals. Counting the maximum numbers of electrons available in each of the four types of orbitals—2 in the $s$, 6 in the $p$, 10 in the $d$, and 14 in the $f$—yields a total of 32.

42. (C) When presented with a generic formula, such as $AB_2$, the best way to answer the question is to use familiar examples that satisfy the conditions of the question. $H_2O$ would satisfy $AB_2$ as a bent molecule, and $CO_2$ would satisfy $AB_2$ as a linear molecule. In $CO_2$, a linear molecule, the two dipoles cancel each other, resulting in a nonpolar molecule. However, in $H_2O$, which also satisfies the $AB_2$ requirement, the two dipoles do not cancel each other out and result in a net dipole moment and a bent molecule. For both $CO_2$ and $H_2O$, we have data on ionization energy, electron affinity, electronegativity, and bond energy, but these are of no use, by themselves, in determining the geometry of the species.

43. (C) Water molecules are neutral. Hydroxide ions ($OH^-$) have a $-1$ charge. The overall charge of the complex is $+1$. Zinc would have to have a $-2$ charge in order for the complex to end up with a $+1$ charge. If you let $x = $ the charge of the zinc ion, then

$$+1 = x + 3(0) + 1(-1)$$
$$x = +2$$

44. (B) To do this problem, you would use the Clausius–Clapeyron equation:

$$\log \frac{P_2}{P_1} = \frac{\Delta H_{vap}}{2.303\,R}\left(\frac{T_2 - T_1}{T_2 T_1}\right)$$

where

$P_1$(132 mm Hg) is the vapor pressure of the liquid at $T_1$(327 K).

$P_2$(x) is the vapor pressure of the liquid at $T_2$(310 K).

$R$ is a universal gas constant: 8.314 joules/(mole · K).

Although the problem does not require you to solve the equation, it is presented below. Substituting the values of the problem into the equation gives

$$\log \frac{x}{132\text{ mm Hg}} = \frac{4.33 \times 10^4\text{ J/mole}}{2.303 \times 8.314\text{ J/(mole} \cdot \text{K)}}\left(\frac{310\text{ K} - 327\text{ K}}{310\text{ K} \cdot 327\text{ K}}\right)$$

Simplifying this problem gives you

$$\log \frac{x}{132} = -0.379$$

Solving for $x$ yields $x$ = 55.2 mm Hg.

Note that the question tells you there are 2.00 moles of the compound. This information is irrelevant to solving the problem since equilibrium vapor pressure is independent of the amount of compound.

45. (C) This problem can be solved by using the factor-label method.

$$\frac{10.\text{ g } C_6H_2O}{90.\text{ g } H_2O} \times \frac{1000\text{ g } H_2O}{1\text{ kg } H_2O} \times \frac{1\text{ mole } C_6H_2O}{90.\text{ g } C_6H_2O} \approx 1.2\text{ m}$$

46. (B) The $Al^{3+}$ has been diluted tenfold:

$$\frac{0.10 \text{ M} \times 1 \text{ cm}^3}{10. \text{ cm}^3} = 0.01 \text{ M}$$

47. (D)   $\dfrac{\text{rate}_1}{\text{rate}_2} = \dfrac{(\text{new conc.})^x}{(\text{old conc.})^x} = \dfrac{8}{1} = \left(\dfrac{2 \cdot \text{old conc.}}{\text{old conc.}}\right) = 2^x$

$8 = 2^x$

$x = 3$

48. (D) All intermediate mechanisms must add up to yield the original, overall balanced equation.

$$NO(g) + O_2 \rightarrow \cancel{NO_3(g)}$$
$$\cancel{NO_3(g)} + NO(g) \rightarrow 2\,NO_2(g)$$
$$\overline{2\,NO(g) + O_2(g) \rightarrow 2\,NO_2(g)}$$

49. (C) Remember that $K_a \times K_b = 10^{-14}$. Therefore,

$$K_b\,\text{Lac}^- = \dfrac{10^{-14}}{1.5 \times 10^{-5}} = 6.7 \times 10^{-10}$$

50. (D) Use the relationship gram-equivalents acid = gram-equivalents base. Solve for the gram-equivalents of acid.

$$\frac{0.700 \text{ liter acid}}{1} \times \frac{3.0 \text{ gram-equiv. acid}}{1 \text{ liter}}$$

$$= 2.1 \text{ gram-equivalents of acid}$$

At neutralization, the gram-equivalents of acid = the gram-equivalents of base. Therefore,

$$\frac{2.1 \text{ \sout{gram equiv. NaOH}}}{1} \times \frac{40.00 \text{ g NaOH}}{1 \text{ \sout{gram equiv. NaOH}}} = 84 \text{ g NaOH}$$

51. (D) $\Delta G°$ represents the free energy at standard conditions: 25°C and 1 atm pressure. $\Delta G$ represents the free energy at nonstandard conditions. In this problem, we have the nonstandard condition of 100°C. In order to solve for the free energy of this reaction, you must use the following equation:

$$\Delta G = \Delta G° + 2.303\, RT \log Q_p$$

where the constant $R = 8.314\ \text{J} \cdot \text{K}^{-1} \cdot \text{mole}^{-1}$ and $Q_p$ is called the reaction quotient. The reaction quotient has the same form as the equilibrium constant $K_p$.

*Step 1:* Write a balanced equation.

$$CaCO_3(s) \rightarrow CaO(s) + CO_2(g)$$

*Step 2:* Determine the value of $Q_p$, the reaction quotient.

$$Q_p = [CO_2(g)] = 1.00$$

*Step 3:* Substitute into the equation.

$\Delta G = \Delta G° + 2.303\, RT \log Q_p$
$\quad = 130{,}240\ \text{J/mole} + 2.303(8.314\ \text{J} \cdot \text{K}^{-1} \cdot \text{mole}^{-1})$
$\qquad\qquad\qquad\qquad\qquad\qquad (373\ \text{K})(\log 1.00)$
$\quad = 130{,}240\ \text{J/mole}$
$\quad = 130.240\ \text{kJ/mole}$

52. **(D)** The positron is a particle with the same mass as the electron but the opposite charge. The net effect is to change a proton to a neutron. Begin by writing the nuclear equation.

$$^{239}_{94}\text{Pu} \rightarrow {}^{0}_{1}\text{e} + {}^{A}_{Z}\text{X}$$

Remember that the total of the $A$ and $Z$ values must be the same on both sides of the equation.

Solve for the $Z$ value of X: $Z + 1 = 94$, so $Z = 93$.
Solve for the $A$ value of X: $A + 0 = 239$, so $A = 239$.

Therefore, you have $^{239}_{93}\text{X}$, or $^{239}_{93}\text{Np}$.

53. (A)

$$Ni(s)\ |Ni^{2+}(aq)||Ag^{+}(aq)|Ag(s)$$

anode (oxidation)        cathode (reduction)

$$Ni(s) \rightarrow Ni^{2+}(aq) + 2e^{-}\ ||2\ Ag^{+}(aq) + 2e^{-} \rightarrow 2\ Ag(s)$$

By convention, in the representation of the cell, the anode is represented on the left and the cathode on the right. The anode is the electrode at which oxidation occurs (AN OX), and the cathode is the electrode at which reduction takes place (RED CAT). The single vertical lines ($|$) indicate contact between the electrode and solution. The double vertical lines ($||$) represent the porous partition, or salt bridge, betwen the two solutions in the two half-cells. The ion concentration or pressures of a gas are enclosed in parentheses.

Take the two equations that decoded the standard cell notation and include the $E°$ reduction and the $E°$ oxidation voltages:

(Change the sign!)

ox: $Ni(s) \rightarrow Ni^{2+}(aq) + 2e^{-}$      $E°_{ox}\ =\ +0.25$ volt

red: $2\ Ag^{+}(aq) + 2e^{-} \rightarrow 2\ Ag\ (s)$    $\dfrac{E°_{red}\ =\ +0.80\ \text{volt}}{E°_{cell}\ =\ +1.05\ \text{volts}}$

By definition, $E°_{cell}$ voltages that are positive indicate a spontaneous reaction.

54. (A) Begin by writing as much of an equation as you can:

$$S_8(s) + M(s) \rightarrow M_aS_b(s)$$

From the information provided, you can determine that the residue, $M_aS_b(s)$, weighed 21.00 grams $(62.00 - 41.00)$ and that the metal M weighed 14.00 grams $(55.00 - 41.00)$. According to the law of conservation of mass, the sulfur that reacted with the metal must have weighed 7.00 grams $(21.00 - 14.00)$. You can now set up a proportion that relates the grams of $S_8$ and M to their respective equivalent weights.

$$\frac{7.00 \text{ grams sulfur } (S_8)}{16.0 \text{ grams/equiv. sulfur}} = \frac{14.00 \text{ grams M}}{x \text{ grams/equiv.}}$$

Solving for $x$, you obtain 32.00 grams/equiv. for metal M. From this information, it would seem reasonable that the unknown metal is copper, forming the compound CuS. Copper, with a $+2$ valence, has an equivalent weight of 31.78.

55. (C) The law of Dulong and Petit states that

$$(molar\ mass) \times (specific\ heat) = 25\ J/mole \cdot {}^\circ C$$

Substituting the given information into this relationship yields

$$(x\ g/mole) \times 0.052\ cal/g \cdot {}^\circ C = 25\ J/mole \cdot {}^\circ C$$

Because you know that 4.184 joules = 1 calorie, convert the 25 joules to calories so that units can cancel.

$$(x\ g/mole) \times 0.052\ cal/g \cdot {}^\circ C = 6.0\ cal/mole \cdot {}^\circ C$$

Solving for $x$ yields $\sim 115$. You can also learn something more about the metal from the concept of equivalent weights.

$$\frac{0.80\ grams\ oxygen}{equivalent\ \#8} = \frac{3.00\ grams\ x}{equivalent\ \#?}$$

? = 30 is the gram-equivalent weight for the metal. However, this assumes that the charge of the metal is +1. Because equivalent weight = atomic weight/valence number,

$$30\ gram\text{-}equivalent\ weight = 120\ g \cdot mole^{-1}/x$$

$x = +4$, which means that the metal, whose atomic weight is approximately 120, has a valence of +4. Thus, the metal is probably tin.

56. (A)

$$\text{Density} = \frac{\text{mass}}{V} = \frac{P \cdot \text{MM}}{R \cdot T} = \frac{\text{atm} \cdot \text{g}/\text{mole}}{1 \cdot \text{atm} \cdot \text{mole}^{-1} \cdot \text{K}^{-1} \cdot \text{K}} = \frac{\text{g}}{1}$$

Many students would choose answer choice (E). The reason molecular mass is the wrong answer is the question did not state the conditions when comparing one gas to another. For example, 1 mole of hydrogen gas at 50 K in a 1.0-liter container might have a higher density than 0.01 mole of uranium hexafluoride ($UF_6$) at 200 K in a 20-liter container, even though the $UF_6$ has a greater molecular mass.

57. (D) Element A keys out to be Al, which, being a metal in Group IIIA, would have a +3 charge. Element B would key out as sulfur, a nonmetal with a charge of −2, giving the formula $Al_2S_3$, or $A_2B_3$.

58. (A) If you missed this question, go back to the rules for naming coordination compounds found in the answer to question 22 (page 356).

59. (C) Raoult's law states that the partial pressure of a solvent over a solution, $P_1$, is given by the vapor pressure of the pure solvent, $P_1^\circ$, times the mole fraction of the solvent in the solution, $X_1$.

$$P_1 = X_1 P_1^\circ$$

A decrease in vapor pressure is directly proportional to the concentration (measured as mole fraction) of the solute present.

60. (E) In dilution problems, we use the formula $M_1 V_1 = M_2 V_2$; therefore, it is necessary to determine the molarity of the initial solution first.

$$\frac{1.50 \text{ g solution}}{1 \text{ ml solution}} \times \frac{1000 \text{ ml solution}}{1 \text{ liter solution}}$$

$$\times \frac{36.45 \text{ g HCl}}{100 \text{ g solution}} \times \frac{1 \text{ mole HCl}}{36.45 \text{ g HCl}} = 15.0 \text{ M}$$

Next we use the relationship $M_1 V_1 = M_2 V_2$:

$$(15.0 \text{ M})(x \text{ liters}) = (5.0 \text{ M})(9.0 \text{ liters})$$
$$x = 3.0 \text{ liters}$$

61. (B) In examining the balanced equation, note that for each mole of $N_2O_5$ gas that decomposes, $\frac{1}{2}$ mole of $O_2$ gas is formed. Therefore, the rate of formation of oxygen gas should be half the rate of decomposition of the $N_2O_5$.

62. (B) Begin by writing the equilibrium equation.

$$PbCl_2(s) \rightleftarrows Pb^{2+}(aq) + 2\,Cl^-(aq)$$

Next, write the equilibrium expression.

$$K_{sp} = [Pb^{2+}][Cl^-]^2$$

In reference to the chloride ion concentration, rewrite the expression for [Cl⁻]:

$$[Cl^-] = \left(\frac{K_{sp}}{[Pb^{2+}]}\right)^{1/2}$$

At any value greater than this expression, $PbCl_2(s)$ will precipitate, removing $Cl^-(aq)$ from solution.

63. (D) Use the equation $N_a V_a = N_b V_b$. Solve the equation for $N_a$.

$$N_a = \frac{N_b V_b}{V_a} = \frac{0.50 \text{ N} \times 50.0 \text{ ml}}{25.0 \text{ ml}} = 1.0 \text{ N}$$

64. (E) This problem can be done using the factor-label method.

$$\frac{1.0 \text{ gram equiv. } HC_2H_3O_2}{1 \text{ liter vinegar}} \times \frac{60.00 \text{ g } HC_2H_3O_2}{1 \text{ gram equiv. } HC_2H_3O_2}$$

$$= 60. \text{ g } HC_2H_3O_2/\text{liter of vinegar}$$

65. (D) This problem can be solved using the factor-label method.

$$\text{wt. } \% = \frac{\text{parts } HC_2H_3O_2}{\text{solution}} \times 100\%$$

$$= \frac{60. \text{ g } HC_2H_3O_2}{1000. \text{ ml solution} \cdot 1.0 \text{ g/ml}} \times 100\% = 6.0\%$$

66. (A) Heat needs to be absorbed when a solid melts; therefore, the reaction is endothermic, $\Delta H > 0$. When a solid melts and becomes a liquid, it is becoming more disordered, $\Delta S > 0$.

67. (C) The question concerns the effect of changing standard conditions of a cell to nonstandard conditions. To calculate the voltage of a cell under nonstandard conditions, use the Nernst equation

$$E = E° - \frac{0.0591}{n} \log Q = E° - \frac{0.0591}{2} \log \frac{[Zn^{2+}]}{[Ag^+]^2}$$

where $E°$ represents the cell voltage under standard conditions, $E$ represents the cell voltage under nonstandard conditions, $n$ represents the number of moles of electrons passing through the cell, and $Q$ represents the equilibrium constant.

Choices (D) and (E) would have the effect of increasing the cell voltage. Choices (A) and (B) would have no effect on the cell voltage.

68. (C) To solve this problem, use the equation

$$\log \frac{x_0}{x} = \frac{k \cdot t}{2.30}$$

with the corresponding half-life $t_{1/2} = 0.693/k$, where $x_0$ is the number of original radioactive nuclei and $x$ represents the number of radioactive nuclei at time $t$. $k$ represents the first-order rate constant (0.693). Substituting into the equation yields

$$\log \frac{x_0}{x} = \frac{(0.693/6.93 \text{ years})(11.5 \text{ years})}{2.30} = 0.5$$

$$\frac{x_0}{x} \approx 3$$

$$\frac{x}{x_0} \approx \frac{1}{3} \times 100\% \approx 33\% \text{ that remains unreacted}$$

69. (D) Begin by writing the equations which define the equilibrium constants.

(a) $AgCl(s) \rightarrow Ag^+(aq) + Cl^-(aq)$     $K_{sp_1} = 1.6 \times 10^{-10}\,mol^2 \cdot L^{-2}$

(b) $AgI(s) \rightarrow Ag^+(aq) + I^-(aq)$     $K_{sp_2} = 8.0 \times 10^{-17}\,mol^2 \cdot L^{-2}$

The $K_{eq}$ is needed for the following equation:

$$AgCl(s) + I^-(aq) \rightarrow AgI(s) + Cl^-(aq) \qquad K_{eq} = \frac{[Cl^-]}{[I^-]}$$

$$K_{eq} = \frac{K_{sp_1}}{K_{sp_2}} = \frac{[\cancel{Ag^+}][Cl^-]}{[\cancel{Ag^+}][I^-]} = \frac{[Cl^-]}{[I^-]} = \frac{1.6 \times 10^{-10}}{8.0 \times 10^{-17}}$$

$$= 2.0 \times 10^6\,mol^2 \cdot L^{-2}$$

70. (D)

Bond breaking $(\Delta H_1)$ = H—H + F—F = 103 kcal · mole$^{-1}$ + 33 kcal · mole$^{-1}$ = 136 kcal · mole$^{-1}$

Bond forming $(\Delta H_2)$ = 2 H—F = 2(−135 kcal · mole$^{-1}$) = −270 kcal · mole$^{-1}$

$\Delta H° = \Delta H_1 + \Delta H_2$ = 136 kcal · mole$^{-1}$ + (−270 kcal · mole$^{-1}$) = −134 kcal/mole

71. (D) Whether you can answer this question depends on whether you are acquainted with what is known as the Maxwell–Boltzmann distribution. This distribution describes the way that molecular speeds or energies are shared among the molecules of a gas. If you missed this question, examine the following figure and refer to your textbook for a complete description of the Maxwell–Boltzmann distribution.

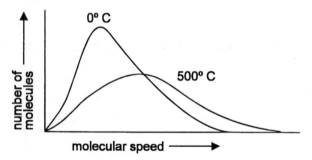

72. (A) Because all choices have 18 electrons in their valence shell, you should pick the species with the fewest protons in the nucleus; this would result in the weakest electrostatic attraction. That species is sulfur.

73. (A) The central metal ion forms only two bonds to ligands, so the coordination number is 2.

74. (C) The body-centered cubic cell looks like this:

The formula that relates the atomic radius ($r$) to the length of one edge of the cube ($s$) for a body-centered cubic cell is $4r = s\sqrt{3}$.

$$s = \frac{4(0.255 \text{ nm})}{\sqrt{3}} = 0.600 \text{ nm}$$

75. (C) $H_3PO_4$ is a triprotic acid; that is, there are 3 moles of $H^+$ ions produced for each mole of $H_3PO_4$ that ionizes. Normality is the number of equivalents per liter. A 1-molar HCl solution is 1 normal. A 1-molar $H_2SO_4$ solution is 2 normal, and a 1-molar solution of $H_3PO_4$ is 3 normal. Because 1 mole of $H_3PO_4$ weighs 97.995 grams, 1 equivalent of $H_3PO_4$ would weigh ⅓ as much, or 32.665 grams. Given this relationship, it is now possible to do this problem by using factor-label techniques.

$$\frac{100.0 \text{ ml}}{1} \times \frac{1 \text{ liter}}{1000 \text{ ml}} \times \frac{0.100 \text{ equiv.}}{1 \text{ liter}} \times \frac{32.665 \text{ g}}{1 \text{ equiv.}} = 0.327 \text{ g}$$

# SECTION II (FREE-RESPONSE QUESTIONS)

## Part A
## Writing and Predicting Chemical Reactions

*The roman numeral in each answer refers to the section in the chapter entitled "Writing and Predicting Chemical Reactions." For example, I is found on page 284.*

1. Restatement: Give a formula for each reaction, showing the reactants and products.

   (a) I. $Sn + Cl_2 \rightarrow SnCl_4$

   (Usually pick the higher oxidation state of the metal ion.)

   (b) II. $C_2H_6 + O_2 \rightarrow CO_2 + H_2O$

   All hydrocarbons burn in oxygen gas to produce $CO_2$ and $H_2O$. ("Air" almost always means oxygen gas.)

   (c) IX. $Cu + HNO_3 \rightarrow Cu^{2+} + H_2O + NO$

   or

   $Cu + NO_3^- + H^+ \rightarrow Cu^{2+} + H_2O + NO$

   This reaction is well known and is covered quite extensively in textbooks. Note how it departs from the rubric.

   (d) XV. $SO_4^{2-} + Hg^{2+} \rightarrow HgSO_4$

   (e) XVII. $SO_3 + CaO \rightarrow CaSO_4$

   (f) XVIII. $CuSO_4 \cdot 5\,H_2O \rightarrow CuSO_4 + 5\,H_2O$

   (g) XX. $Zn(OH)_2 + NH_3 \rightarrow Zn(NH_3)_4^{2+} + OH^-$

   (h) XXI. $C_2H_6 + Br_2 \rightarrow C_2H_5Br + HBr$

383

## Part B

2. Given: $C_2H_5NH_2(\ell) + H_2O(\ell) \rightleftharpoons C_2H_5NH_3^+(aq) + OH^-(aq)$

   $K_b$ for $C_2H_5NH_2 = 5.6 \times 10^{-4}$

(a) Given: 65.987 ml of 0.250 M $C_2H_5NH_2$

   Restatement: Find $[OH^-]$

   *Step 1:* Rewrite the balanced equation for the ionization of ethylamine.

   $$C_2H_5NH_2 + H_2O \rightleftharpoons C_2H_5NH_3^+ + OH^-$$

   *Step 2:* Write the expression for the base-dissociation constant.

   $$K_b = \frac{[C_2H_5NH_3^+][OH^-]}{[C_2H_5NH_2]} = 5.6 \times 10^{-4}$$

   *Step 3:* Create a chart showing initial and final concentrations (at equilibrium) of the involved species. Let $x$ be the amount of $C_2H_5NH_3^+$ that forms from $C_2H_5NH_2$. Because $C_2H_5NH_3^+$ is in a 1:1 molar ratio with $OH^-$, $[OH^-]$ also equals $x$.

| Species | Initial Concentration | Final Concentration (at equilibrium) |
| --- | --- | --- |
| $C_2H_5NH_2$ | 0.250 M | $0.250 - x$ |
| $C_2H_5NH_3^+$ | 0 M | $x$ |
| $OH^-$ | 0 M | $x$ |

*Step 4:* Substitute the equilibrium concentrations from the chart into the equilibrium expression and solve for $x$.

$$K_b = \frac{[C_2H_5NH_3^+][OH^-]}{[C_2H_5NH_2]} = 5.6 \times 10^{-4} = \frac{(x)(x)}{0.250 - x}$$

You have a choice in solving for $x$. The first method would require the quadratic equation—not a good idea because compared to the magnitude of 0.250, the value of $x$ is negligible. If you used the quadratic, you would be wasting time. The second method would assume that $[C_2H_5NH_2]$ remains constant at 0.250 M; $5.6 \times 10^{-4} = x^2/0.250$.

$$x = [OH^-] = \mathbf{0.012 \ M}$$

By the way, the 65.987 ml is not needed because concentration is independent of the amount of solution measured.

(b)  Restatement: Find pOH of solution.

$$pOH = -\log[OH^-]$$
$$pOH = -\log[0.012] = \mathbf{1.92}$$

(c)  Restatment: Find % ionization of ethylamine

$$\% = \frac{part}{whole} \times 100\% = \frac{0.012}{0.250} \times 100\% = \mathbf{4.8\%}$$

(d)  Given: 15.000 g $C_2H_5NH_3Br$ + 250.00 ml 0.100 M $C_2H_5NH_2$

Restatement: Find pH of solution.

*Step 1:* Note that when $C_2H_5NH_3Br$ dissolves in water, it dissociates into $C_2H_5NH_3^+$ and $Br^-$. Furthermore, $C_2H_5NH_3^+$ is a weak acid.

*Step 2:* Rewrite the balanced equation at equilibrium for the reaction.

$$C_2H_5NH_3^+ \rightleftharpoons C_2H_5NH_2 + H^+$$

*Step 3:* Write the equilibrium expression.

$$K_a = K_w/K_b = \frac{[C_2H_5NH_2][H^+]}{[C_2H_5NH_3^+]} = 10^{-14}/5.6 \times 10^{-4}$$

$$= 1.8 \times 10^{-11}$$

*Step 4:* Calculate the initial concentrations of the species of interest.

$[C_2H_5NH_2] = 0.100$ M (given)

$$[C_2H_5NH_3^+] = \frac{15.000 \text{ g } \cancel{C_2H_5NH_3^+}}{1} \times \frac{1 \text{ mole } C_2H_5NH_3^+}{46.15 \text{ g } \cancel{C_2H_5NH_3^+}}$$

$$\times \frac{1}{0.250 \text{ liter}} = 1.30 \text{ M}$$

$[H^+] = 0$

*Step 5:*

| Species | Initial Concentration | Final Concentration (at equilibrium) |
|---------|----------------------|--------------------------------------|
| $C_2H_5NH_2$ | 0.100 M | $0.100 + x$ |
| $C_2H_5NH_3^+$ | 1.3 M | $1.30 - x$ |
| $H^+$ | 0 M | $x$ |

$$\frac{(0.100 + x)(x)}{(1.3 - x)} = 1.8 \times 10^{-4} \sim \frac{(0.100)(x)}{(1.3)} \qquad (5\% \text{ rule})$$

$$x = 2.3 \times 10^{-3} = [H^+]$$

$$pH = -\log [H^+] = -\log [2.3 \times 10^{-3}] = \textbf{2.6}$$

(e) Given: 0.125 g AgBr$(s)$ is added to solution (a).
$K_{sp}$ AgOH = $1.52 \times 10^{-8}$

Restatement: Will AgOH precipitate?

*Step 1:* Write the equation in equilibrium for the dissociation of AgOH.

$$AgOH(s) \rightleftarrows Ag^+(aq) + OH^-(aq)$$

*Step 2:* Calculate the concentration of the ions present.

$$[Ag^+] = \frac{0.125 \text{ g AgBr}}{0.065987 \text{ liter sol'n}} \times \frac{1 \text{ mole AgBr}}{187.772 \text{ g AgBr}}$$

$$\times \frac{1 \text{ mole Ag}^+}{1 \text{ mole AgBr}} = 0.0101 \text{ M}$$

$$[OH^-] = 0.012 \text{ M} \qquad \text{(from part a)}$$

*Step 3:* Solve for the ion product, $Q$.

$$Q = [Ag^+][OH^-] = (0.0101)(0.012) = 1.2 \times 10^{-4}$$

$$K_{sp} \text{ AgOH} = 1.52 \times 10^{-8}$$

$Q > K_{sp}$, so **AgOH will precipitate.**

## Part C

3. Given: $H_2O$ + 2.51 g $SbCl_3$ → 1.906 g $Sb_xO_yCl_z$

    0.802 g gas, 97.20% Cl, and 2.75% H

   (a) Restatement: Simplest formula for gas.

   If you had 100. grams of the gas, 97.20 grams would be due to the weight of chlorine atoms, and 2.75 grams would be due to the weight of hydrogen atoms.

   97.20 grams Cl/(1 mole Cl/35.453 g/mole) = 2.742 moles Cl
   2.75 grams H/(1 mole H/1.00794 g/mole) = 2.73 moles H

   Because this is essentially a 1:1 molar ratio, the empirical formula of the gas is **HCl**.

   (b) Restatement: Fraction of chlorine in the solid product and in the gas phase.

   1. The mass of chlorine in the original compound:

   2.51 ~~g of SbCl₃~~ × 106.36 g Cl/228.10 ~~g SbCl₃~~ = 1.17 g Cl

   2. Fraction of chlorine in the gas.

   According to the law of conservation of mass, if you have 1.17 grams of chlorine in the original compound, you must account for 1.17 grams of chlorine on the product side. Because the gas is 97.2% by mass chlorine, the fraction of chlorine in the gas can be found as follows:

   $$\frac{part}{whole} \times 100\% = \frac{0.802 \text{ g gas } (0.972)}{1.17 \text{ g total chlorine}} \times 100\%$$

   $$= \textbf{66.6\% gas}$$

   fraction of chlorine in the solid product

   $$= 100.00\% - 66.6\% = \textbf{33.4\% solid}$$

(c) Restatement: Formula of solid product.

You know from the question that the solid product contains Sb, Cl, and O atoms. The weight of Sb can be found by taking the weight of antimony chloride (which has all of the antimony atoms in it) and getting rid of the weight of chlorine atoms, which you have determined to be 1.17 g. Therefore, 2.51 g $SbCl_3$ − 1.17 grams of chlorine atoms = 1.34 grams of antimony.

The weight of chlorine in the solid product can be determined by taking the weight of chlorine in the original compound (which has all of the chlorine atoms in it) and multiplying it by the percent of chlorine found in the solid product. This becomes 1.17 grams of chlorine × 0.334 = 0.391 g chlorine in the solid product.

The weight of oxygen in the solid product can be found by taking the total weight of the solid product and subtracting the amount of antimony and chlorine previously determined. This becomes 1.906 g solid product − 1.34 g antimony − 0.391 g chlorine = 0.175 g oxygen atoms in the solid product.

Expressing these weights as moles yields.

$$1.34 \text{ g Sb} \rightarrow 0.0110 \text{ mole Sb}$$
$$0.175 \text{ g O} \rightarrow 0.0109 \text{ mole O}$$
$$0.391 \text{ g Cl} \rightarrow 0.0110 \text{ mole Cl}$$

Thus, they are in essentially a 1:1:1 molar ratio, which indicates the molecular formula **SbOCl**.

(d) Given: Empirical formula is true formula.

Restatement: Balanced equation.

$$\textbf{SbCl}_3(s) + \textbf{H}_2\textbf{O}(\ell) \rightarrow \textbf{SbOCl}(s) + 2\ \textbf{HCl}(g)$$

4. Given: $CH_3OH(aq) + O_2(g) \rightarrow HCOOH(aq) + H_2O(\ell)$

   Data shown in the table

   (a) Restatement: $\Delta H°$ for the oxidation of methyl alcohol.

   $\Delta H_f° \ HCOOH(aq) = -409$ kJ/mole

   $\Delta H_f° \ H_2O(\ell) = -285.84$ kJ/mole

   $\Delta H_f° \ CH_3OH(aq) = -238.6$ kJ/mole

   $\Delta H° = \Sigma\Delta H_f°$ products $- \Sigma\Delta H_f°$ reactants

   $= (\Delta H_f° \ HCOOH + \Delta H_f° \ H_2O) - (\Delta H_f° \ CH_3OH)$

   $= [(-409$ kJ/mole$) + (-285.83$ kJ/mole$)]$

   $\quad - (-238.6$ kJ/mole$)$

   $= \mathbf{-456 \ kJ/mole}$

   (b) Restatement: $\Delta S°$ for the oxidation of methyl alcohol.

   $\Delta S° \ HCOOH(aq) = 129$ J/mole $\cdot$ K

   $\Delta S° \ H_2O(\ell) = 69.94$ J/mole $\cdot$ K

   $\Delta S° \ CH_3OH(aq) = 127.0$ J/mole $\cdot$ K

   $\Delta S° \ O_2(g) = 205.0$ J/mole $\cdot$ K

   $\Delta S° = \Sigma\Delta S°_{products} - \Sigma\Delta S°_{reactants}$

   $= (\Delta S° \ HCOOH + \Delta S° \ H_2O)$

   $\quad - (\Delta S° \ CH_3OH + \Delta S° \ O_2)$

   $= (129$ J/K $\cdot$ mole $+ 69.94$ J/K $\cdot$ mole$)$

   $\quad - (127.0$ J/K $\cdot$ mole $+ 205.0$ J/K $\cdot$ mole$)$

   $= \mathbf{-133 \ J/K \cdot mole}$

(c) (1) Restatement: Is the reaction spontaneous at 25°C? Explain.

$$\Delta G° = \Delta H° - T\Delta S$$
$$= -456 \text{ kJ/mole} - 298 \text{ K}(-0.133 \text{ kJ/mole} \cdot \text{K})$$
$$= -416 \text{ kJ/mole}$$

**Reaction is spontaneous because $\Delta G°$ is negative.**

(2) Restatement: If the temperature were increased to 100°C, would the reaction be spontaneous? Explain.

$$\Delta G = \Delta H - T\Delta S$$
$$= -456 \text{ kJ/mole} - 373 \text{ K}(-0.133 \text{ kJ/mole} \cdot \text{K})$$
$$= -406 \text{ kJ/mole}$$

**Reaction is spontaneous because $\Delta G$ is still negative.**

(d) Given: $\Delta H_{\text{fus}}$ HCOOH = 12.71 kJ/mole
$= 8.3°C$

Restatement: Calculate $\Delta S$ for the reaction

$$HCOOH(\ell) \rightarrow HCOOH(s)$$

The temperature at which liquid HCOOH converts to solid HCOOH is known as the freezing point; it is also the melting point. Because at this particular temperature a state of equilibrium exists—that is, $HCOOH(\ell) \rightleftarrows HCOOH(s)$— you can set $\Delta G = 0$. Substituting into the Gibbs–Helmholtz equation yields

$$\Delta G = \Delta H - T\Delta S$$
$$0 = -12.71 \text{ kJ/mole} - 281.3 \text{ K}(\Delta S)$$

(Did you remember to make 12.71 negative, because you want $\Delta H$ for freezing, which is an exothermic process?)

$$\Delta S = \frac{-12.71 \text{ kJ/mole}}{281.3 \text{ K}}$$

$$= -0.04518 \text{ kJ/mole} \cdot \text{K} = -45.18 \text{ J/mole} \cdot \text{K}$$

(e) (1)  Given: $S° \text{ HCOOH}(\ell) = 109.1 \text{ J/mole} \cdot \text{K}$

Restatement: What is the standard molar entropy of $\text{HCOOH}(s)$?

$$\text{HCOOH}(\ell) \rightarrow \text{HCOOH}(s)$$

$$\Delta S° = \Sigma \Delta S°_{\text{products}} - \Sigma \Delta S°_{\text{reactants}}$$
$$= S° \text{ HCOOH}(s) - S° \text{ HCOOH}(\ell)$$

$$-45.18 \text{ J/mole} \cdot \text{K} = S° \text{ HCOOH}(s) - 109.1 \text{ J/mole} \cdot \text{K}$$

$$S° \text{ HCOOH}(s) = \textbf{63.9 J/mole} \cdot \textbf{K}$$

(2)  Restatement: Is magnitude of $S° \text{ HCOOH}(s)$ in agreement with magnitude of $S° \text{ HCOOH}(\ell)$?

**The magnitude of $S°$ HCOOH($s$) is in agreement with the magnitude of $S°$ HCOOH($\ell$)** because the greater the value of $S°$, the greater the disorder; the liquid phase has higher entropy than the solid phase.

(f)  Given: $(K_a = 1.9 \times 10^{-4})$

Restatement: $\Delta G°$ for the ionization of methanoic (formic) acid at 25°C.

$$\Delta G° = -2.303 \, R \cdot T \log K_a \qquad R = 8.314 \text{ J/K}$$

$$= -2.303(8.314 \text{ J/K})298 \text{ K}(-3.71)$$

$$= 2.1 \times 10^4 \text{ J} = \textbf{21 kJ}$$

## Part D

*Of the choices available for answering essay questions, the outline format would work best for this type of question.*

5.  Given: 1.00 mole HCl + 1.00 mole NaOH; 13.4 kcal released.

    Restatement: Describe a laboratory experiment to explain the data.

    I.  Equipment needed

       A. Coffee cup calorimeter (2 Styrofoam coffee cups)
       B. Balance able to be read to 0.01 gram (for measuring NaOH)
       C. Graduated cylinder able to be read to nearest 0.2 ml (for measuring HCl)
       D. Thermometer able to be read to nearest 0.5°C (for measuring temperature change)

    II. Laboratory technique

       A. Measure out 40.0 grams of NaOH (1 mole).
       B. Depending on molarity of acid given, use the relation Volume = moles/molarity to measure out 1.00 mole of HCl in liters.
       C. Take initial temperature of HCl.
       D. Mix NaOH and HCl together in insulated coffee cup calorimeter.
       E. Immediately measure total mass of solution. Do not include mass of calorimeter.
       F. Read and record highest temperature of reaction.

III. Calculations

    A. Because HCl is dissolved in water, use 4.184 J/g · °C as the specific heat.

    B. Using the relation $Q_{water} = 4.184 \text{ J/g} \cdot °C \times \text{mass}_{water} \cdot \Delta t$, determine $Q_{water}$.

    C. $\Delta t$ = highest temperature reached − initial temperature of HCl

    D. $\Delta H_{reaction} = -Q_{water}$

    E. Answer will be in joules for the 1.00 mole of HCl and the 1.00 mole of NaOH mixture. To convert to kilocalories, use the relationship 1 kilocalorie = 4.184 kilojoules.

*For the following answer, try using the bullet format.*

6. Restatement: Explain each of the following:

(a) Water can act as either an acid or a base.

- Water can provide both $H^+$ and $OH^-$.

$$H_2O \rightleftharpoons H^+ + OH^-$$

- According to Brønsted–Lowry theory, a water molecule can accept a proton, thereby becoming a hydronium ion. In this case, water is acting as a base (proton acceptor).

$$H_2O + H^+ \rightarrow H_3O^+$$

- When water acts as a Brønsted–Lowry acid, it donates a proton to another species, thereby converting to the hydroxide ion.

- According to Lewis theory, water can act as a Lewis base. Water contains an unshared pair of electrons that is utilized in accepting a proton to form the hydronium ion.

- According to Lewis theory, water can act as a Lewis acid because the water molecule can accept an electron pair.

(b) HF is a weaker acid than HCl.

- Fluorine is more electronegative than Cl.

- The bond between H and F is therefore stronger than the bond between H and Cl.

- Acid strength is measured in terms of how easy it is for the H to ionize. The stronger the acid, the weaker the bond between the H atom and the rest of the acid molecule; measured as $K_a$ or, if the acid is polyprotic, $K_{a1}, K_{a2}, K_{a3}, \ldots$

(c) For the triprotic acid $H_3PO_4$, $K_{a1}$ is $7.5 \times 10^{-3}$, whereas $K_{a2}$ is $6.2 \times 10^{-8}$.

- $K_{a1}$ represents the first hydrogen to depart the $H_3PO_4$ molecule, leaving the conjugate base, $H_2PO_4^-$.

- The conjugate base, $H_2PO_4^-$, has an overall negative charge.

- The overall negative charge of the $H_2PO_4^-$ species increases the attraction of its own conjugate base $HPO_4^{2-}$ to the departing proton. This creates a <u>stronger</u> bond, which indicates that it is a weaker acid.

(d) Pure HCl is not an acid.

- An acid is measured by its concentration of $H^+$ (its pH).

- Pure HCl would not ionize; the sample would remain as molecular HCl (a gas).

- In order to ionize, a water solution of HCl is required:

$$HCl(aq) \rightarrow H^+(aq) + Cl^-(aq)$$

(e) $HClO_4$ is a stronger acid than $HClO_3$, $HSO_3^-$, or $H_2SO_3$.

- As the number of lone oxygen atoms (those not bonded to H) increases, the strength of the acid increases. Thus, $HClO_4$ is a stronger acid than $HClO_3$.

- As electronegativity of central atom increases, acid strength increases. Thus, Cl is more electronegative than $S$.

- Loss of $H^+$ by a neutral acid molecule ($H_2SO_3$) reduces acid strength. Thus, $H_2SO_3$ is a stronger acid than $HSO_3^-$.

- As effective nuclear charge ($Z_{eff}$) on the central atom increases, acid strength is likewise increased. Thus, a larger nuclear charge draws the electrons closer to the nucleus and binds them more tightly.

7. Restatement: Explain how MW measured just above boiling point deviates from its ideal value in terms of the ideal gas law.

The ideal gas equation, $PV = nRT$, stems from three relationships known to be true for gases:

   i) The volume is directly proportional to the number of moles:
   $V \sim n$
   ii) The volume is directly proportional to the absolute temperature: $V \sim T$
   iii) The volume is inversely proportional to the pressure:
   $V \sim 1/P$

$n$, the symbol used for the moles of gas, can be obtained by dividing the mass of the gas by the molecular weight. In effect, $n$ = mass/molecular weight ($n = m/MW$). Substituting this relationship into the ideal gas law gives

$$PV = \frac{m \cdot R \cdot T}{MW}$$

Solving this equation for the molecular weight yields

$$MW = \frac{m \cdot R \cdot T}{PV}$$

Real gas behavior deviates from the values obtained using the ideal gas equation because the ideal equation assumes that (1) the molecules do not occupy space and (2) there is no attractive force between the individual molecules. However, at low temperatures (just above the boiling point of the liquid), these two postulates are not true and one must use an alternative equation known as the van der Waals equation, which accounts for these factors.

Because the attraction between the molecules becomes more significant at the lower temperatures, the compressibility of the gas is increased. This causes the product $P \cdot V$ to be smaller than predicted. $PV$ is found in the denominator in the equation listed above, so the **molecular weight tends to be higher than its ideal value.**

*Question 8 might best be answered in the bullet format.*

8. Restatement: Interpret using bonding principles.

(a) Restatement: Compare carbon-to-carbon bond lengths in $C_2H_2$ and $C_2H_6$.

   • Lewis structure of $C_2H_2$:

$$H-C\equiv C-H$$

   • Lewis structure of $C_2H_6$:

   • $C_2H_2$ has a triple bond, whereas $C_2H_6$ consists only of single bonds.

   • Triple bonds are shorter than single bonds.

(b) Restatement: Bond angle of $H_3O^+$ is less than 109.5°.

   • Lewis structure of $H_3O^+$:

$$\left[ H \underset{\underset{\ddot{O}}{|}}{\overset{H}{}} H \right]^{+}$$

   • $H_3O^+$ is pyramidal in geometry due to a single pair of unshared electrons.

   • Angle of tetrahedron is 109.5°; this exists only if there are no unshared electrons.

   • Repulsion between shared pairs of electrons is less than repulsion between an unshared pair and a shared pair. This stronger repulsion found in the shared-unshared pair condition, as seen in $H_3O^+$, decreases the bond angle of the pure tetrahedron (109.5°).

(c) Restatement: Compare C—O bond lengths as found in CO and $CO_3^{2-}$.

- Lewis structure of CO:

$$:C\equiv O:$$

- Lewis structures of $CO_3^{2-}$:

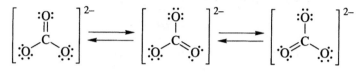

- $CO_3^{2-}$ exists in three "resonant" forms. C—O bond length is considered to be the average of the lengths of all single and double bonds.

(d) Restatement: $CNO^-$ ion is linear.

- Lewis structure of $CNO^-$:

$$\left[\ddot{C}{=}N{=}\ddot{O}\right]^{1-}$$

- There are no unshared pairs of electrons around the central atom N, resulting in a linear molecule.

- The molecule is polar because O is more electronegative than C.

*Question 9 could be answered by using the bullet format. You should try to arrange your points in logical order, but because time is a consideration, you may not be able to organize all of your bullets in perfect sequence.*

9.  Given: $F_2 < PH_3 < H_2O$

    Restatement: Discuss boiling point (BP) order.

    General Trends

    - BP is a result of the strength of intermolecular forces—the forces between molecules.

    - A direct relationship exists between the strength of intermolecular forces and the BP: The stronger the intermolecular force, the higher the BP.

    - Relative strength of intermolecular forces: H bonds > dipole forces > dispersion forces.

    - BP is directly proportional to increasing MW-dispersion force (van der Waals force).

    - Greater MW results in greater dispersion forces.

    - Strength of dispersion force depends on how readily electrons can be polarized.

    - Large molecules are easier to polarize than small, compact molecules. Hence, for comparable MW, compact molecules have lower BP.

    - Polar compounds have slightly higher BP than nonpolar compounds of comparable MW.

    - Hydrogens bonds are very strong intermolecular forces, causing very high BP.

Lowest BP: $F_2$

- $F_2$ is nonpolar; the <u>only</u> intermolecular attraction present is dispersion forces.

- $F_2$ has a MW of 38 g/mole.

- $F_2$ is covalently bonded.

Intermediate BP: $PH_3$

- $PH_3$ is polar; geometry is trigonal pyramidal; presence of lone pair of electrons.

- $PH_3$ is primarily covalently bonded; two nonmetals.

- There are dipole forces present between $PH_3$ molecules because $PH_3$ is polar.

- $PH_3$ has a MW of 34 g/mole (even though $PH_3$ has a lower MW than $F_2$ and might be expected to have a lower BP, the effect of the polarity outweighs any effect of MW).

Highest BP: $H_2O$

- $H_2O$ is covalently bonded.

- $H_2O$ is a bent molecule; hence, it is polar.

- $H_2O$ has a MW of 18 g/mole.

- Between $H_2O$ molecules there exist hydrogen bonds.

- Even though $H_2O$ has the lowest MW of all three compounds, the hydrogen bonds outweigh any effects of MW or polarity.

# THE FINAL TOUCHES

1. Spend your last week of preparation on a general review of key concepts, test-taking strategies, and techniques. Be sure to review the key terms and key concepts for each subject-matter chapter in this preparation guide.

2. Don't cram the night before the test! It's a waste of time.

3. Remember to bring the proper materials: three or four sharpened number-2 pencils, an eraser, several ballpoint pens, a calculator, and a watch.

4. Start off crisply, answering the questions you know first and then coming back to the harder ones.

5. If you can eliminate one or more of the answers in a multiple-choice question, make an educated guess.

6. On the test, underline key words and decide which questions you want to do first. Remember, you do not have to do the essay questions in order in your answer booklet. Just be sure to number all of your essays properly.

7. Make sure that you're answering the question that is being asked and that your answers are legible.

8. Pace yourself; don't run out of time.